A New Perspective on Education in the Digital Age

Also available from Bloomsbury

Digital Governance of Education: Technology, Standards and Europeanization of Education, Paolo Landri
Digital Technologies in Early Childhood Art: Enabling Playful Experiences, Mona Sakr
Education and Technology: Key Issues and Debates, Neil Selwyn
Literacy, Media, Technology: Past, Present and Future, edited by Becky Parry, Cathy Burnett and Guy Merchant
Transforming Teacher Education with Mobile Technologies, edited by Kevin Burden and Amanda Naylor

A New Perspective on Education in the Digital Age

Teaching, Media and Bildung

Jesper Tække and Michael Paulsen

BLOOMSBURY ACADEMIC
LONDON • NEW YORK • OXFORD • NEW DELHI • SYDNEY

BLOOMSBURY ACADEMIC
Bloomsbury Publishing Plc
50 Bedford Square, London, WC1B 3DP, UK
1385 Broadway, New York, NY 10018, USA
29 Earlsfort Terrace, Dublin 2, Ireland

BLOOMSBURY, BLOOMSBURY ACADEMIC and the Diana logo are trademarks of Bloomsbury Publishing Plc

First published in Great Britain 2022
This paperback edition published in 2023

Copyright © Jesper Tække and Michael Paulsen, 2022

Jesper Tække and Michael Paulsen have asserted their right under the Copyright, Designs and Patents Act, 1988, to be identified as Author of this work.

Cover image © YinYang / iStock

This work is published open access subject to a Creative Commons Attribution-NonCommercial-NoDerivatives 3.0 licence (CC BY-NC-ND 3.0, https://creativecommons.org/licenses/by-nc-nd/3.0/). You may re-use, distribute, and reproduce this work in any medium for non-commercial purposes, provided you give attribution to the copyright holder and the publisher and provide a link to the Creative Commons licence.

Bloomsbury Publishing Plc does not have any control over, or responsibility for, any third-party websites referred to or in this book. All internet addresses given in this book were correct at the time of going to press. The author and publisher regret any inconvenience caused if addresses have changed or sites have ceased to exist, but can accept no responsibility for any such changes.

A catalogue record for this book is available from the British Library.

A catalog record for this book is available from the Library of Congress.

ISBN: HB: 978-1-3501-6717-9
PB: 978-1-3502-1675-4
ePDF: 978-1-3501-6718-6
eBook: 978-1-3501-6719-3

Typeset by RefineCatch Limited, Bungay, Suffolk

To find out more about our authors and books visit www.bloomsbury.com and sign up for our newsletters.

To our children and grandchildren

Contents

List of Illustrations	viii
Preface	ix
Foreword *Stephen Dixon*	x
Note on Copyright	xi
Introduction	1
1 Teaching, Media and Bildung	13
2 The Digital Revolution	43
3 The Three Waves	75
4 Bildung in the Digital Age	105
5 Big Data	135
6 Filter Bubbles and Lockdowns	157
References	181
Index	195

Illustrations

Figures

1.1	Media epochs and the possibility of teaching	23
1.2	The external understanding of Bildung	33
1.3	The internal understanding of Bildung	35
1.4	The dimensions of critical Bildung	37
1.5	The critical understanding of Bildung	39
1.6	The experimental understanding of Bildung	41
2.1	Teaching practices and critical Bildung	73
3.1	The three waves of responses to digital media in education	79
3.2	The SME second wave strategy model	83
3.3	Different variants of responses to digital media	96
4.1	An analytical model of how to work with Bildung in the digital age	107
5.1	A Big Data Machine	139
5.2	Citizen Big Data Machine as state or corporate medium	141
5.3	The New emerging Big Cyborgs	142
5.4	The inside of the new Big Cyborgs	145
5.5	The totalitarian state Big Data Cyborg	147
5.6	Student Big Data Machine as a medium for producing the desired citizen.	150
5.7	Democratically controlled SBDM	153

Tables

4.1	New aims and means in the single subject matters	124

Preface

In this book, we present a comprehensive theory of digital media and education, including a chapter on COVID-19 lockdowns, in which we all, as professionals, students and institutions, were seriously tested in our capacities to be online. The book is the fruit of our appropriation of continental thought and our own action-based research on new digital media and teaching, which we have carried out in the period 2006–2020. It is with great gratitude that we thank our Danish publisher *Unge Pædagoger* (UP) for permission to use content from our five books in Danish (Paulsen and Tække 2013; 2015b; 2016e; 2018 and 2019). We also thank *The Journal of Communication and Media Studies* for letting our English publisher buy the rights for us to use the article *Acting with and against Big Data in School and Society: The Big Democratic Questions of Big Data* (Paulsen and Tække 2020). In addition, we thank the many other journals that we have published in and referred to in this book.

We would also like to thank Aarhus University for providing funding to support this book's publication and make it available as Open Access through Bloomsbury's Open Access programme on www.bloomsburycollections.com.

Our biggest thank you goes to our English publisher Bloomsbury for publishing this book and especially to our editor Alison Baker who trusted in us and our book from the beginning and who have helped us all the way through the process. Also thank you to Evangeline Stanford who has assisted Alison with great talent. We also want to thank Dr Stephen Dixon for writing the excellent Foreword to the book with all his insight and knowledge of the field. Last, we want to thank our many colleagues for their critical and helpful comments during the years, the many teachers and students that we have observed and interviewed, and to our families for backing us through our research. With all this help and valuable critique, we now provide a comprehensive presentation of our suggestions on how to critically understand education in the present media environment.

Jesper Tække and Michael Paulsen

Foreword

I am writing this on a grey February Sunday during the third national lockdown in England. In a physical sense, I have not seen my students or colleagues, or indeed been on campus, for almost a year. Like many working in education, my days are filled with technology – Zoom, Google Meet, Microsoft Teams, recorded PowerPoints, Google Classroom, Loom… the list goes on. Whilst it is undeniable that the impact of COVID-19 has highlighted (and even exacerbated) the inequalities in western society, it remains to be seen whether it has imposed this adoption of technology in learning and teaching, or merely accelerated its use. Over the past year, education professionals have very quickly had to adapt, and not only re-consider the relationship between education and technology, but also their understanding of both the nature and purpose of education itself, particularly through finding new ways to teach, but also to engage, connect with and challenge learners.

In this sense, the authors Jesper Tække and Michael Paulsen, through a well-structured discussion, have written an important book, and I am delighted to have been asked to write this brief Foreword. Drawing on a wealth of experience within Denmark, and with an emphasis on education as an interactive and dialogical process in which students are encouraged and supported, the book can be seen as a critique of (and an argument to re-orientate away from) the current dominant discourse of a *technical* understanding of education. Here they both draw upon and develop the Bildung tradition, with the emphasis on a critical and constructive understanding of both teaching and media, the importance of both community and support and the understanding that Bildung is itself both a creative and inventive process. This critical and constructive understanding of education allows the authors to focus their discussion in a completely non-deterministic manner and is one of the books major strengths. This is a timely and fascinating study and will be of interest to both academics and practitioners alike.

Stephen Dixon
Newman University, Birmingham, UK

Note on Copyright

Every effort has been made to trace copyright holders and we apologise in advance for any unintentional omission. We would be pleased to insert the appropriate acknowledgement in any subsequent edition.

Introduction

Over the last 30 years, digital media, computers and the internet have become embedded in almost every branch of social life in affluent western societies. However, in every sector of society people have struggled – and are still struggling – to invent and apply rewarding responses to the new media situation. The same can be said for educational institutions. If you walk into any western classroom today, 'you'll find a mix of smart phones, tablet computers and smart boards' (Livingstone 2014) and/or other digital media (Paulsen and Tække 2018) depending on the degree of digitalisation (Fu 2013). Also, many researchers have discussed the general impact of the digitalisation of education (Erstad et al., 2015; Islam and Grönlund, 2016). Yet it is seldom emphasised that this impact depends on how teachers and other school-actors struggle, understand and choose to use and/or modify new digital media (Paulsen 2020).

The New Media Situation

This is not to say that it is only up to teachers to decide how they want to use digital media and control the effects. Like many media researchers, we agree that digitalisation has transformed the basic premise of teaching – its communicative infrastructure (Dede, 2016; Jenkins et al., 2013; Paulsen and Tække, 2019c). The digitalisation of society has created what media theory calls 'a media revolution', comparable to former societal alterations triggered by the invention of speech, writing, printing and electronic media (Eisenstein 1983, Finneman 2008). Yet, media revolutions do not have a specific, certain or predictable impact. Rather they alter/expand the (im)possibility space of human activities: they afford us new options by enabling us to do things differently (Wegerif 2013), but they also imply coverings, oblivions, challenges and problems and make concepts, norms and solutions developed in former media ecologies obsolete (McLuhan 1967, Paulsen and Tække 2013). They close down 'old worlds' and open up 'new worlds', but do not determine how we should respond to and shape these transformations (Luhmann 2012 vol 1). The same is true for the digital revolution.

In Chapter 1, we outline a theory of teaching, media and Bildung that takes account of this. Further, in Chapter 2 we describe how the old classroom with its four walls becomes communicatively contaminated when teachers, students and others are equipped with computers, tablets, smartphones and a wireless network and how new opportunities, but also new problems, arise in connection with this new technology. For instance: normlessness, plagiarism, lack of attention, futile multi-tasking strategies, new control systems and surveillance, and nudging and platform capitalism colonising the classroom. But, as we show, in Chapter 3, it is also possible to understand, respond to and modify this new space of possibilities and impossibilities in different ways, shaping the situation differently. And, as we demonstrate in Chapter 4, it is even possible to develop genuinely new ways of teaching in the new media matrix, actualising educational and humanistic aspirations to a higher degree than ever. This, however, is not to say, that paradise on earth will finally be realised, if only schools and teachers learn to make use of new media. On the contrary, as we exemplify with Big Data in Chapter 5 and with *filter bubbles* and *lockdowns* in Chapter 6, new serious problems have arisen with digital media, which call for answers and responses not yet in sight. The upshot is that the new media situation is more open than any earlier media epoch has been, and that it is both possible and desirable that societies, schools, teachers, and students develop and *experiment* with different responses to this openness. Or to make our claim bold: digitalisation does not have – or need to have – one univocal effect on education.

A Non-Deterministic Approach to Media and Teaching

Nevertheless, it is often taken for granted that digitalisation has a certain impact, X, on education as if digitalisation and education were like two billiard balls. What is discussed and disagreed upon is often only what the impact of X is (whether positive or negative, big or small). We argue in this book that another basic approach is needed, to create a better battleground for the the debates about technology and education. This approach could be called *a non-deterministic perspective* (Nørreklit 2017; Paulsen 2020). We do not suggest this to add just another type of research. However, what we are pointing out is the need for a non-deterministic approach, whatever specific position that might take (hermeneutics, pragmatism, constructivism, etc.).[1] Our argument for this is simple, namely that digitalisation and education are not like billiard balls. Instead, they should be understood as part of human action. This is most obvious when it comes to education. To educate and teach is a human affair. It means that a teacher does something more or less freely and inventive together with other human beings – the students (Hansen et al., 2019). Yet, teaching is not possible without technology. To teach, you need to communicate and interact, and to do this, you need media like language, which can be seen as technology (Paulsen and Tække 2013).[2]

For instance, with the invention of writing, it became possible to communicate and interact not only through spoken words but also with written language, hereby unfolding *a writification of education*, still going on, every time teachers and students decide whether they should communicate and interact using oral and/or written language. The digitalisation of education implies a similar issue. Should you choose to interact and communicate through analogue and/or digital media? Such choices are not absolutely free, but are complex, influenced from the outside (e.g., by laws, expectations, political values and capitalism) but limited by the willingness of others (e.g., students, parents, school leaders and colleagues) to accept them. Yet they are more-or-less free (Sen 2005).

That human action is free means that we can begin something new (Arendt 1998). Further, to act means to select from possibilities based on one's values and understanding (Nørreklit 2017). Thus, an action and response can transform a situation (Deleuze 1983). If, for instance, one walks down an airplane, turns around and says, 'this is a hijack', it alters the sense of the situation (Deleuze 1990; 2014). In a similar manner, the sense of digital media may change depending on how teachers and other actors respond. All this implies that humans can respond differently to the same and transform and modify their surroundings Thus, human beings have *a transactional relation* to their environment, meaning they co-create the situation they respond to (Dewey 1997). And it is exactly by using technology like language that human beings become capable of doing this

---

[1] We are not arguing that 'a non-deterministic approach' is something completely new. Over the years many non-deterministic alternatives have been developed, in very different variants (e.g., social construction of technology) (Bijker et al., 1987), social shaping of technology (MacKenzie and Wajcman 1999) and distributed cognition (Hutchins 1995), some of which have been applied to education (e.g., activity theory)(Engeström 1987). To this line of research, we add and develop in this book Bildung theory as one among other non-deterministic approaches to media and education/society.

[2] The North American medium theory tradition (Innis, Eisenstein, McLuhan, Ong, Postman, Meyrowitz) has convincingly demonstrated that the unfolding of society (including education) depends on communication and information technology (media) but, unfortunately, it often wrapped this insight into a technology deterministic outlook. We return to this in Chapter 1.

(Cassirer 1970). Human beings can also create *alliances with technologies*, for instance with social media, becoming social media (empowered)-wo/men (Latour 1999; Paulsen and Tække 2013). Without these alliances, humans cannot do much, and teaching is impossible. To interact and communicate using oral language (i.e., using a specialised phonetic sign system) is to create an alliance.

Seen from a non-deterministic and media-reflective perspective, it is therefore incorrect to talk about the impact of digitalisation in an unconditional deterministic way. Rather, one should ask how human actors, like teachers, can (re)create, respond to, and modify their partly self-created media environment, including digital media. Also, one should trace what specific choices and technology alliances teachers make and with what consequences. What matters is how teachers (and other actors) develop and choose between different possibilities that they try to actualise.

Different Understandings of Teaching and Media

Thus, digitalisation should be understood as something that teachers and other educational actors in principle (if not necessarily *de facto*) can respond to, recreate, and modify in different ways. In this book, we therefore want to analyse and discuss how teachers and schools with different outlooks are likely to respond differently to the new digital situation. Yet, we are not neutral observers. Even though we analyse different outlooks and responses, we also pay special attention to one educational understanding that we find more plausible than others (or at least better than mainstream understanding), both in general and with regard to how one could and should respond to the new media situation. The aim of this book is to explain, defend, and elaborate on this understanding. In short, we call this understanding *the critical-constructive Bildung approach to teaching and media*.

This Bildung understanding differs from two mainstream understandings of education. On the one hand, a *technical and causal understanding* of teaching and media, constraining education as a pure techno-bureaucratic space (Roy 2004). On the other hand, a *voluntaristic* and *facilitating* understanding of teaching and media, constraining education as a totally free and safe space for pure individual self-development (Biesta 2017). Against these two, we defend a third way, a *critical* and *constructive* – understanding of teaching and media. Here a teacher's main task is not only to use different media to produce certain outcomes, externally determined (as in the technical understanding) or to facilitate internal self-development (as in the voluntaristic understanding), but also to *challenge* their students' understanding of themselves and the world. That is (1) *what* students think they can do, know, and what they need to know, (2) *how* they relate to others and think they ought to relate, and (3) *who* they think they are, who they want to become while encouraging them to explore and create new ways of being in the world.

This 'critical and constructive' Bildung approach to teaching and media, is further distinguished in Chapter 1 as two distinct Bildung approaches: (1) a critical Bildung approach, relying mainly on enlightenment thinkers like Kant, and (2) an experimental Bildung approach, relying mainly on post-modern thinkers like Deleuze. Sometimes in the book we call (and thus theoretically construe) a teacher who relies on the critical approach *a challenger* and a teacher relying on the experimental approach *a creator*. Similarly, we call a teacher relying on the technical mainstream approach, *an engineer*, and one relying on the voluntaristic approach, *a gardener* (see especially Chapter 3). Yet, in most of the book, we treat the challenger and the creator as 'two sides of the same coin' that we together call *the critical-constructive Bildung approach to teaching and media*; in contrast to the two mainstream approaches – the technical and the voluntaristic understandings. We explain all approaches in Chapter 1.

For the present, only two points are important: (1) that we are defending the thesis that the digitalisation of education can be understood, responded to and modified in different ways, depending on what basic understanding one is assuming; (2) that we more specifically defend a certain basic understanding, which we call the critical-constructive Bildung approach to teaching and media, being preferable to mainstream understandings in ways not yet specified, but discussed throughout the book.

The Bildung Tradition

The German Bildung concept goes back to the thirteenth century and can be seen as a further development of the ancient educational concepts *Humanitas* and *Paideia* (Gadamer 2013; Klafki 2005; Straume 2017; Paulsen 2020). In English, the Bildung concept is often translated as *Self-Cultivation* (e.g. Bruford 1975) or *Self-Formation* (e.g. Sorkin 1983). Yet, these translations are partly misleading. However, there have been several conflicting theories around Bildung and several different ways of using the term in German literature. So, it's a term with many different definitions. Literally 'Bild' means 'image' and Bildung can broadly be seen as the process of becoming similar to an image, and as the result thereof. In a teaching context, the Bildung approach raises *the question* of what image(s) (i.e., ideals, role models, pictures and ideas about 'the good man') students should, as much as possible, become similar to.

In modern Bildung literature, two different kinds of answers can be found (Koselleck 2007). On the one hand, vulgar and common ideas of Bildung understood as a process in which a student is formed either from outside, externally to conform to a preconceived image (decided by the society and the teacher – what is taken to be the preferred good citizen), or formed by itself internally to conform to an innate, also preconceived image (thus actualising its own human potential) only facilitated by the teacher. As one can see, these two vulgar variants correspond to what we have called the 'the technical' and 'voluntaristic' understanding of education. On the other hand, philosophical ideas of Bildung, developed by Kant and others (e.g., Humboldt, Hegel and Schleiermacher) understand Bildung as a pedagogical process, in which the teacher encourages and challenges the students to think, critically and reflectively, about what image(s)/ideals they could set up for themselves and also those around them in terms of action and development. The crucial point is, that here the image is not given in advance, either from outside (society) or from inside (the individual). Bildung is a way to critically explore one's assumptions and ways of being in the world; critically examining all kinds of groundless socialisations, images, natural habits, egoism, social conformism and immediate inclinations. It is therefore a process where one is challenged to leave one's home, i.e., what is taken for granted, to attain an attitude of doubt, reflexivity and homelessness, with the final goal of rebuilding a better home; that is, a true sense of one's position in the world (Gadamer 2013).

Bildung, in this critical variant, suggests that, through teaching, students should be encouraged, supported and challenged to (1) think and act critically-reflectively but to be *autonomous*; (2) think and act *rationally*, i.e., from the point of view of humanity; and (3) think and act in an *historically and contextually conscious* manner. And, to this we will add: (4) to think and communicate *through different media in critical-reflective-conscious ways*. As we argue in Chapter 1, this fourth point is crucial, in line with the critical aspiration of the Bildung tradition. Yet, media is often not emphasised in the Bildung tradition, which this book is an attempt to rectify. Moreover, inspired by post-modern thinking and its critique of the Bildung tradition, we will also stress that Bildung is – or ought to be – a creative process.

Finally, it should be mentioned that Bildung, in the critical-constructive variant, diverges from contemporary mainstream educational ideas about *digital literacy* and *twenty-first century skills*, insofar as the latter implies that education is reduced to *delivering* certain skills, abilities, competences and/or *forming* the students and changing their behaviour and values in certain ways. Seen from 'a critical Bildung perspective' this amounts to the technical variant of the vulgar model of Bildung, that *instrumentalises* education, while the critical-constructive variant instead emphasises education as an interactive and dialogical process, in which students are *encouraged* and *supported* to explore, transform and develop their ways of being in the world critically and reflectively.

Bildung and the Media

Although we do not assume that there is a direct correlation between media revolutions and the development of Bildung theory, we propose that the ancient ideas of Bildung, i.e. *Paideia* (in the Greek antiquity) and *Humanitas* (in the Roman republic), can be seen as reflected responses to the expansion of the social (im)possibility space, afforded by the invention and development of writing techniques, while the modern idea of Bildung (in the age of Enlightenment) can be seen as a reflected response to the even greater social complexity afforded by the invention and development of the printing press. However, what we have called the technical and voluntaristic understandings of education can be seen as non-reflective, re-active and defensive responses; trying to control/limit the increasing social complexity or escaping from it (or simply ignoring it).

We can exemplify with the concept of knowledge. In the wake of the printing press, the amount of accessible knowledge increased enormously. Yet, in earliest days of modern time, the *encyclopaedists* (see Gustavsson 2017) still thought that it would be possible for one single human being to acquire all aspects of important knowledge. However, eventually this becomes impossible and one was forced to a narrow selection of the most important. Now, the technical response was to determine politically, with arbitrary references to societal functions, what narrow corpus of knowledge students should acquire. Rousseau in his *Emile*, suggested the opposite solution: one should not read anything before the age of 12, and everything one learned should come from practical activities linked to one's local surroundings, ideally outside and protected from the complexity of modern society. However, modern reflective Bildung theory suggested a third solution: students should become (1) reflective-critically autonomous; (2) rational-ethical; and (3) historical-contextually conscious readers and actors, with the ability and will to confront, by themselves, the problem of selecting relevant and important knowledge.

There are more nuances, but the main point we want to make here, is that with electronic and digital media, social complexity has once again increased and we have not only witnessed defensive responses (totalitarianism or escapism), but also the need for reflective Bildung responses. There is much more to say about Bildung and the media, but we will return to that in Chapter 1. Further, in Chapter 2, we elaborate why the new media situation calls for Bildung, while in Chapter 3 we conclude our argument that Bildung responses to the situation are preferable to mainstream responses, ranging from control, prohibition and technical regimes to laissez faire, media ignorance and voluntaristic reactions.

Theoretical Framework

To understand the new digital situation to which educational actors today must respond, we put forward *a new interpretative framework* (Caputo 2018) in which we link three concepts: teaching, media and bildung. Firstly, this framework consists of a sociologically and descriptive understanding of the complexity of *teaching and society*. This allows us to answer the question: what is the case today? Secondly, it entails a media theoretical subscriptive understanding of how *all teaching is mediated* through media-like speech, printing, and electronic and digital media. This allows us to answer the question: what is behind or underneath? Thirdly, and finally, it consists of a Bildung theoretical prescriptive understanding of education. This makes it possible to answer the question: what should be done? All three questions are examined in Chapter 1. Our theoretical framework for understanding and describing the complexity of society, school and the teaching we find primarily in sociological systems theory (Luhmann 1995, 2006, 2012) but also by drawing on insights from Foucault and other social thinkers. Our examination on the mediation of teaching is primarily cultivated by medium theory (McLuhan 1967; Eisenstein 1983; Ong 1982; Postman 1993; Finnemann 2005; Baym 2010; Boyd 2014; 2010; and especially Meyrowitz 1985). But we also integrate media concepts, ideas, and insights from Bryant (2014), Latour (2008), Deleuze (2006), Bauman (2009), Bruns (2008) and Jenkins (2016; 2008; 2006). In relation to Bildung theory, we draw on Kant (1803), Gadamer (2003), Klafki (2005), Koselleck (2007) and Biesta (2017, 2015; 2014; 2011; 2006), but we also provide our own model of Bildung on the basis of other philosophers (e.g., Straume 2017) and our own thoughts (Paulsen and Tække

2018; 2019; Paulsen 2020) and other educational thinkers (Dewey 1997, Dysthe 2013, Roy 2004, Beck 2014, Hansen 2019).

Empirical Basis

During the last 15 years we have done research on digital media and education. We have conducted case studies and three larger action-based research projects funded by Danish public authorities like the Ministry of Education. We have published five books in Danish, and a number of journal articles and conference papers. This book aims to provide an international public with a compilation of our findings and theories. It is not a huge book, so there will not be space for many intermediate reflections, mistakes, subprojects, transcriptions of observations and interviews etc. Nor will there be space for a long account of methodology. Therefore, we here only present some headlines from and about the two most important research projects we have conducted, and that we rely on respectively in Chapters 3 and 4.

(1) *Socio Media Education* experiment (SME) was an action research project about how a Danish upper secondary school class experimented with their media culture. The background was that we earlier had conducted research in a number of upper secondary schools in Denmark and written a series of critical articles about how digital media and wireless networks altered the premises of classroom teaching (Paulsen and Tække 2009, 2010a, 2010b). Our findings showed that the new digital media situation gave rise to a series of problems: among other distractions, ambivalences and conflicts. They also showed that teachers either reacted to the new media environment with prohibition (control and surveillance strategies) or indifference (laissez-faire strategies), but without great success. Applying medium theory (Meyrowitz 1985) and sociological systems theory (Luhmann 1995; 2006), we came to the conclusion that new forms of classroom culture and educational practice were required. Following on from this, the teachers in a three-year SME experiment class (existing from 2011–2014) agreed to neither prohibit nor to be indifferent to any use of media. Instead they committed themselves to find, develop and actualise the potential of the new media situation, and simultaneously reduce the obstacles that the new media environment implied for teaching. The teachers would try to fill out gap between prohibition and indifference with interventions that aimed to improve students' media-related reflexivity (especially encouraging them to become attentive to their own media use) and they had to use social media

critically in their teaching. The method behind the experiment was basically a circular step-wise process where (1) we, as researchers, provided input, reflections and suggestions to the teachers; (2) teachers responded and designed how they would carry out interventions and media experiments in the class; (3) the researchers conducted field studies (interviews, data analysis, observations and questionnaires) to observe how the teachers and students acted and evaluated the ongoing experiments; (4) the researchers and the teachers met and discussed things; and (5) the teachers redesigned new experiments and interventions consecutively in the class (Paulsen and Tække 2013; 2016). The main result of the project is our *theory of the three waves* and we present this in Chapter 3.

(2) *In the research project called DUFA* (digitally mediated Bildung in different school subjects), we worked with two Danish upper secondary schools (Rødkilde Gymnasium and Silkeborg Gymnasium) and a group of 12 teachers teaching in different subject areas. Each teacher had to design two teaching courses in which they used (and experimented with) digital media to support academic work in the subject and Bildung in general. We provided the teachers with a research overview and a theoretical framework, fleshing out an agenda within which they could design their own courses. We reworked this into an analytical framework, selected 10 of the courses and analyzed them and pointed out potential difficulties, shortcomings and extrapolated four different scenarios for the future of the school that we present in Chapter 4 (2018; 2019).[3]

The Structure of the Book

In Chapter 1 we present our theoretical framework and the main concepts of Teaching, Media and Bildung, their connections and our arguments for this conceptual nexus. In Chapter 2 we *use* our conceptual framework to analyse *the new digital situation* – especially the differences before and after the internet; identifying what is new and what is not new about the contemporary situation. This forms our diagnosis of the historically framed situation we stand in today regarding media and education. Also, we outline major educational challenges

---

[3] In both projects – SME and DUFA – we have documented interviews (with students, groups of students, teachers and school managers), observations, schedules, photos, descriptions made by the teachers and online resources from social media (especially more than 30.000 tweets from the SME-class), mails, wikis, blogs, 3D-drawings, etc. All our projects have been almost only qualitative research and the books and journal articles has been through review and the conference papers discussed at conferences (Paulsen and Tække 2013, 2016, 2018, 2019).

and opportunities of this situation. In Chapter 3 we apply our theory to analyse how societies/schools/teachers with different understandings of the aim of education will most likely develop different responses to digitalisation (the new media ecology) and thus frame and modify the new situation differently. We show that societies/schools/teachers with the critical-constructive Bildung-understanding of education will develop the situation differently than 'actors' with other understandings. Also, we argue that the critical-constructive Bildung-understanding is preferable from a democratic point of view. In Chapter 4 we present *how* it is possible for schools and teachers to work in practice with the critical-constructive Bildung understanding. We explore four options using examples from different subject matters. In Chapter 5 we discuss Big Data, as an example of the dark side of digitalisation, something that schools and societies will have to deal with in the future and which makes critical-constructive Bildung-orientated teaching necessary. Finally, in Chapter 6 we analyse two more current challenges: (1) filter bubbles – the polarisation of society related to social media and (2) teaching during the lockdowns as a result of the COVID-19 pandemic, which lead us to the final conclusion of the book, at the end of Chapter 6, namely that a critical-constructive Bildung approach to teaching, in our view is challenged, but is still possible and also desirable, in the digital age in which we are now living. It is, of course, up to the reader to judge for themselves whether the present book provides convincing arguments.

1

Teaching, Media and Bildung

In this chapter we present an interpretive framework that connects three theoretical concepts – Teaching, Media and Bildung. The framework makes it possible to generate *a non-deterministic* understanding of education and digital media (see the introduction to this book). This in opposition to mainstream thought in which media is either ignored or the relationship is understood to be more or less deterministic, as if technology and media have a certain unconditional impact on education and teaching, either good or bad, big or small; or hold a certain potential that ought to be realised by schools (to adapt to digital society). Instead of such mainstream views we want to pursue the thesis that the relationship between media and teaching should be thought of as more open, uncertain and unfixed. We understand and develop the German concept Bildung as a way of reflecting on the relationship in a non-deterministic way (see also Kergel 2017). In the tradition of Bildung we find a distinction between *vulgar* (i.e., common) ideas about education, in which the formation and cultivation of students is determined from pregiven (internal or external) ideals, and *reflective* ideas, in which formation/cultivation is considered more openly (explorative and/or experimentally) (Koselleck 2007). Yet, in the tradition of Bildung, this is mostly not linked explicitly to a deeper consideration of media and technology. What we want to do in this chapter is, however, exactly this: to develop the concept of Bildung into a reflection about the open and non-deterministic relationship between teaching and media. Thus, we will understand Bildung theories as reflections about how societies, schools and teachers can and should link teaching and media; where the vulgar Bildung theories think the relationship is a given, the reflective theories do not believe it is already fixed. Or to put it differently: we use and develop the Bildung semantic to compare different educational theories in relation to the rise of digital media and ask how one ought to respond educationally to this new media situation.[1] Through this, it becomes possible to acknowledge and understand how societies, schools, teachers and students can respond to and modify the new digital situation, inventing different strategies and transforming the situation differently. Only then does it become fully understandable that very different norms, societies and practices can be developed through more or less the same technical media matrix; e.g., democratic or totalitarian actualisations. We therefore regard our proposed framework as both necessary and superior to mainstream thought. Basically, we argue that teaching is impossible without media, but also that media, though a necessary condition of teaching, does not determine teaching; rather it opens up a field containing problems that can be solved in different innovative ways, depending on how one cultivates the teaching-media relationship (Deleuze 1994).

The chapter is divided into three main parts: the first two deal with teaching and media respectively, while part three deals with Bildung and the relationship between teaching and media. The upshot is a theoretical distinction between teaching and media, reflected through the Bildung concept. This whole trinity – Teaching, Media and Bildung – we regard as the main theoretical contribution of this book. It is an invented theoretical framework, contingent, but not arbitrary, insofar as we garnish it with arguments and validation. Following the idea of radical hermeneutics (Caputo 2018) it can be understood as an interpretive framework or a perspective that makes possible new understandings of education in the digital age; creating novel conceptual and interpretative capacities which we actualise in the following chapters.[2]

---

[1] See the introduction to this book for a short and concise explanation of the Bildung concept and why we use this German concept in an English text. Simply put the concept denotes both *what* education should be about and *how* it should proceed; often translated into English as *Self-Cultivation* (e.g., Bruford 1975) or *Self-Formation* (e.g., Sorkin 1983); where 'self' in both cases underlines the necessity of active engagement of the student in the process of forming and cultivating 'one self', through support from others. Literally, the term Bildung means *imaging*, which raises the most basic question in education: what ideal image(s) of an educated man should guide educational activities? But also, how can one replicate this image, through a journey, in which one moves through three stages: (1) *Home* (a non-educated state, the starting point); (2) *Away* (going through a Bildung-process, becoming different by moving through an unfamiliar region; and (3) *New Home* (ending up in an educated state, in which one has become 'an educated man') (Gadamer 2013).

[2] Our distinction between teaching and media is both *theoretical* and *reflective* because we (a) mark both sides of the distinction Teaching AND Media; but also (b) through the Bildung concept reflect on the unity of the two sides. This is in opposition to everyday distinctions where one only marks one side of a distinction while leaving the other unmarked and also carries out no reflection of the distinction itself. This is the case when one says: 'Oh, how beautiful!'. In such a claim one draws a mere distinction between beautiful and non-beautiful, but it is only beautiful that is marked, while the non-beautiful remains a non-thematised 'void', left unmarked as a non-clarified 'rest of the world'; but also, nothing is said here of the validity or character of the distinction itself, between beauty and non-beauty and the criteria of beauty. Yet, as Spencer Brown (1969) and Luhmann (1995) both stress, all distinctions, including those that are theoretical and reflective, inevitably leave an 'outer space' unmarked; implying that there is something non-thematised and non-reflected in all

The Teaching Concept

In this section we put forward a *descriptive* analysis of the teaching concept.[3] In the next section about media, we pursue what we call a *subscriptive* analysis; dealing with what lies behind or underneath teaching (i.e. what makes teaching possible at all). And finally, in the last section of this chapter, which deals with Bildung, we bring out a *prescriptive* and thus a pedagogical understanding of teaching, considering what schools and teachers ought to do, not merely what they can do or what they actually do, or have done. Thus, what we propose is a new ontological understanding – or what could be called an *onto-cartography* (Bryant 2014) – *of Teaching, Media and Bildung*. The cornerstone of this new ontology is that instead of a David Humean absolute distinction between facts (what is) and values (what ought to be), we make room for values and freedom in the descriptive and subscriptive understanding of mediated teaching reality –thereby showing why value-based stances (based on Bildung theories) towards teaching and media are necessary.

Historically, teaching has been developed on three different levels (micro, meso and macro): firstly, and primordially it has been established as *interaction* between teachers and students who communicate with each other via reciprocal roles; the teachers as those with the expected responsibility of educating the students, the students as those who are intended to be educated. Secondly, these interactions have been institutionalised through the invention of schools, being the *organisations* where formal teaching is framed organisationally. Thirdly, the schools have not fall from heaven but has been developed as part

---

distinctions. When one, for instance, distinguishes between teaching and media, one also distinguishes between 'teaching and media' AND everything else – where 'everything else' is left unmarked. If we try to be specific about this 'everything else', the problem recurs; no matter how many distinctions we make, there will always be an outer unmarked void. Thus, even a theoretical and reflective distinction is only a limited and contingent perspective, cleaving the world in a specific way, making some of the world seen/understandable, but only from this narrow perspective, while also concealing what could be seen/understood with other distinctions. In the language of systems theory this means that observation is a paradox because invisibility is the condition of visibility (Luhmann 2018: 381). In hermeneutical terms it means that there is always something we don't understand when we understand something *as* something (Heidegger 2002). The implication of such a *multi-perspective epistemology* is that each new *drawn* distinction is also a *creative* act in a world making this 'ontologically' possible (Deleuze 1994).

[3] We base our descriptive understanding of teaching mainly on sociological systems theory. We do this, because it brings out a clear and general theoretical reconstruction of teaching as a socio-historical phenomenon. This general conceptualisation of teaching makes it possible for us to analyse and discuss how teaching can be arranged very differently depending on (1) what media it relies on (before and after the arising of the internet era) and (2) what kind of Bildung (i.e. idea of education) it aims for.

of the education systems of modern *society* (Luhmann 2006). For instance, secondary schools in Denmark, function in relationship with primary schools on the one hand, and higher education on the other hand; supported by and controlled by the Danish state. To grasp teaching adequately one must take account of all three contextual levels. In the following we describe each of the three levels.

The Interaction Level

Teaching can basically be understood as social interaction between teachers and students, *aiming at* educating the students. Such social interaction can take on many forms, ranging from teacher-dominated and dictatorial instruction to student led and democratic arrangements. But whatever format teaching takes, it is a kind of communication and interaction in which symbolic meaning content is produced and exchanged *between* teachers and students (Biesta 2006). Teaching must therefore take the form of interaction systems that are maintained and developed through the participants' mutual observations and contributions, bringing out an educational complexity that students can benefit from in different ways and that teachers can reflect on and reconsider their contribution to. It is important to stress, that there is no strict causal relationship between teaching as *social* interaction and *individual* learning and development of the students (Luhmann 2006). Just because something is said in the social interaction, it does not imply a given effect on each student. If the teacher has the necessary competence, she can perhaps lead the educational interaction in a way that promotes opportunities for students' learning, but she cannot directly control the learning of the individuals (Luhmann 1998, Tække 2011, 2014). Punishments, rewards, motivation, encouragement, challenges, instructions, role models, tricks etc. *might* convince the singular student – but not necessarily – that she should participate in activities, which *might* imply some learning and development effects, but these effects are uncertain and *might* have some unintended and unwanted effects. Thus, the teacher can, with some *risk,* contribute to the social interaction and perhaps dominate it by organising it, but she cannot carry out the *individual* learning operations of each student. She can try to convey something to the students by speaking to them, drawing for them, etc., but this only contributes to the class' educational interaction – it does not have certain and necessary effects on the students. It is up to the students, to make inferences, think about them, remember them, put them in context and thereby, perhaps, learn and develop.

The Organisational Level

Schools constitute the organisational level of teaching. They function as decision systems deciding how educational aims are interpreted and realised organisationally (Luhmann 2018). *School classes, classrooms, lessons* and *subjects* are the historically developed and institutionalised *general frames* for organising formal teaching, limiting *who* can attend (e.g. qualified teachers and students at certain ages or levels of competences), *where* teaching can be expected to take place, *when* and how long, and *about* what. Different schools have different programmes to 'fill out' these general frames for organising teaching (and even experimental schools usually use one or more of these general formats, if not anarchically and informally). For instance, how many students should be in a classroom, which type of teacher should be hired, how many meetings should the teachers have and in what groups should the teachers engage. The school, as an organisational system, makes decisions that work as decision premises for the teachers teaching in the classes. However, the schools as organisation systems not only make educational decisions, but also economic decisions, mass media decisions, political decisions and so on. They thereby reduce societal complexity "around" teaching and make *structural couplings* between the education system and other functional systems of the society.

The Societal Level

The education system constitutes the societal level of teaching. By this we mean that each teaching interaction and each school function as a part of and make a contribution to the education system of society *as a whole*. Following Luhmann (2006), the modern education system is an out-differentiated functional system in line with other (but different) functional systems such as the political system, the economic system and the legal system. Luhmann defines the binary communication code of the education system as *teachable/not teachable*, which is what *all* schools and teachers supposedly are reflecting on while they plan, initiate and evaluate teaching. The knowledge focused on in the education system is not the same as in the science system, where possible untruths can be tested, but a form of knowledge that creates opportunities for the students which, over time, can participate 'more and more' and 'better and better' in the society including their own life sphere. According to Luhmann, the education system has also developed general educational 'reflection theories' consisting of pedagogy that helps teachers to reflect on the aim of teaching and how the communicative selections in the classroom interaction system can increase the chances of successful/fruitful teaching.

The Role of Education

In the functionalist tradition, from Durkheim to Parsons (drawing on Kant and especially Hegel), it is argued that the main role of education – and thus formal schooling and teaching – is to lift children and young people from the family sphere to the wider sphere of the whole society. Thus, school is said to take over the role of socialisation, as a bridge between family and society as a whole, preparing new generations for adult roles in society (and also allocating human resources within the role structure of adult society; i.e., fulfilling the selection function). While children in the family sphere, are assessed by particular standards (i.e., through what parents think is best for the family and/or the particular child), they are met by (more) universal standards in the school (i.e. the same standards are applied to all pupils and the standards is about what is good for society as a whole). By this shift, the school prepares children to participate in wider society. Thus, the school is based on meritocratic principles, sustaining a modern society, characterised by merits, rather than tradition and innate positions.

Yet, there are at least three major problems with this story. The first is that the functionalist tradition confuses descriptive and prescriptive levels of analysis. In Kant, for instance, it is still clear, that he – based on his theory of Bildung – argues that schools *ought* to be based on universal standards but, at the same time, criticizes contemporary upbringing, schooling and education for being, *de facto*, too particularistic, because it relies on the interests of particular families or states, thus not on an idea of what would be good for humanity as such (and good for the individual as a human being which, for Kant, is not in opposition to what is good for humanity).

Secondly, many, especially Marxists, but also thinkers like Bourdieu (1977), Foucault and others have criticised the functionalistic picture of education. According to this critique it is basically wrong that actual education systems of the modern society pertain to universalistic values. Rather, modern schools tend to transmit and sustain the values of the ruling class and/or the ruling structures, orders and hierarchies of the society and thus reproduce inequality and the status quo. The idea that the school (and society as a whole) is meritocratic is at least partly a myth, because, in reality, chance equality has never been realised (which we will return to in Chapter 2).

Thirdly, it has been argued that education is able to fulfil several functions. If education only has one function, namely to help children to make the transition from the 'family sphere' to the 'sphere of adult civic society', then adult education would be pointless (because adult education is not about helping children). Biesta (2010) argues, therefore, that education can have at least three important functions: (1) qualification; (2) socialisation; and (3) subjectification. However, the status of these is unclear in Biesta's own educational theory and, again, the descriptive and the prescriptive level of analysis are blurred. Our theoretical solution to all this has been to leave it open on the descriptive level, what the educational aim of teaching more precisely ought to be. Or, to put it differently: In our descriptive account of the concept of teaching, we have conceptualised education as generally as possible and have thereby also emptied the concept – so far – for more specific normative values (i.e., educational aims and specific understandings of education). Only then will it be meaningful to compare different educational understandings and aims as different solutions to the same problem; the problem of what it can mean – or rather ought to mean – to 'educate through teaching'.

Summing up: Thus, we suggest that teaching is a historically invented social phenomena, especially developed in modern societies, taking the form of social interaction between people ascribed the reciprocal roles of teachers and students, with the general aim of contributing to the education of students, organised typically as classroom teaching taking place in schools, as part of the wider education system of the whole society. This general and open format can be 'filled out' differently by different societies, schools and teachers/students; and can also be developed and deviated from, in all kinds of experimental and alternative forms of schooling and teaching. The main point is, that teaching is a historical-social phenomenon, with its own complexity, so teachers can only try to contribute to, modify and alter this social complexity by interacting *with* students, without any certainty that they will have any direct educational effects on the students. Finally, this concept of teaching not only leaves open as to *how* teaching as a social interaction is possible, but also *what* education – as the aim of teaching – basically ought to be about. The next main section about media attempts to answer to the first of these two questions; while the subsequent and final section, about Bildung, reflects pedagogically about what it can mean – or rather *ought to mean* – to 'educate through teaching'.

The Media Concept

We now move to the next concept in our theoretical framework – the *media* concept. Our motivation for this is that teaching is impossible without media.

Thus, media is the core concept at the subscriptive level of analysis; answering the question: what is behind or beneath the development and possibilities of teaching. Such an analysis and theoretical resource can help us to understand how all teaching is mediated, and later in Chapter 2, can be used to analyse and clarify the new media situation – how it differs from the situation before the rise of digital media and the internet.

Media of Teaching: Semiotic Accessibility and Flexibility

Our focus is on teaching as mediated and, therefore, the *media of teaching*. In the previous section we argued that teaching could be understood as communicative sense-making and social interaction taking place *between* teachers and students. This demands a *materiality* (different than only each of the interacting bodies taken separately) which is (1) *accessible* for both parties; and (2) semiotic *flexible*. It must be intersubjectively accessible, to make it possible for both parties to *perceive* the and take advantage of the shared activities (and figure out how to respond to and initiate new activities). But it must also be semiotic *flexible*, to make it possible for both parts to *contribute* to – and modify – the shared activities in a manner that continuously creates new informative expressions, *formed* by the participants.

Both semiotic accessibility and flexibility are relative notions. Stones and runes are, for instance, less flexible than paper and ink, but stones and runes have been used as writing media. In a similar manner, sounds are not accessible to deaf people, while visual gestures are not to blind people. Harold Innis (1951), one of the pioneers of Canadian medium theory, has proposed that all media have either a bias toward time or space. We would add that this can be understood in terms of different degrees of accessibility and flexibility of different media. Time-bias media, which include stones, are media that are durable in character. They have a high accessibility in time, meaning that the same signs can be accessed by different generations, but at the same time they have a low material flexibility, insofar they are hard to make inscriptions on and carry fixed meanings. Yet, according to Innis they, for the very same reason, favour societal stability and tradition. Space-bias media, on the other hand, which includes modern mass media such as newspapers, television and radio, but also writing on papyrus, and later printing, are more ephemeral. They have a higher accessibility in space, meaning that they are easy to spread across a large area but also, because of their ephemerality, are highly flexible and changeable thus, according to Innis, favour innovation and large empires. Yet, as Innis also indicates, each historical situation is unique and relies on a specific matrix of media, calling for concrete, not abstract, analysis.

Yet, the basic idea we want to stress is that communication, sense-making and social interaction between teachers and students is not a kind of mere spiritual being-togetherness, a kind of direct mental contact between them, during which teachers and students without further ado, would be able to solve mathematical equations and other things together (Luhmann 1995: 158; 1990: 87). Rather, teaching as social interaction takes place in and though the media of communication and sense-making (Luhmann 1995: 271, 2012, vol 1: 120). The advantage of such a setup – compared to a kind immediate contact or mind reading (if that was possible) – is that it allows for greater degrees of freedom on both sides (alter and ego can interpret the same social event differently and can thus also bring forth a greater surplus of perspectives and original innovations and thoughts expressed socially).[4]

Expansion of the Capacity of Teaching Trough Media

The most basic media of teaching is *bodily oral language*, understood as a kind of phonetic sign system, which develops and becomes accessible to both parties by being articulated through spoken *sounds* (phonemes) and *visual* gestures/facial expressions that both teachers and students can perceive and (learn to) decode. Also, bodily oral language is relatively flexible, because it allows both parts to combine (and invent) words and gestures in many different ways, forming different language games, to use Wittgenstein's phrase.

Yet, underneath bodily oral language are even more basic media – brains, memory, perception, behaviour, bodies, sounds and lights. But with bodily oral language this basic media matrix is transformed and each of these media achieve a new status. Brains are raised to consciousness, memory to remembrance, perception to experience, behaviour to action and bodies, sounds and lights to faces, voices and signs of meaning.

---

[4] Our concept of media is based on a combination of systems theory (Esposito 1999; Luhmann 2000, 2002, 2012; Brauns 2002; Paulsen and Tække 2010c), medium theory (McLuhan 1967; Eisenstein 1983; Meyrowitz 1985; Postman 1993; Finnemann 2005) and our own thoughts (Paulsen 2006; Tække 2006) as well as others (Heider 1959, Deleuze 1994; Latour 1994; Krämer 1998; Bryant 2014, Krutka 2015). Our application of media theory within educational theory runs contrary to those of Arendt (1998) and later Biesta (2006), who claim that teaching understood as action can take place directly and non-mediated, as activities that are not materially mediated. But it also diverges from media theories (e.g., Brügger 2002) claiming that media has a certain effect or gives rise to certain possibilities that only need to be realised, without changing the media; which makes teaching into a passive residual.

During the last (approximately) 7,000 years (but especially the last 3,000 years), other media have also been invented, which have *expanded* both *accessibility* and *flexibility*; that is, first of all: *writing, printing, electronic analogue media*, and now also *digital media*. Through these media, the *capacity* of communication, sensemaking, social interaction and thus also teaching has been transformed and expanded.[5] Thus, modern teaching – as described in the previous section – has been developed and made possible through the invention of these media (before the invention of bodily oral language, teaching is hardly thinkable). Yet, with the advent of new media, the impossibilities of teaching has also increased; because the media cannot just be used to mediate ever-advanced forms of teaching, but also other activities, some of which can counteract, obtrude or undermine certain kinds of teaching (see Chapter 2).

What We Can Learn from Media History

Since McLuhan (1967), there has been a historical media view that has identified a number of phases that can be understood as *historical media societies, media ecologies or media matrices*.[6] According to Finnemann (2005; 2008) six distinct epochs are suggested in the medium theoretical literature:

I. Societies based on Prelinguistic media (e.g., mere perception, behaviour[7])
II. Societies based on Prelinguistic media + Oral language

---

[5] We use the term *capacity* throughout this chapter to make it clear that a given 'media society ecology' (e.g. the contemporary media-based society) should *not* be understood in Aristotelian terms like a gigantic seed, with a pregiven finality and potentiality (set of possibilities), just waiting to be actualised and thus fully realised. Rather it should be understood as a field of capacities, powers or differences, from which can be invented and created *new* expressions, social activities and media, that also might transmute the capacity of the media society ecology. Only then can one understand, how new and unpredictable things can be created, including new media. The main inspiration for this theoretical maneuver is – of course – Deleuze (1994) and his concept of the virtual as a field of difference. Yet, we have chosen here the less technical term 'capacity' for the sake of clarity.

[6] *Media matrix* (matrices in plural) is a term for all the media a society relies on at any given time and which gives it its capacity for communication and sensemaking (including, for instance, the ability to store and retrieve information). Cf. Meyrowitz 1985: 339. Media theorists have often focused on historical studies of the shift from one epoch to the next; e.g. the transition from societies based on only orality to societies also based on writing (Havelock 1982, Ong 1982, Innis 1951, McLuhan 1995, 1994) or the further transition to 'the printing revolution' (Eisenstein 1979) or the age of electronic media (Meyrowitz 1985).

[7] For instance: Alter learns from Ego, *vaguely* that something is forbidden, because every time Alter tries to do X it is followed up by being hit by Ego. This is a kind of *non-linguistic teaching*, based on the media of perception and behaviour. In a wider sense, however, this might also be called a kind of (semi)linguistic activity, insofar as Alter takes the hit not simply as a hit, but as a *sign of something else* – the forbidden thing. Thus, the prelinguistic media epoch should not literately be understood as absolutely non-linguistic, but as a 'border concept' – indicating something hypostasised before the invention of doubly articulated oral and gesture language games. Ong (1982) is one of the few media theorists taking account of this prelinguistic media epoch.

III. Societies based on Prelinguistic media + Oral language + Writing
IV. Societies based on Prelinguistic media + Oral language + Writing + Print
V. Societies based on Prelinguistic media + Oral language + Writing + Print + Analogue electronic media
VI. Societies based on Prelinguistic media + Oral language + Writing + Print + Analogue electronic media + Digital media

A crucial point is that old media do not necessarily disappear when a new one arises. Instead, the media matrix of each new epoch is an expansion of the former. Therefore, old media are *refunctionalised* in each new epoch (Finnemann 2005). When, for instance, writing is invented, orality is partly relieved from the function of social memory, giving rise to more dialogical and free forms of speech. What matters in each epoch is therefore the media matrix or media ecology of that epoch and thus the total capacity of the whole media environment. This is not to suggest that concrete technics always survive from one epoch to the next; on the contrary: old techniques might be substituted by new ones, but on the most general media level, orality did not disappear with the advent of writing and, still today, in the digital age, we have not stopped talking to each other.[8] Generally speaking, the communicative infrastructure has, from the

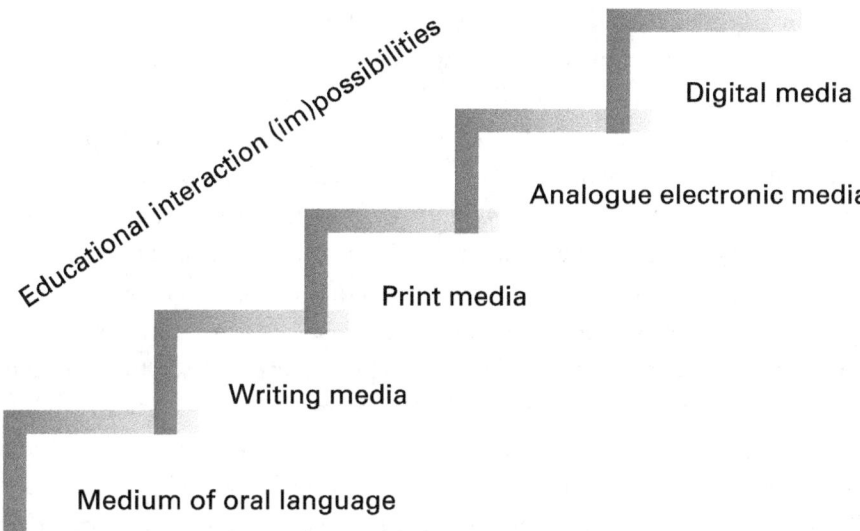

Figure 1.1 Media epochs and the possibility of teaching.

---

[8] The capacity of spoken language increases with each new medium. Thus, it is estimated that spoken language before writing had only a few thousand words, while grapholects have tens of thousands of words, a capacity which has again increased with the printing technology (in English there are as many as one-and-a-half million words) (Ong 1982).

invention of language until today, been both transformed and expanded meaning, in this context, that the capacity of teaching has become altered and expanded throughout the last five media epochs. Before the invention of speech, teaching, as a concept, was inconceivable and teaching as social interaction had hardly any meaning, other than limited prelinguistic practises. We can, therefore, as illustrated in Figure 1.1, state that with each new media epoch, a new infrastructure of teaching with transformed and expanded capacities, problems and (im)possibilities evolves.

Beyond Media Determinism

Within medium theory one often finds a tendency to suggest that each new media matrix leads to a certain kind of society, and thus also affects education and teaching in a certain way (e.g., Innis 1951; McLuhan 1995, 1964; Toffler 1980, Ong 1982, Debray 1996). Or, more abstractly, that each epoch gives rise to a new increased space of possibilities for communication, sensemaking and/or other cognitive activities (e.g., Brügger 2002; Finnemann 2005). This way of thinking implies either a strong or weak kind of determinism, in which one is inclined to think that new media affects society and human history in certain ways. It thereby does not pay enough attention to the fact that all media are invented creatively by people and societies, thus transforming themselves and the media. Also, some different cultures and societies have relied on pretty much the same media, indicating no strict cause-and-effect-relationship (e.g., China versus Europe). Thus, one must take account of the specific societal and cultural ways media are selected, innovated, understood and used within a given society (Finnemann 2008). The connection between media and society/teaching should therefore not be thought of in terms of a one-way 'cause-and-effect' relationship – not even on the level of 'potentiality'. What we can learn from media history is that each new media environment and society brings forth a unique creative and self-transforming/open *capacity* for creating social activities like teaching (Pool 1983). Such capacity is not something fixed or pregiven; because it includes the power to invent and create new things, new kinds of teaching, new media it tends to transmute. Following Deleuze (1994), we could say that each media and society environment can be regarded as *a problematic field*, to which different transformative 'solutions' might be invented and actualised, transforming the environment in different unpredictable 'directions'. Thus, each new environment implies a transformation and refunctionalisation of former media – their properties, relations and uses. With the rise of oral language for instance behaviours and perceptions are transformed into actions and experiences; that is, into the possibility of linguistic articulated and reflected understandings (instead of mere perception) and decided doings (instead of mere behaviour). The same goes for print and other media. But only non-deterministic thinking makes it understandable that one cannot foresee new media or the consequences of an invention of a medium; only retrospectively can media history be theorised. Thus, we agree with medium theory that media matters, but disagree that new media has certain effects on society (the strong version of determinism) or that new media give rise to a certain new set of possibilities waiting to be realised (the weak version of determinism).

A Post-Human Media Ecology

Bryant (2014) proposes a post-human media ecology that can help us to clarify the idea that a medium environment and society possesses an open capacity for teaching and other things. To begin with, Bryant follows the idea of McLuhan that a medium extends human organs or abilities. For instance: a car extends the human feet, television extends the eye, radio extends the ear, and so on. Thus, Bryant says, more generally, that *something functions as a medium when it modifies and extends the powers and capacity of something else*. To do this, the *materiality* of the medium matters. Cars, for instance, can only extend and modify human abilities and activities, or way of life, because of the internal properties that cars possess; wheels, seats etc. Yet, Bryant also adds to McLuhan in two ways. Firstly, McLuhan focuses on media extensions of *sensory organs*. Bryant expands this to the more general claim that anything that extends and modifies something else – its powers, activities and becomings – function as a medium (for that other thing). Thus, vitamin B functions as a medium for our human body because it can modify our mood. Secondly, McLuhan only pays heed to the extension of *human* abilities, while Bryant suggests a more general media concept. Thus, for instance, electric light not only expands the power of human beings, their sight, it also modifies and extends the powers and activities of some non-humans, whose environment is changed because of it (e.g., bringing forth new hunting conditions). Also, a cat-owner can be the medium of a cat, whose conditions and capabilities are expanded and modified by being taken care of. Further, a shark can be a medium for other beings living on it. This implies that media can be regarded as anything that, through being structurally coupled to something else, can modify its capacities, activities and becomings. The implication is that human beings, function in a wider 'more than only human' media ecology; that is, an environment consisting of many different things mediating each other. To map and understand such an environment Bryant has developed *onto-cartography*, which we will return to in Chapter 5.

Yet, it is not explained by Bryant, how it can be that media, like language, printing etc., has developed and has become so important in human society. What is not sufficiently accounted for, is that (some) media becomes important only when they are invented, selected, used, modified and applied by human actors. Bryant claims that media modifies human activities but does not acknowledge that such modifications are only realised when human beings decide to use such media in specific ways. Or, to put it differently: Media does not directly modify human actions; rather the modifications are 'mediated' through how human beings relate to, understand, use and modify media. Thus, something does not become a medium by directly modifying something else; rather it becomes a medium by being used by *someone*, an actor, to transform the latter's capacities, activities and becomings (whether this is conscious or unconscious, controlled or experimental).

In the context of contemporary teaching, the upshot is that teachers and students can modify and transform their capacity through many different things (i.e., media) – the architecture of the classroom, blackboards, books, social rules, norms, bodies, vitamins, energy flows, outdoor surroundings, field trips, projects, writing, electronic light, digital media etc. – all are potentially modifiable parts of the media environment of teaching today. What kind of teaching is actually possible and what effects – positive or negative – it can lead to, is therefore an open question depending on how the whole media environment is understood, used and experimented with and thus is also a question of how a specific society, school, class and concrete encounter between teachers and students *develops* and *transforms* the environment and thus *the capacity of teaching*.

The Transformation of Social Norms and Structures

McLuhan (1967) understood transitions from one media society to another (within which we initially seek to solve new problems with old solutions) as *media revolutions*. According to McLuhan, and with him many other media theorists, the whole of society and culture has been changed as a *result* of the rise of this new media revolution. Or, as Postman (1993:18) put it, the medium changes *everything*. It is often said that newer medium theorists like Meyrowitz (1985) still see the new media as triggering the mechanism of social change, but he is not as deterministic when it comes to causality giving away explanatory power on the level of micro sociology. Yet Meyrowitz also put forward a (weak) deterministic account of the media revolution that he has analysed most profoundly: the invention of electronic analogue media, especially television. According to Meyrowitz, new media, exemplified by television, changed the information situation of society, triggering the development of new norms for *social behaviour*; a development which, according to Meyrowitz, runs though *effect loops*, towards a new equilibrium, where norms again adequately function, in this new information situation. Thus, the point is, that norms for social behaviour *adjust*, over time, to the new media environment. The problem with this account, however, is that it is caught up in a deterministic and behaviouristic way of thinking. It is claimed that new media *causes* social change and that new norms and social behaviour will simply *adjust* and find a new equilibrium. This leaves no room for genuine innovation – for creativity and human actors taking the new situation in different, unpredictable and transformative directions. It takes for granted that the new medium has a specific effect. It is as if the medium brings forward a fixed set of possibilities and a certain new information situation, in relation to which the adequate norms already exist as 'the right solution', which only need to be found, applied and developed and then everything will be stable again.[9]

Instead, we wish to propose, that each new media society ecology makes up a new problematic field, tendentially opening up new information and communication situations that call for new norms, tools, theories, practices etc, and also make former norms and theories *more or less* obsolete. But also, we propose: (1) There is not necessarily just one set of possible new norms waiting to be realised, which will adequately work. (2) When and if one specific 'solution' is developed and actualised, it alters and transmutes the whole ecology, what is possible and not possible, what is needed and what is now obsolete. (3) The new media is developed in and out of the old media society environment, indicating that there is always a level of continuance between different media epochs. (4) The core of media of teaching and society – social complexity per se – is, as we have argued, semiotic accessibility and flexibility; but if the development of society simply, in each media matrix, runs towards a new equilibrium, then increased flexibility would be pointless. If there is any immanent kind of telos within societal media, such as writing, it is not a fixed equilibrium of social norms, at each stage of human development, but only increased practicable semiotic accessibility and flexibility, enlarging and transforming the capacity of humanity, for good or for bad.

---

[9] For a critique of equilibrium theory see Deleuze (1994) and Luhmann (2002).

Yet, there is one final point which Meyrowitz (1985) and medium theory make clear, and which we want to stress and take account of: if we want to understand the relationship between teaching and media – we have to acknowledge that new media like writing and printing, not only open up new teaching capabilities, but also new capabilities, possibilities and impossibilities *for society as a whole indirectly* having importance for the education system and teaching. This can be exemplified by television. Selwyn (2017: 57) says that television, despite huge levels of investment, never became a big success *directly* when it comes to teaching. However, the point here is that *indirectly* television changed society at large. According to Meyrowitz (1985) it was because of television – and the new information situations it created – that the teacher's position of authority was diminished in the 1960s, when it became illegal to beat the school students, and mixed classes were introduced. The whole of society was changing, through the women's liberation movement, children's rights and the youth movement. According to Meyrowitz, the more a medium supports the relationship between physical isolation and informational isolation, the more it supports the separation of people into distinct positions. The more a medium allows people to gain access to information without leaving old places and without severing old affiliations, the more it fosters homogenous positions (Meyrowitz 1985: 61). The rigorous school hierarchy became more fluid because information could no longer be given drip-by-drip, year-by-year. The younger students already knew secrets that they had not been told before – if ever – before they were older. The older generation's inconsistency on issues such as sex, drugs and politics was revealed, the authorities were on the decline and young people marched under the slogan 'don't trust anyone over 30' to general outrage (Meyrowitz 1985:139).[10]

We agree with Meyrowitz that it is important to look at how a society as a whole transforms through a new medium and how this might have consequences for the education system, the school and what is taught (content) and which social rules and role models are accepted. But we disagree that television without further ado has had certain and specific effects – for all the reasons we have already outlined above – criticising media determinism.[11] The upshot is that the great media revolutions are open media society experiments that imply that the capacity of teaching and other social activities are transformed into new open

---

[10] Those over 30 were, in fact, those who had not grown up with television (Meyrowitz 1985: 137).
[11] Television, in itself, did not trigger the same consequences in places like China and the Middle East as in the western democracies.

problematic fields, of unfixed possibilities and impossibilities, without pregiven effects or developments towards pregiven equilibriums or specific finalities. Thus, revolutions are not something external that just happen to people in society which they just passively adapt to, until everything is once again brought into balance. Instead of such a mechanical metaphysical account we suggest that revolutions are better understood immanently as societies and people (e.g., teachers and students) experimenting, though media, with their capacities, transformations and actualisations.

Does a Medium Revolution Change What It Is To Be a Human?

In Postman's book, *Technopoly*, he presents a famous passage from Plato's dialogue Phaedrus, in which an Egyptian king, Thamus, by the god Theuth, who was the inventor of many things, is presented for letter writing. Theuth argues that this invention will improve both memory and wisdom. However, Thamus is not so easy to convince and points to the opposite conclusion, that 'Those who acquire it will cease to exercis their memory and become forgetful' (Postman 1993: 4). There is no doubt that Plato has a point, as human memory became poorer because of letter writing (Ong 1982).[12] But as we left the long rhythmic memory-friendly verses in favour of alphabetic writing, we gained a much greater vocabulary and the ability to make longer and much more complex coherent arguments, etc. The philosophy that Plato and the other ancient philosophers exposed could never have been developed without the letter writing that can be distributed in time and space and constitutes a medium through which one can include oneself in the social sphere while still being alone (Luhmann 1995: 87). So yes, we lost something as we relieved the mind and the oral communication with the script, but we gained something else that at the time of the introduction was impossible to predict, which allowed for many fundamental changes in society: what it mean to be a human being.

Viewed from such a media-ecological mindset, we think it is important to develop an educational thinking that can respond wisely and innovatively to the new. We must take Postman's and others' scepticism with us, and not leave the development of schools to technocratic efficiency agents and commercial interests. However, we must also not identify the medium with the negative

---

[12] Where Plato is perhaps the first western media-pessimist, Postman (1992) is one of the biggest, in *Technopoly* which examines the technologically determined development of society steering directly towards total instrumentalisation.

examples, but as already stated, seek to influence the development in a positive direction. And here, it is necessary for the school, as an important community-creating institution of society, to become involved and help citizens to experiment with and shape the society of the future. In the next and final section of this chapter, about Bildung, we reflect about this project, comparing four different educational stances towards teaching and media.

The Bildung Concept

The German Bildung concept goes back to the thirteenth century and can be seen as a development of the ancient educational concepts *Humanitas* and *Paideia* (Gadamer 2013; Klafki 2005; Straume 2017; Paulsen 2020). In English, the Bildung concept is often translated as *Self-Cultivation* or *Self-Formation* (Bruford 1975, Sorkin 1983). Yet, these translations are partly misleading. The matter is difficult, because different, conflicting theories have developed around Bildung and the ways of using the term in German literature. So, it's a term with many senses. Literally 'Bild' means 'image' and Bildung can be seen as the process of becoming similar to an image, and as the result thereof. In a teaching context, the Bildung tradition raises *the question* of what image(s) students should become similar to and how the teacher could and should support such a process and reflection. Bildung theory therefore addresses the two most important questions of teaching and education: *What* should it be about and *How* should it proceed?

The descriptive and subscriptive framework put forward in the two previous sections showed that teaching through media is normatively 'open' and calls for prescriptive and value-based understandings and answers to what it *ought to* mean to educate through mediated teaching. In the modern and post-modern Bildung literature (accounted for in Koselleck 2007, Klafki 2005, Luhmann 2006, Straume 2017, Paulsen 2020, Biesta 1995, Gustavsson 2017, Gadamer 2013 and Andersen 1999) we mainly find four different answers to this. On the one hand, *vulgar* (i.e., common) ideas of Bildung as a process in which a student is formed either from outside, externally to conform to a pregiven image (decided by the society and the teacher – what is taken to be the preferred good citizen) or formed by itself internally to conform to an innate, pregiven image (and thus actualising its own human potential) only facilitated by the teacher. On the other hand, *reflective* (i.e., more philosophical) ideas of Bildung, developed by Kant and others (especially Humboldt, Hegel, Schelling and Schleiermacher), basically understand Bildung as a pedagogical process, in which a teacher (or someone else) encourages and challenges the students to think through, by themselves, critically and reflectively, what image(s)/ideals they could wish to set up and, at the same, could desire that everybody else also set up for their doings and developments. The crucial point here is, that the image is not pregiven, neither from outside (society), nor from inside (the individual). Bildung is a way to critically explore one's assumptions and way of being in the world; critically examining all kinds of ungrounded socialisations, natural habits, egoism, social conformism and immediate inclinations. It is, therefore, a process where one is challenged to leave one's home, what is taken for granted, to attain an attitude of doubt, reflexivity and homelessness, but with the final goal of rebuilding a better home; that is, a true grounding of one's being in the world (Gadamer 2013). This reflective and critical understanding of Bildung is further developed in postmodern thinking (Paulsen 2020, Hansen 2019), focusing on Bildung as an infinitely transcending process, in which the aim is to create and experiment with *new* expressions and ways of being in the world, that transcend the existing order and stratified way of life. Thus, we can distinguish between two vulgar variants and two reflective variants of Bildung theory:

1. Vulgar Bildung thinking:
   (a) Bildung as an external shaping of someone by the society and culture; and
   (b) Bildung as a facilitated internal development of innate potential.
2. Reflective Bildung thinking:
   (a) Bildung as a critical exploration of different ways of being in the world; and
   (b) Bildung as an experimental and creative transgression of existing order.

In the following text, we elaborate on each of the four variants in turn. In relation to the first two variants, we are mostly rejective and sceptical. First of all, neither of these vulgar variants pay enough heed to the contingent and mediated character of teaching and education. Rather they reify human beings and take for granted that they ought to conform to certain (external or internal) standards. With regard to the two reflective variants, we are more positive and endorse these as genuine and valuable Bildung theories because both variants take account of the open and mediated character of human beings, education and society. Thus, when we talk of Bildung in the following chapters, we rely mainly on a combination of the two reflective theories of Bildung – the critical and the explorative experimental, in contrast to the more common – but inadequate – ideas around education. This, however, does not imply that we completely dismiss the two vulgar variants. What we propose is rather to subsume these into the two reflective variants.

(1) Bildung: External Shaping of the Individual by the Society

The first and, perhaps, most common view of Bildung is that it is a kind of shaping of an individual to conform to a pregiven normative image of 'the good citizen' established by society and or certain authorities and executed by the school and its teachers or other educational institutions. Here, Bildung and education is seen as something that can be delivered. Everybody (or only a certain 'privileged' segment of society) growing up is required to attain as much Bildung as possible – that is to conform, as much as possible, to a pregiven image of what is taken as the ideal of an 'educated man'. In this view it is possible to distinguish clearly between people with and without Bildung (educated and uneducated people). The specific content of what it means to be an educated man, a good citizen, can be very different from one society to another; the image can be religious or secular, nationalistic or bureaucratic, broad or narrow, consisting of knowledge, social norms, morality or mere skills. Whatever the specific content, this view on Bildung gives the school and teachers the task of influencing and shaping students to conform with a predetermined ideal image 'X' of a good citizen – with certain specific knowledge, manners and values. Such a view assumes that some already educated adults (normally at the top of the societal order) have the ability, power and legitimate right to recognise and decide what it means to be a 'good citizen'. Teaching is then seen as a causal relationship, where the teacher's job is to select efficient methods in relation to pregiven goals and optimise certain effects, adding something externally to students (e.g., knowledge) or removing something from them (e.g., bad manners). The aim of teaching and education is therefore to produce good citizens. The teacher functions as an engineer, who ensures that all students achieve the same 'X' or come as close as possible to the ideal. In this way, teaching is seen as an input-output system. What the teacher wants to produce is basically determined before they start teaching (by the curriculum). Dewey (1997) calls this *traditional education*. The main task is to pass on X (knowledge, skills, etc.). This means that it is determined from above and from outside of teaching what the students do and what they should become. Biesta (2006) calls this *a technological expectation of education*. The core idea is that one wants to produce and control a certain output. In educational literature, variations of this view are not difficult to find. An example is positivistic and behaviouristic approaches, like Skinner and his idea of a complete program, to determine

Figure 1.2 The external understanding of Bildung.

desired behaviour that educational systems should produce (Beck et al., 2014). But this view is also presupposed when one argues that students should be made into good citizens through education (Biesta 2017). Also, in non-Western educational traditions, the idea of education as passing on something specific features heavily (Reagan 2017). Bildung is consequently regarded as coming from 'outside' and 'above' the student and consists of shaping the student so that they conform to the X-ideal. The school's various subjects function as moulds, in which students are shaped (mathematically etc.) into becoming identical to this X-ideal. Thus, the role of the school is to adapt the students to a given (religious, nationalistic, bureaucratic or other) order. Yet, there are basic problems with this view of Bildung. It reifies human beings and naturalises certain standards, that might lead to exclusion, loss of meaning and reproduce an unjust social order. But, most importantly, it conflates Bildung with mere socialisation and indoctrination and does not pay heed to the contingent and open character of mediated teaching. It assumes both that it is possible and legitimate to effect and control students in certain pregiven ways and priorities society's existing order over the individual and the new. Also, in this view of Bildung, media is seen only as a controlling remedy for optimising effects. We will return to this in chapter 2.

Figure 1.2 outlines the external understanding of Bildung as an approach which assumes there is assumed a cause-and-effect relationship between a controlling teacher, representing society, and their affected students. Our point is not that such a causal nexus exists, but only that it is taken for granted in this view.

(2) Bildung as Facilitated Internal Self-Development

In opposition to this external understanding of Bildung, progressive thinkers have put forward an internal understanding (Beck 2014). Bildung is here understood as the self-development of inner potential. The main pedagogical task of the teachers is therefore only to secure and facilitate students' free self-development of their own innate potential. The task is not, as in the external understanding of Bildung, to produce certain effects, but rather to create a protective, safe, meaningful and facilitating environment for the free self-development of each individual. The goal of this environment is that each student will become able to unfold and actualise all their human potential and develop a true and sound character. The function of the teacher is to be a 'gardener', who cultivates and 'fertilises the soil' that makes it possible for each student to grow without being distorted and alienated by the society they grow up into. Thus, Bildung, in this view, is regarded as free and personal self-development of human potentials coming from 'inside' and already waiting to be actualised. School subjects are used to cultivate and facilitate aspects of such human self-development (e.g, the ability to bring out the potential musical talent that lies dormant in each individual student). The role of the school is to protect the students from society (and its distracting ideas and images) thereby making it a 'free space' for unspoiled self-development. In this space it is the task of pedagogical agents to create a good environment for each individual's self-development using activities like games, projects and quests. The assumption is that everyone within themselves possesses talents, and abilities that can grow, unfold, and become actualised if one is cared for, protected and placed in the right environment with the right activities. Thus, the role of the teacher is not to influence the students from outside but to facilitate each student's own active inner self-development. Dewey (1997) calls this *the progressive model of education*. Different variations can be traced at least back to Rousseau and progressive education. However, it is also a widespread model within Western humanism – going back to ideas about active learning and education as actualisation of potential (Beck 2014). It can also be found in non-Western educational thoughts. An example is Confucianism, where Mencius famously argues that education must awaken the innate abilities of the individual through social activities – abilities that, he argues, are directed toward goodness and which he calls 'the four sprouts' (Paulsen and Garsdal 2017). However, there are also problems with this view on education. Firstly, it is assumed that human beings – independently of media and society – are born with only good-natured potentials, described and understood only as some kind of living organisms. Secondly, the school and the teacher are likewise only understood as protectors and facilitators; they are reduced to instrumental roles. The idea that the school ought to be a free space, protecting students from society, also ignore the fact that the school and its social activities always will be part of a given society. Thus, in this view, Bildung in the end is conflated with some kind of hypostasised natural self-development, where society and the media do not have a constitutional role. Media is only seen as facilitating and protecting instruments in relation to the development of independent potential.

Figure 1.3 outlines the idea that Bildung is about protecting students and creating a good environment – like cultivating plants in a greenhouse – facilitating each student's self-development. The point is not that this potential necessarily exists or can be awakened but only that it is assumed in the internal view of Bildung.

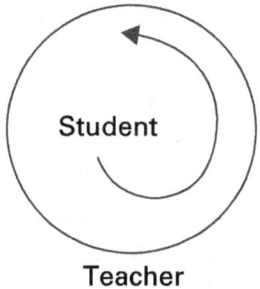

Figure 1.3 The internal understanding of Bildung.

(3) Bildung as a Critical Exploration of Ways of Being in the World

The classical variant of reflective Bildung theory has been developed as a critical alternative to both the external and internal view. In this alternative and reflective view, Bildung is instead seen as a critical exploration of ways of being in the world. This understanding was developed in the period 1770–1830 by Kant and other German thinkers, mostly idealists, attached to enlightenment, democratic and secular movements (Klafki 2005). According to Luhmann (2006: 205) it was a societal response to the situation that occurred after the introduction of printed books, where the idea of one fixed definition of man was finally undermined. When we do not know for sure what man is or should be, we do not know what education should aim for. In the literature of the eighteenth century so many versions of the 'ideal human being' were circulating, that none of them could really convince fully. However, the critical alternative to one fixed image had roughly been hinted at by Plato in ancient times and later on also by renaissance thinkers such as Pico (Paulsen 2020). Yet, the Bildung thinking that the German idealists developed was an explicit critical response to the vulgarised pedagogical educational literature of the eighteenth century (Koselleck 2007). Against this literature, Kant and others argued that Bildung should not be understood as something that has been initiated 'from the outside in' or from 'the inside out'. Here, Bildung is reduced to either (a) socialisation/indoctrination (man as a *tabula rasa*, which must be shaped in the best way for society, see Locke) and/or (b) actualisation (man as a seed, who just has to have good growth conditions, see Aristotle; but also Rousseau's *Emile*, by whom Kant was both inspired and challenged). Instead, the reflective Bildung thinkers proposed that it should be understood as the development of critical consciousness, that reflects on and eventually transgresses the social and historical context that makes this development possible. Bildung, in this critical variant, suggests that, during teaching, students should be encouraged, supported and challenged to (a) think and act critically-reflectively *by themselves*, (b) think and act *rationally* (i.e., from the point of view of humanity as such), and (c) think and act *historically and contextually consciously*. And, to this we will add: (d) think and communicate *using different media in critical-reflective-conscious ways*. The pedagogical task of the teachers is then to encourage and challenge the students to relate critically to their ways of being in the world. Thus, the function of the school is neither to influence the students, nor to protect them from society, but instead to support their critical engagement in and with society. Bildung is, therefore, about critically exploring one's ways of being in the world, how one relates to oneself, others and the world. The teacher's task is to question the student's presence in the world, encouraging and challenging them to explore their ways of being by confronting them with challenging otherness – other ways of being and thinking – which allow them to question what they might otherwise take for granted .

This critical challenging of students' ways of being in the world concerns (a) knowledge; (b) attitude; and (c) existence which, in our eyes, marks the three most central Bildung dimensions.[13] With regard to 'knowledge' the teacher should make it a living question among the students whether *what* they think they know is actually something they know and not just a belief and also think about whether what they actually know offers a sufficient foundation for creating a good life together with others. In other words: the teacher should encourage and challenge students to critically explore their knowledge and ignorance, the limit and value of what they know – their cognitive way of being present in the world and its assumptions, validity, drawbacks and possibilities for improvement. With regard to 'attitude', the teacher should try to make *how* they are present a living question among the students. Do they, for instance, relate naively or critically, egoistically or altruistically, short-term or long-term. According to Kant and most other classical Bildung thinkers this means that teachers should encourage students to attain the viewpoint of 'humanity' as such, i.e., Is my way

---

[13] The three classical dimensions of Bildung (that we propose as a reconstruction of classical Bildung theory) – *knowledge, attitude* and *existence* – apparently correspond with the three main functions of education that Biesta (2010) proposes: *qualification, socialisation* and *subjectification*. Yet, only subjectification is conceptualised by Biesta as a genuine Bildung dimension and qualification so socialisation is therefore not identical with what we call knowledge and attitude but is understood by Biesta to be more in line with the external view of education. This makes his educational theory unclear, as seen from the point of view of classical Bildung thinking. Biesta, however, seems to only have a reduced understanding of 'Bildung' (because he mainly understands it, as a failed attempt to form an educational theory of subjectification but, in reality, ending up with what we, in this chapter, call either an 'external' or 'internal' understanding of education).

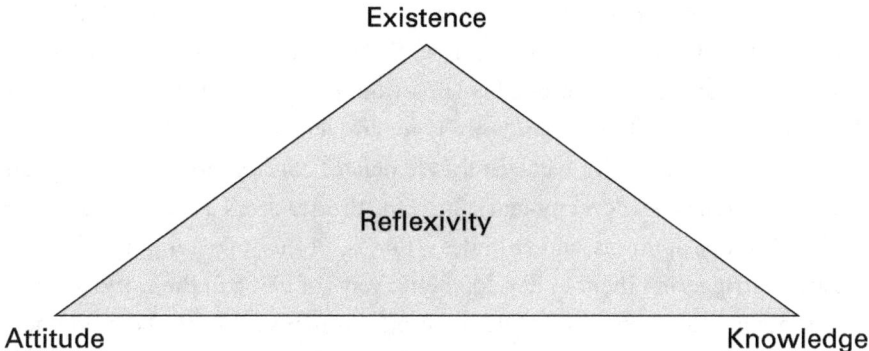

Figure 1.4 The dimensions of critical Bildung.

of being present in the world not only good for me, my fellow beings or the state I live in, but also good for humanity? (or, we would add today, for the whole life of this planet). Bildung is about encouraging the students to raise their reflectivity to this general level. Concerning 'existence' it amounts to the question of *who* the students think they are and want to become (i.e., questioning their self-image). Again, the point is not to impose certain images on students, but to challenge their self-understanding and encourage them to explore critically who they really are, can be, and want to become in the world in which they live.

Thus, the task of the teacher is to appeal to critical explorations of our ways of being in the world, with regard to both knowledge, attitude and existence. Bildung is, accordingly, about becoming critical-conscious about how we are present in the world, what assumptions about a good life we rely on, where these assumptions come from and what consequences they have. The school subjects are frames, that make it possible to explore these assumptions using different perspectives (e.g., a biological perspective in relation to environmental consequences). Thus, the function of the school is to *challenge* the students to become critically engaged world citizens (Paulsen and Tække, 2019a). Biesta (2017) calls this *a world-orientated view on education*. However, it can be traced back to the modern idea of *Bildung* (Klafki 2005; Koselleck 2007) but also features some aspects of Socratic Midwifery Art (Beck 2014). Also, it could be argued that part of Dewey-derived ideas about *problem-based learning* support the idea of the teacher as a challenger (Beck 2014; Dewey 1997). The same holds true for *critical hermeneutics*, when Gadamer (2003) insists that new knowledge and learning is only possible through negative experiences. Also, some parts of Bakhtin-derived forms of *dialogical teaching* (Dysthe 2013) stress that true learning and knowledge can only appear through the confrontation of different voices challenging one another. In this strain of thinking, the goal is neither to influence the students from outside (this would imply what Bakhtin calls 'the dominance of the authoritarian voice'), nor to facilitate students' internal self-development (because this will lack the element of confrontation which triggers critical self-reflexive development). Instead, the teacher's role is to question students' voices, opinions, and attitudes – that is, all they take for granted – with the aim of triggering them to develop better ways of being in the world.

The assumption behind this Bildung project is that such critical development is boh possible and necessary (Gustavsson 2017). Simply put, no one is perfect or lives a perfect life; all of us can benefit from being challenged on our basic beliefs. Yet the point is not that our beliefs are necessarily false, but that they should be maintained only if they somehow can resist being challenged; furthermore, that such challenges are likely to trigger further critical self-reflexive development (Straume 2017), in the direction of more comprehensive world-views and self-understanding (also a necessary condition for a well-functioning democracy, which we will touch on in Chapter 5).

The basic problems with the critical variant of reflective Bildung is, however, that it is too intellectual, placing too much emphasis on argument and thought reflection, without necessarily making it possible to create new and better alternatives. Likewise, it puts too much emphasis on negative aspects, critique and scepticism, challenging the students more than helping them to create and sustain new things. One could even accuse the critical and modern variant of Bildung of valorising a 'hidden curriculum', based on a certain pregiven image of the good citizen – the critical and reflective man – to which the school tries to make its students adjust; making the critical variant close to the external understanding of Bildung. In a similar way, one could argue that the critical variant relies on a philosophical anthropology in which each human – like in the internal variant – is seen as having a rational potential, which is waiting to be actualised. Thus, the critical Bildung understanding is better seen as complementing and modifying the vulgar understanding in a critically direction, than being a completely other view. Yet, with regard to media and society and human beings, the critical Bildung theory is a more elaborate response to the contingency of the modern world and the complexity and unfixed capacity opened up successively by new media. Instead of forcing students to adapt to totally fixed ideals or just facilitating their own self-development, uncritically, the critical Bildung understanding advocates for an ongoing examination of our mediated being in the world.

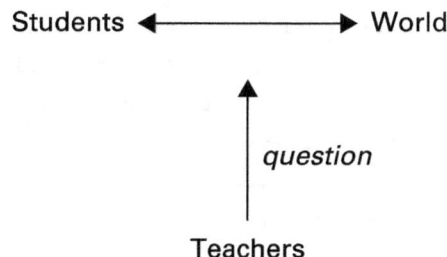

Figure 1.5 The critical understanding of Bildung.

Figure 1.5 outlines the idea of Bildung as one in which the teacher sets up questions in relation to how the students are in the world. Here, the teacher not only tries to pass on something specific to their students or influence them in certain ways but they also try to protect and facilitate the student's own self-development; on the other side, the critical teacher disapproves of self-development and confronts the students with difficult foreign voices, disturbing otherness and resistance.[14] Whether such challenges are a good thing, or are even possible, is taken for granted in this critical understanding of Bildung.

(4) Bildung as Experimental and Creative Transgression of the Existing Order

Post-modern thinking is generally sceptical about modern Bildung thinking and thinks it comes too close to both the external and internal understanding of Bildung, as described above (Lyotard 1979; Løvlie 2003, Biesta 2006). As a response to this, ideas of a more 'open' way of thinking about humanity and society has been proposed by post-modern thinking (Paulsen 2020). In this response, Bildung is seen as 'pure becoming', never coming to an end, not even in principal or teleologically speaking. In this view, Bildung is understood *as transgression* and, thus by definition, negating any finality. Yet, we regard this fourth variant of Bildung as only complementing the critical understanding of Bildung. While critical Bildung theory emphasises reflection, understanding and argumentation, the experimental understanding of Bildung that can be derived

---

[14] See Plato's Meno, where the 'passing over' model of education is rejected but so, also, is pure self-development. This is developed further by Plato in his reconceptualisation of *Paideia*, especially in the Republic, being a forerunner to the Bildung concept (and the concept of *Humanitas* – the Latin translation of Paideia by Cicero – developed further in the renaissance and then finally transformed into the Bildung concept (Jaeger 1993, Andersen 1999, Paulsen 2020).

from post-modern educational thinking (Roy 2003, Paulsen 2020), emphasises creativity, action and experiments. Both variants are critical of the existing and prevailing order and try to bring out images of education different from vulgar educational theories (Hansen 2019). What distinguishes the two reflective variants is mostly a matter of emphasis.

Yet, the fourth variant is relevant as a complement to the too-intellectualistic critical understanding. In the experimental understanding of Bildung, the task of the teacher is first to initiate and support experiments through connecting differences, which might prove to be productive and result in *new and different ways of acting, perceiving and creating* (Roy 2003). Thus, teaching is seen as a workshop, in which potentially new things can be created experimentally by putting differences together in unique ways – different teachers, students, materials, problems and other alterities. The goal is to find out which differences can resonate with each other to create something new and valuable. The teacher functions as a creator and sorcerer, who experiments with getting new things to happen in the encounter between powerful texts, beings and materials that can be capable of more together than separately (Roy 2003, Deleuze 1994, Deleuze and Guattari 2000, Braidotti 2011; 2013). In this view, Bildung is capable of perceiving, acting and creating in new and different ways that surpass the world, society and oneself in their current state, i.e. transcending the existing order and stratification of the earth, society and way of life.

The school subjects are seen as potential remedies that can be combined and used to create something new, that also recreates and transcends the borders of the subjects themselves. Thus, the school is seen as a place in which experiments ought to take place and in which the world/society/individual 'opens up' and becomes something else than it is currently positioned (Lyotard 1979, Deleuze and Guattari 2000, Ranciere 2007, Roy 2003).

Yet, if teaching is based solely on this post-modern view of education, one could object that it is not certain that students will learn what is required according to the prevailing order – the political-technocratic-bureaucratic education system of the state (specified through laws and state curriculum). The post-modern thinkers might reply that this is actually also the point – in post-modern Bildung theory students should learn *something else* – something more transversal and transformative than that already specified by the state. Yet, some post-modern thinkers would agree that the post-modern view of education is only meant to complement, not substitute, other views (e.g., Roy 2003). Thus, they will see basic schooling (e.g., learning to read and write, calculate, play, draw etc) as necessary conditions of more transgressive Bildung (edification) but pinpoint that, in the end, the latter ought to be the final task of education, while the former only should be instrumental to this undertaking (Klafki 2005, Rorty 1989 and 1999, Larsen 2014).[15]

When it comes to media and society, the post-modern Bildung theory is the most media-elaborated educational theory (of those we deal with in this book), because it basically reflects on the contingency and capacity that new media opens up, in relation to the societies that develop and are then transformed by using them (Deleuze 1994, Bryant 2014). Thus, media are seen as constitutive in developing new productive educational spaces (i.e., new possibilities of resonance and creation of new ways of perceiving, acting and creating (Latour 1999).

Figure 1.6 outlines the idea of Bildung as one in which *different* teachers together with *different* students try to create *resonance between differences* and thus produce new transformative and transversal differences – that is, new ways of being in the world. Here the teacher does not try to influence the students directly, nor facilitate their internal self-development, but neither do they try to challenge the students to reflect on their ways of being in the world. Rather the post-modern teacher tries to be an affective and creative force, who *becomes* different to anyone else and, together with different students, tries to create something anew, experimentally and rhizomatically (Deleuze and Guattari 2000), without being totally sure of what this is, and allowing everyone to pick up what they are capable of and wish to 'follow' (Deleuze 1994, Roy 2003).

Figure 1.6 The experimental understanding of Bildung.

---

[15] Luhmann (2006) observes this as a general paradox within classical Bildung thinking. It is also called the most *basic pedagogical paradox* by Oettingen (2001) in his exposure of classical Bildung thinking. On the one hand, the classical Bildung thinkers like Kant think that students must learn to think for themselves *independently of others* but, on the other hand, they must be educated to do this *by others, effecting the students from outside*. Yet, in post-modern theory, paradoxes are not theoretical calamities, but basic conditions of thinking (Deleuze 1994), moreover, the boundary between external and internal is only a contingent product of a certain way of thinking. Also, already in the classical variant of Bildung thinking, the paradox is 'solved' by giving the teacher not the role of an external determinator, but also the role of one who only ought to appeal to and encourage the individual. After all: an invitation 'to think for yourself' should not be interpreted as an external determination.

Conclusion

In this chapter we have outlined our educational theory of teaching, media and Bildung. We have argued that teaching is a historical and social invention, that opens up for contingent and risky interactions and relationships between teachers and students, taking place in schools (or other educational institutions) within the system of education. Also, we have argued that teaching only becomes possible through media such as speech, writing, printing, electronic media and now, also, digital media. Before the first great media revolution – the invention of oral language – teaching was hardly imaginable and did not exist in any similar form to what is understood by teaching today, but also with each new media revolution the capacity of teaching has increased, letting teaching come to fore as we know it today. Finally, we have argued that the open and contingent character of mediated teaching calls for a prescriptive and value-based pedagogical understanding of what it ought to mean to educate through mediated teaching. With recourse to the German Bildung tradition, but including post-modern thinking, we have outlined, compared and discussed four basic pedagogical understandings and answers. On the one hand, two vulgar or common ideas of what it ought to mean to educate through mediated teaching. These two answers – the external and internal understanding of Bildung and education – we have mainly rejected as being not sufficiently elaborated with regards to the mediated and contingent character of teaching, society and the human being. On the other hand, we have discussed two reflective and more philosophically elaborated answers and variants of Bildung – respectively, a critical and explorative and an experimental and creative understanding of education. It seems to us that these variants, together, take sufficient account of the mediated and contingent character of teaching, society, humans and other beings. Also, we have argued that only these views can be assessed as genuine Bildung theorical understandings. Together they bring out an image of education as a critical and experimental affair, in which teachers, through the media ought to encourage, challenge and support the students to become capable of exploring, critically and passionately, their mediated ways of being in the world – their knowledge, attitude and existence – but also become capable of experimenting with and creating new alternative ways of being in the world, i.e. new and potentially valuable ways of perceiving, acting and creating, which transcend the prevailing repressive world order. Taken together, we call this a critical-constructive Bildung approach.

2

The Digital Revolution

Over the last 30 years, digital media, computers and the internet have become embedded in almost every branch of social life, as well as in educational institutions. If you walk into any classroom today 'you'll find a mix of smart phones, tablet computers and smart boards' (Livingstone, 2014, p. 1) or other digital media (Paulsen and Tække, 2019b). Like other media researchers, we agree that this digitalisation has transformed the basic communicative infrastructure of teaching and society (Dede, 2016; Jenkins et al., 2013; Paulsen and Tække, 2020) and has thus sparked a media revolution comparable to those triggered by the inventions of speech, writing, printing and electronic media (Eisenstein 1983, Finneman 1997). Such media revolutions alter and expand the (im)possibility space of human activities: they afford us new options (i.e., enabling us to do things differently) (Wegerif 2013), but they also bring about challenges and problems and make concepts, norms and solutions developed in former media ecologies obsolete (McLuhan 1967, Tække and Paulsen 2016).

In this chapter, we analyse how the old classroom with its four walls becomes communicatively contaminated when teachers, students and others are equipped with computers, tablets, smartphones and a wireless network and how both new obstacles and possibilities arise in connection with this openness. Thus, the aim of the chapter is to bring forward an account of how digital transformation alters the premises of teaching, in both good and bad ways. Yet, what we provide in this chapter is only a structural analysis of the transition to digital age. In Chapter 3 we examine more extensively how actors with different educational understandings are likely to respond to and modify the new situation differently. What we intend to do in this chapter is to sketch out what the media environment initially brings forth about new educational obstacles and possibilities. Our exposure is based on the theoretical framework outlined in Chapter 1. The core of this is, that teaching is a historical and social invention, that opens up for contingent interactions between teachers and students, but also, that teaching only becomes possible through media, such as speech, writing, print, electronic media and now also digital media. With each new media revolution, the total media environment – and thus also the communicative infrastructure of teaching and society – is altered and the capacity of teaching has changed. In this chapter we flesh out this first phase of the digital media revolution with regard to education. Yet, as we also argued in Chapter 1, the contingent character of mediated teaching – especially the radical openness of contemporary media environments – can be responded to and modified differently by societies, schools, teachers and students, depending on their understandings of what it ought to mean to educate through mediated teaching. In Chapter 3 we analyse such responses and the different value-based educational stances toward the general obstacles and possibilities of digital media, that we account for here in Chapter 2.

The chapter is divided into three main parts. In the first part we sketch out our historical understanding of the educational situation *before* and *after* the arrival of digital media. This part provides us with a general framework to understand the transition to digital age.[1] Parts two and three discuss whether the digital situation gives rise to new obstacles and/or possibilities by reviewing the research. Part two examines 'media panics' and obstacles that new digital media gives rise to with regard to teaching and education, while Part three discloses to what extent new teaching practices – with new educational possibilities – can be developed through embedding digital media. We close the chapter by summarising what is educationally new when it comes to the digital situation compared with that 'before digital media'.

The School in a Historical Medium Perspective

First, the spoken language defines humans as human beings and creates the basis for society since knowledge can now not only be stored in genes, but also in the spoken language (Tække 2011). With scripture, knowledge can be communicated

---

[1] The distinction between 'before' and 'after' Internet and digital media is, to some extent, analytical. There is no single day that separates 'before' and 'after'. Yet, in, e.g., the 1990s, no schools in Denmark made use of the Internet, but, by 2020, it is now the law that every school must use IT in school (Elf and Paulsen 2020). Thus, we use the distinction 'before' and 'after' to analyse *the structural change* that has taken place as if from a distance, not noticing all the small alterations and deviations and not caring about when exactly the change happed, which is not much different to distinctions between premodern and modern times. This implies that 'before' and 'after' can be different in different countries/contexts; some in which classroom teaching might still take place today as what we structurally call 'before'. In other words: 'before' and 'after' denote two structurally different media ecologies: one without the internet and digital media and one with.

over longer periods of time and longer geographical distances than is the case of spoken language, which enabled great empires such as those of Egypt and Rome (Innis 1991; 1986). With writing we also see the first schools and the prototypical forms of Bildung as described in Chapter 1, but not before printing education began to gain the forms and structures we know today (Luhmann 2006). Printing enabled a multiplication and dissemination of the same text (via copies), which meant that, eventually, the majority of the civilised world learned to read and write. The Czech pedagogue and theologian Iohannes Amos Comenius (1592–1679) was perhaps the first to use both text and pictures in his educational book *Orbis Sensualium Pictus* (Frau-Meigs et al., 2017: 93). The advent of printing technology allowed society to revolutionise itself. In Europe the new media was used to propel phenomena such as the reformation, enlightenment and modern science (Eisenstein 1983) and eventually the public sphere and democracy (Habermas 1976). As discussed in Chapter 1, the visions of Bildung were a part of the enlightenment project and schools for ordinary people were founded from the eighteenth century onwards (e.g. in Denmark from the beginning of the nineteenth century (in 1814) all Danish children had to go to school) (Drejer 2014: 60). Typically, like in the US, this was a one-room rural schoolhouse, later replaced with the industrial-era schools we have today (Dede 2016: 105).

Since this foundation of the educational system the interactions between students and teachers has taken place within a closed classroom fenced by four walls. This is a specific type of architecture including both social and physical technology. The school is one of the societal institutions built on what Foucault (2002) calls the 'power of discipline'. We have a closed room with a teacher sitting in front of a class of students, monitoring them, asking them questions, noting marks in a protocol, etc. During the teaching time there are no interruptions from the outside: 'The interaction takes place in a closed room that is not public, so that distraction from the outside world can be minimized' (Luhmann 2006: 131). The teacher has an authoritative power over the interpretations of the printed textbook and great power over the educational interaction. The closed classroom ensures that 'the education system can control its own thematic and decide for itself when to begin, alternating or quit themes' (Luhmann 2006: 132). This closed classroom system was structured around the principle of one teacher, one book, one subject, one curriculum, one class (based on students around the same age) – and all the communication within the school-class made up a self-referential structure from lesson to lesson, allowing only students and their teacher to participate (as inside members of the communication). The students could think about their relationships outside the classroom but had no interactional access to them (while in school). In this way the teacher became not only the one held all the power as the educational leader but was also the person who decided the truth within the classroom setting.

The Main Structure of Teaching Before Internet and Digital Media

Thus, first of all, the teaching situation before the arrival of the Internet was characterised by a clear-cut distinction between classroom teaching and the outside world.[2] Interaction between teachers and students was restricted to the classroom: between teacher and students (and among the students). Here they could communicate about the outside world through representation media such as textbooks, blackboards and the assumed all-knowing teacher (functioning as the absolute Other). There were exceptions – like field trips – but these were exceptions. Before the advent of the Internet, the main structure of teaching was therefore *a two-chamber system*: on the one hand, the homes of students and what happened there were more or less different for everyone. Some got help with schoolwork, while others didn't. On the other hand, the school – that is, the classroom teaching – was mainly the same for everyone (if one was placed in the same class, with the same teacher, attending the same lesson). The consequences of this structure were chance inequalities, exclusion mechanisms and the reproduction of social classes. By this, we do not mean that these were objective results like gravity effects – rather, they were problems that different teachers (and other actors) dealt with in different ways, thus shaping the two-chamber system differently. Outside school, the students were left to their own personal networks, with created inequality because some came from highly literate and cultivated homes where the parents were educated, read books and were used to the doxa of the school system; while others came from homes with little or no education and a doxa that matched very poorly with the culture of the school. Also, it seems that teachers tended to better accept students with a more prominent social position who, through their receptions, attitudes, language codes, elegance and personality were given more weight than students who communicated in other codes (Bourdieu 1977).

---

[2] In Paulsen and Tække (2013, 2017, 2019b) the teaching situation before the advent of the Internet is analysed in detail. The following is based on Paulsen (2020).

Shapes of the Closed Classroom

Yet, societies, schools and teachers with different educational understandings shaped the closed classroom very differently.[3] To simplify matters, we suggest that the mainstream shaping developed in the old rural and later industrial era was identical with what we, in the introduction to this book, called a 'technical and causal understanding of teaching'. Before the arrival of the Internet, societies, schools and teachers with this mainstream understanding framed the closed classroom in such a way that it could be used to produce an input-output machine – or what could be called *an echo-chamber* (Paulsen and Tække 2016). The idea was to stimulate students to learn as much as possible of the same X (curriculum). A typical way of doing this would take this form: First, the students should read X in the textbook, then talk about X in the class, then write X on the blackboard and then write X down in personal notes, perhaps also making exercises or other activities about X. Finally, the students took a test where it was seen to what degree they could reproduce X. Many variations and deviations from this standard were worked out. The point here is only that, before the advent of the Internet, mainstream schools and teachers developed ways of framing teaching in the closed classroom to control the production of outputs. The implication was that the closed classroom was understood, used and modified into a control and steering technique. Interaction in this old rural and later industrial-era schools' classroom then took the form of sequences of echoes. Thus, we propose that the echo room has been the main institutional form of educational interaction called classroom teaching for the last two or three centuries. The foundational infrastructure of this has been the four walls, the blackboard, the teachers' authority, the printed book and later also copies from books, newspapers and e.g. tape recordings of native language speakers. This educational and social technology inside the classroom was developed and refined over centuries and fitted the industrial mass production where society needed many people with exactly the same qualifications and not so much autonomous thinking.

Yet, there have also been other understandings of teaching than just the technical-bureaucratic mainstream understanding (Roy 2003, Paulsen 2020). According to Drejer (2014) the mainstream 'positivistic' understanding had been challenged, especially in the twentieth century (in Denmark and similar

---

[3] The analysis of different educational responses and thus different restructurations of the basic teaching situation before and especially after the arrival of digital media and internet, is elaborated further in Chapter 3.

countries), by more 'deliberative' and democratic understandings of education but, from the beginning of the twenty-first century, the positivistic understanding of education had regained the upper hand. What we want to do here, however, is to sketch out how the closed classroom was also shaped differently than into an echo chamber – and was thus 'made sense of' by alternative understandings of education (see Chapter 1). Let us call these alternatives: (a) a facilitating and voluntaristic understanding; (b) a critical and challenging understanding; and (c) an experimental and creative understanding of education. Our aim is to show that these alternative understandings relied on the same main structure (i.e. the closed classroom, but shaped it differently). We will examine here and in Chapter 3, that because all educational actors – despite operating on the basis of different educational understandings – relied on the same main structure, they all reacted – more or less – with the same initial perplexity to the arrival of digital media and the Internet, which undermined this structure, but later began to develop different variants of the new open classroom of the digital age.

One alternative shaping of the closed classroom was carried out by societies, schools and teachers who affirmed a more facilitating and voluntaristic understanding. As an alternative they used the closed classroom to *protect* the students from the outside world and to facilitate students' *own* self-development in a safe environment. Here, teaching activities were based on students' own interests and experiences but supported by the teachers, who encouraged them to undertake projects and explore the world within their reach. The students produced posters, their own books, experiments, projects, plays, artworks, gardens, constructions, music performances, roleplays and so on. They used their bodies, instruments, pen and paper and other analogue media. The classroom/school was constructed as a secure space for all this, without interference from outside society.

Another alternative to the mainstream echo chamber was teaching developed by societies, schools and teachers who wanted to critically challenge and encourage students to become transformative citizens. Before the arrival of the Internet, these shaped the closed classroom into a place where they selectively confronted students with the strangeness of the world (e.g., using books, films, tapes, pictures of ancient artwork, clips from newspapers, or from experimental settings). The students worked in the classroom with epochal key problems such as environmental issues (Klafki, 2005), analysing the problems and discussing possible solutions critically.

Finally, there were also schools and teachers who developed even more experimental and creative forms of teaching in which students, together with their teachers, were supported to create and develop new expressions, thoughts, constructions, potentially creating new ways of perceiving, acting and being in the world.

All these variants of using the closed classroom for different educational purposes are important to take account of and remember, when it comes to discussing the consequences of the shift to digital age, to which we now turn.

The Main Structure of Teaching After Internet and Digital Media

With digital media and wireless networks, the classroom is communicatively opened. This produces both a new space and a new time. Students can access educational communication from almost everywhere and at any time. Teachers can contact and interact with their students while they are at home or elsewhere. Other people 'from the whole world' can contact students and teachers sitting in a classroom. The upshot is that communication[4] in and out of the schoolroom has increased massively, while the communication inside the classroom between the students has increased by using written interaction. Thus, with the arrival of the Internet, digital media and wireless networks (in Denmark mainly at the beginning of the twenty-first century[5]), teachers and especially students began to use digital media (in school time) to interact and communicate not only with one another but also with outsiders from the surrounding world, through interaction media like Messenger. This opened up the classroom: The clear-cut distinction between inside and outside of teaching was *deconstructed*. In the pre-Internet classroom it was impossible or very unlikely that students (and teachers) communicated with outsiders – friends, parents, politicians, sellers and so on – and also it was almost impossible to participate in other communities. However, with this new media, students can now be sitting in the classroom playing online games, participating in online communities, being politically active, sending and receiving private messages, collecting information quickly and being in touch with people from across the globe. However, they are also vulnerable to exposure to those whose commercial interests have other aims than education. All this means that the fixed boundary of classroom teaching has been destabilised:

---

[4] Communication in the most broadly sense: interaction, film watching, gambling, gaming etc.
[5] In the Danish upper secondary schools, school reform from 2005 stated that IT should be used in all subjects and daily teaching practice. Around that time, upper secondary schools began to buy wireless networks but also computers, digital blackboards etc. At the same time, it became normal for students to bring laptops to school, using them to carry out non-educational activities, like sending private messages. See Paulsen and Elf (2020) and Paulsen and Tække (2013).

Teaching can, in principle, take place anywhere and anytime, with students and teachers being in different places and the teaching situation is nowhere safe from outside influences. This implies a more complex, contingent and open teaching situation than before with new obstacles and possibilities and a lack of adequate social norms and teaching methods.

Educational Understandings of the Open Classroom

We described above how the closed classroom of the pre-Internet era was shaped and modified differently by societies, schools and teachers with different educational outlooks. We think the same is – and will be the case – when it comes to the open classroom of the digital age. Yet, based on our analysis of the development of teaching in Denmark the last 15 years (see Paulsen and Tække 2013, 2016, 2019) it seems to us that most schools and teachers, with only few exceptions, have responded with the same level of perplexity to digital media and the new radical openness. When digital media appeared – and changed everything, as described above – the first response of teachers in mainstream schools can be seen as a reaction to what the new digital media situation did to their closed classroom: it made it open and (to begin with) uncontrollable. At first, this new open room implied distraction, loss of control and loss of authority and teachers responded with frustration. They wanted to prohibit the new disturbing world: 'Shut down the Internet' they cried. While students' attention was drawn away from teaching to other things, the functioning of the mainstream teaching machine declined. Media platforms like Facebook were more likely to catch students' attention than mainstream teaching machines (Paulsen and Tække, 2016).

Even schools and teachers who based teaching on more facilitating, progressive and voluntaristic outlook were concerned. For them, opening up the classroom meant that their safety and protection was lost. Other people now had direct access to students' mental processes, 24 hours a day. Thus, actors with non-educational goals could interrupt and influence the students using glamourous content, commercials, games and so on – undermining educationally framed self-development. The first response to all this from the progressive teachers was ambivalence. On the one hand, they wanted to protect the students by trying to shut down the Internet or prohibiting the use of smartphones and/or other new media during teaching hours. On the other hand, they also wanted to respect their students' ability to make their own choices. Thus, these schools and teachers oscillated between protecting students (by trying to prohibit the use of new media during school hours) and ignoring the new situation (being too kind to prohibit media use). The result was ambivalence, confusion and conflict (Tække and Paulsen 2013).

Schools and teachers who were even more critical in their outlook and who usually used the closed classroom to challenge the students, saw, that, in the new digital environment their students were focused on other things that were more appealing but with less educational value, making it harder to challenge them. In the eyes of the students, the old analogue material looked outdated and community and dialogue within the classroom was undermined. The first response to the new media for these teachers was resignation and despair. To really challenge students and encourage them to think deeply seemed to be mission impossible in the digital age. The art of Ancient Greece, novels, classical music, difficult mathematical problems, philosophy and 'heavy' books like *Das Kapital* appeared to be impossible to bring within reach of most students' attention and interest. The frustrating thing was that more than ever before, challenges to prevailing thought and practice were required, but these were not likely to become meaningful to most students.

However, teachers in experimental and creative schools where less perplexed, after all, the shift to the digital age appeared to them like one great experiment. Yet, it also took some time for these schools and teachers to really make valuable educational use of the new media.

Thus, it can be shown that all teachers reacted with concern to the arrival of the Internet, wireless networks and digital media, because they all relied on the same basic infrastructure of teaching – the double-chamber system. Therefore, first responses to the digital age were not quite different: All were confused: Should we ignore new media, or should we prohibit them?. On the other hand, as we elaborate in Chapter 3, when societies, schools and teachers – with different educational outlooks – began to develop more advanced responses, they also begin to distinguish themselves more and more from one another. Nevertheless, there are some common features in all their different responses/strategies. They all react with frustration. This was their shared first response. Then, after a while, they began to incorporate and imbed digital media in the classroom teaching. This was their shared second response. Finally, they all begin to use digital media to make educational use of the new openness outside of the classroom, by using the Internet and digital interaction media. This was their shared third response. These similarities point to a common way of responding to the new, despite their differences. It shows a general cultural pattern in which, sooner or later, digital media was integrated educationally. That being said, it might be that we are only describing the initial phases of a digital revolution; it cannot be excluded that the future will bring different and also more rejective responses (see Chapter 5).

The Media Environment of the Digital Age

We now move on to review and discuss research literature both in relation to obstacles and possibilities and in the next chapters look from the perspective of our own research at the responses to digitalisation in the educational system. We begin by looking at the debate, then go on to assess students' competencies, then focus on the obstacles of distraction and multi-tasking before – in the third and last main section of the chapter – examining research that indicates new possibilities when digital media are embedded and integrated into everyday teaching practices.

The Debate

The present debate regarding digital media and education including children and young people's use of media is polarised; on the one side we find *IT-boosters* (e.g., politicians, tech companies and big organisations like OECD (2001, 2009) and the European Commission (2014)) but also researchers who, for instance, have suggested and promoted concepts like *digital natives* (Tække 2021). From this point of view, digital media and technology is predominantly a good thing and also necessary to implement if one wants to be in the driver's seat of the modern way of life, the global economy and the knowledge society of the future (see Elf and Paulsen 2020 about the it-boosting discourse). However, we find *IT-sceptics* (e.g., self-professed experts, parents, school leaders and teachers (Tække 2021). Yet, this debate and dichotomy is based on the common view that digital media has a unilateral impact on education; the only disagreement is whether it is positive or negative. In the research literature about media and education that relies on a deterministic view on education (speaking of impact) one can both find deterministic researchers who are mainly positive (i.e., media is changing education for the best) and deterministic researchers who are mainly negative (i.e., media is changing education for the worse) (Paulsen and Tække 2013). However, from a non-deterministic point of view this debate is almost senseless, because media does not have certain effects on education (see the introduction to this title). More non-deterministic media and education researchers therefore also tend to offer a more complex, but also more critical (in the Kantian sense – indicating both possibilities and limitations) view of media and education thus, for instance, warning against *uncritical* embedding of digital technology that are linked to commercial interests and/or new forms of surveillance, nudging, increased control, capitalism, but also techno-idealism (Livingstone 2012, Cuban 2003, Selwyn 2014, Han 2016, Sims 2017, Williamson 2017, Frischmann and Selinger 2018, Zuboff 2019). On the other hand, some IT-sceptics forward arguments about the *unconditional* harmful effects of the digital media on the biological systems level (brain damage, lack of sleep and exercise and addiction), the psychic systems level (loneliness, narcissism, low self-esteem and self-harm) and the social level of systems formation (bullying, asocial behaviour, normlessness or countercultural norms, unwanted photo sharing, echo chambers and the sharing of fake news) (Tække 2021).[6]

Our own position is in accordance with the critical and non-deterministic position outlined above, to go beyond the debate between IT-boosters and IT-sceptics. Thus, we would argue that the questions of new media and technology are important but call for nuanced answers that take account of the pros and cons of the new media, but also take account of the 'dynamic' situation; meaning that positive and negative effects are never 'unconditional' but depend on the specific societal and cultural ways media are selected, innovated, understood and used within a given society (Finnemann 2008). This implies that the advantages and disadvantages of new media cannot be determined in any simple way, neither speculatively nor empirically. Thus, we reject all simple answers like (a) new digital media has only negative effects; (b) only positive effects; or (c) completely definite effects (negative and/or positive). Instead, we propose that societies, schools, teachers and students transform themselves in unpredictable ways, when they begin to act in new media environments that include digital media, responding to and modifying the new media situation, together or in conflict with other actors (e.g., companies and politicians). If we go back in media history, the inventors of the alphabet, for instance, could not in any way foreshadow the many different real consequences of the new transformative capacity that the alphabet afforded together with other media (Luhmann 1995, Paulsen and Tække 2009). This implies that we must be careful and avoid general and deterministic statements and acknowledge that effects and consequences depend on how different actors use, respond to and continuously modifies the whole media environment (e.g. in democratically or totalitarian directions and also are being transformed at the same time) by these activities. In other words: media and society/school are tightly intertwined, almost as a seamless web and

---

[6] We return to the IT and generally media-sceptic research and provide the research in children's sleep later in this section as an example.

can only analytically be separated. Thus, it would be more adequate to describe and understand society and media/school as 'media using people' who transform themselves and the media – and their capacities – in unpredictable ways into 'new media using people', configured differently.

Also if we, as critical media scholars, observe the debate one thing that stands out is that it is an old debate re-actualised every time a new medium comes into use (Frau-Meigs et al., 2017: 93–98). Drotner (1999) defines the debate as media panic or even as moral media panic (see the classical works on 'moral media panic' by McLuhan 1967 and Cohen 2002) and, according to her, every time a new mass medium has entered the social, it has spurred public debates and: 'In some cases, debate of a new medium brings about [...] heated, emotional reactions: in that case we have to do with what may be defined as a media panic. It may be considered a specification of the wider concept of moral panic and it has some basic characteristics: the media is both instigator and purveyor of the discussion; the discussion is highly emotionally charged and morally polarised (the medium is either "good" or "bad") with the negative pole being the most visible in most cases; the discussion is an adult discussion that primarily focuses on children and young people' (Drotner: 996). Drotner's oldest example is from 1795 where a group of evangelical philanthropists in Britain launched a zealous campaign against women reading short stories: 'the poison continually flowing thro' the channel of vulgar and licentious publications' (Drotner: 599). According to Luhmann (2000b: 139 n 23; 142 n 12) the concept of the authentic first came with the print and mass media. Not before printed books, the distinction between those who experienced the world at first hand and those who experienced it second hand through reading books came into language. In relation to digital media Drotner (1999: 595) writes that cases from the USA were reported in Denmark as early as 1998 by the Danish newspaper *Berlingske Tidende* (17 March 1998) under the headline: 'The Internet is addictive like narcotics.' This sounds like the headings in today's debate about smartphones and social media. An example of a media moral panic, which seems to come back with every new medium, is one in relation to sleep. When we look into the topic like Matricciani et al. (2012), who made a systematic review of 32 sets of medical recommendations for sleep from 1897 to 2009 the problem seems to be a permanent public conflict: 'Recommended sleep duration consistently exceeded actual sleep duration by about 37 minutes . . . as if children always needed extra sleep, no matter how much they were actually getting. The rationale for sleep recommendations was also strikingly consistent for more than 100 years: children were overtaxed by the stimulation of modern living, although that stimulation was embodied in whatever the technological avatar of the time was.' The stimulations included schoolbooks, radio, television and the Internet. The review also highlighted the 'consistency with which authors acknowledged the lack of empirical foundation for their recommendations, despite extremely detailed and quantified guidelines. It is remarkable that after more than 100 years, sleep recommendations are still being issued in the acknowledged absence of meaningful evidence' (Matricciani et al., 2012: 553).[7] The situation today is that the mass media listens more to researchers if they can come up with a conflict angle like: 'It's "digital heroin": How screens turn kids into psychotic junkies.'[8]

The New Media Situation

Instead of deterministic statements and beliefs, we suggest that one should analyse the concrete new media situation (i.e. the whole media environment, including both digital and non-digital media and also analyse how different actors understand, respond to and modify this situation and what effects and consequences such understandings, actions and modifications seems to have). As suggested above, our own analysis indicates that the most important feature of the new media environment is the radical openness that is afforded by digital media. We have noticed that some initial and visible implications with regard to teaching in schools in the Danish upper secondary school context are:[9]

1. The classroom has become more *uncertain* than ever before, because the possibilities of communication both inside the class and with outsiders increases with digital media.
2. Students seem to have problems with being attentive to the teaching and being present in the classroom *and* also 'answer back' and being attentive to outsiders and online fora.
3. Some students describe themselves – or are being attributed – as *digitally addicted*, meaning that they cannot control themselves and do what they really want in the new alluring and appealing media landscape with online games and other temptations.

---

[7] Here quoted in in line with the latest OECD report Burns and Gottschalk (2019).
[8] *New York Post*, 27 August 2016.
[9] It should be noted that this is not a list of general consequences, but only consequences that we found in the Danish upper secondary school context. Not all schools in other contexts have the same equipment, not all students and teachers can be supposed to use the media they have access to in the same way and not all schools will have the same laws and political and educational infrastructure as Denmark, for better or for worse. Nonetheless, we think that the six consequences that we outlined in the Danish context tells a story about how it is likely that schools and teachers might respond initially, given similar contextual constraints.

4. Some students think the right strategy in the new media environment is to *multi-task*, that is simultaneously being attentive to the teaching and other things, made accessible through digital media. As we elaborate, such a strategy is not advisable.
5. The awareness of students is also interpellated and caught by social media, advertisements, commercial companies and others who, through digital media, can capture their attention even when they are in school. The initial result is a 'war over students' attention', declining attention in school and a weakening of the power of the mainstream teaching machine.
6. Teachers initially – as described earlier in this chapter – tend to respond either with ignorance of these problems or try to prohibit non-educational relevant media use, without great success.

See Paulsen and Tække 2013

Yet, our point is not that these and similar problems of the new open classroom and teaching in digital age are totally unavoidable facts. Rather they are concrete and *exemplary* problematic aspects of the *initial* phase of the new situation. Also, as we argue later in this chapter, but even more in Chapters 3 and 4, these six obstacles can all be responded to in different ways and modified, to some extent, even into being educationally valuable. For instance: social media use can draw students' attention away from teaching *but* if teachers begin to use social media to mediate teaching, the same media can also be used to draw their attention back again. Also, the six problems, we have indicated, are related primarily to an initial situation, in which digital media and the internet has become available, both in school and outside school, but in which normal teaching does not yet make use of the media to any great extent, when it comes to fulfilling educational aims. Likewise, the problems are tied to a situation in which most student's understanding of and experience and success with acting and developing a good school life in the new media environment is very limited (in opposition to the belief that they are digital natives and therefore have great digital skills).

Students' Competencies – The Present Situation

Peruvian scientist Eliana Gallardo Echenique, in a review article based on reading 355 publications, has sought to find out what we should put into concepts such as digital natives, net generation and millennials (Echenique 2014).[10] It

---

[10] This section is based on Paulsen and Tække (2018).

turns out that those who praise digital natives base their view on anecdotes and not on scientifically valid methodology (see also Helsper and Eynon 2009). They induce a picture of young digital natives (vs. immigrants) who are team-orientated, collaborative and capable of multi-tasking between many different media (Helsper and Eynon 2009: 169). Critical empirical research rejects this view. There is no significant difference to immigrants and so-called digital natives usually have a superficial understanding of the new technologies and have only limited capabilities for very specific purposes and only superficial knowledge of, for example, search and analysis. Only a few can manage more advanced new technologies. Their abilities are less advanced than the teachers think, and they do not form a homogeneous group in terms of their technological ability. Therefore, one should not assume that they can manage much, on the contrary, they must learn it through a teaching that takes this upon itself. Only a small group knows anything special about technology. The conclusion is that the concept of digital natives (and similar concepts) is merely anecdotal (Helsper and Eynon 2009: 169–72).

Researchers Cinque and Brown (2015) take up the story by pointing out that young people, here under the label 'generation next', are not necessarily good at managing new media. The empirical basis put forward by Cinque and Brown is from Australia, where several hundred students who had just started at the university answered a questionnaire. What is being studied is what screens the students are looking at for how long and for what purposes. The researchers conclude that young people are not very skilled in their IT use and almost always try to 'google' themselves out of problems 'over the development of research skills via electronic databases and scholarly journals'. To this end, they spend little time using IT in pursuit of their studies (Cinque and Brown: 2015).

The researchers Gretter and Yadav (2016) find a big gap between those who can deal with technical subjects and those who cannot; here, the researchers believe that the schools must close the gap. This by combining science (programming) and the humanities (critical thinking). They refer to Jenkins (2008, 2006) who thinks we should become participants and learn to work in networks. The point is that through the scientific programming skills we can practice our media literacy (Gretter and Yadav 2016). However, Iversen et al. (2018) do not believe that everyone should learn how to program and that for those who nevertheless do it, that education in programming cannot stand alone because a basic knowledge of algorithms and pattern recognition does not entail a critical and reflexive attitude towards the digital society. For this, programming alone does not give students the prerequisites to make informed choices regarding technology and participation in technology development. Instead, Iversen et al. (2018) propose 'computational empowerment' that shifts the focus from programming as an end in itself, to imparting the necessary characteristics and resources to students to participate in technological development. This is done through participatory design where students are supported to develop skills, competencies and critical understanding (Bildung) and are also encouraged to engage in creating improvements for the digitalised society. Of course, we agree that programming itself does not develop critical thinking. It would probably be too difficult for non-mathematically orientated classes to have to learn it (to a greater extent). In this context we find it important to consider Iversen et al.'s (2018) methods to help students who do not directly learn to program, to be able to reflect critically on, for example, Facebook's functional infrastructure regulated by algorithms. The important thing is that no student should go through high school without being challenged to reflect critically on technology and to learn to express themselves, to participate in the digital society on an enlightened level.

This indicates that there is a need to rethink the scientific, technical and mathematical education fields, but perhaps also the interdisciplinary connection between educational areas. One may well consider whether a new subject such as *Informatics* would be a solution or the IT competencies should be addressed in single subjects, including interdisciplinary courses where students work together across subjects, such as literature, mathematics and social studies.

Fu (2013) speaks about three sets of problems that constrain the digital education of students. The first set is that many teachers do not have the necessary ICT skills and experience, have technology prejudices and lack the time and support to acquire skills in the new media. To this end, many teachers are under pressure from national tests, exams and the like. Second, many teachers use new technology as an extension of existing ways of teaching that they do not change. The third set of barriers is organisational and administrative. School leaders focus more on quantity and student test results than on how ICT is used. For this, schools do not always provide adequate support, hardware, software, continuing education, etc. To this end, a review of Norwegian conditions points to an overall problem regarding rules and guidelines (Engen et al., 2015).

All in all, students' capabilities are overestimated and teachers lack the skill, experience and an adequate understanding of the new situation, that are not developed because of prejudice, lack of time, tests, management and regulation.

The Obstacles and Possibilities for Attention

Research on multi-tasking clearly seems to reject its use in learning situations.[11] If students do multi-task, the research shows that the tasks in question will be performed more poorly and take longer, with students learning and remembering less about what they have done than when tasks are performed one at a time (Pashler, 1994; König, 2005; O'Brien, 2011; Rekart, 2012; Lee et al., 2012). One mitigating factor is that young students, to some extent, learn to cope with media activities occurring at the same time as teaching (Bardhi et al., 2010). After all, multi-tasking is not a pathology (Aagard, 2018).

For more than 100 years, psychologists have been interested in the (in)ability to perform two or more activities at the same time (Pashler, 1994). In general, research shows that our attention is disturbed if we try to do several things at the same time (Pashler, 1994). However, 'attention' is a term that covers several sub-areas of consciousness, perception, memory functions, etc., implying metaphysical/philosophical discussions and ambiguities (Pashler, 1994). However, others (e.g, König, 2005) do not define multi-tasking as performing different activities simultaneously, but as the ability to achieve multiple action goals within the same time period, by switching between individual activities to achieve certain goals. In this definition, multi-tasking is perceived as the ability to switch rapidly between different activities – rather than being able to perform these activities strictly simultaneously.

It can be concluded that students may not be able to multi-task effectively in the strict definition of the word, but that they can learn to switch more effectively between different activities. In a study of 132 undergraduate students, König (2005) shows that it is not possible to multi-task effectively, in the sense of simultaneously performing several tasks at the same time, but that we do have the ability to switch between different activities, depending on how good our short-term memory or working memory is. However, this individual ability is not just something that can be learned – it can also be unlearned. For instance, older people are typically less able to switch between different activities that require decisions, actions and reflection than young people. But no matter how good your working memory is, it seems to be weakened by multi-tasking (in the strict sense of performing different tasks simultaneously) (O'Brien, 2011). One test of 130 students shows that we absorb less information when we do more than one thing at a time (e.g., watching a video and reading, then answering

---

[11] This section is based on Paulsen and Tække (2019b).

questions) (Lee et al., 2012). Also, Kuznekoff et al. (2015) show how damaging multi-tasking is for learning in teaching situations in a research set up where they distract students during teaching. Yet, such laboratory experiments are both reductionistic and damaging for the debate about digital media in relation to education (Paulsen and Tække 2019b). According to Aagard (2018) such experiments (like those by Lee et al., 2012, König 2005 and Kuznekoff et al., 2015) only cover situations in which students attend classes and are simultaneously asked to perform tasks which have nothing to do with the teaching. Such studies only deal with cases where digital media was used exclusively and explicitly to distract the students and the result is hardly surprising: students cannot concentrate fully when they are distracted.

Single-Tasking, Multi-Tasking and Multiplexing

Following Paulsen and Tække (2019b) the counter concept to multi-tasking is single-tasking. Single-tasking does not imply that people are thinking of only one thing for a certain period of time. Logically, if a person reflects on a topic, the topic involves (most often if not always) several objects, concepts and causalities. As a result, creative thinking implies a kind of multi-perspectivism but is still a kind of thinking in which topics and concepts from completely irrelevant fields do not intervene. Using a Husserlian term, the intentional object is given in a horizon that enlightens it as a meaningful context (Pietersma, 2000). One borderline case could be what Pierce calls abduction, defined as a situation in which a concept from another domain enlightens our thinking like a metaphor (Jørgensen, 1993). In our definition of single-tasking, abduction involves single-tasking if this technique of reasoning is used to inform and understand only one single intentional learning object. Another borderline case is group work, in which a polyphony of different meanings meet each other in discussions. Again, we draw a distinction by saying that if a class or group only discusses one single object (e.g. how to understand X, we refer to this as single-tasking). If some people in the group begin to discuss other objects (Y, Z etc.) in an unrelated way, we refer to this as multi-tasking.

Now the question is if single-tasking in this definition is possible and perhaps more useful and better suited to the present environment. This is a very old discussion because as mentioned in Chapter 1, Plato made it clear that writing harms our memory. What Plato could not know is that history has shown that, because of writing, arguments have grown longer and more consistent and our vocabulary has grown much bigger (Ong, 1982). The start of printing means that this process continued and new developments took off like the invention of the index and the possibility of comparing arguments (Eisenstein, 1983). Even so, Plato is still right in one sense because our ability to remember things by heart has declined as we have learned to write things down, look things up in an encyclopaedia etc. On the other hand, this also means that humans began to use more than one medium when performing activities like studying, thinking, communicating, reflecting, learning etc. This combined use of several media with different and supplementing intellectual affordances has produced a new version of homo sapiens with much larger cognitive capacities. Inspired by Fahey and Meaney (2011), we call this phenomenon *multiplexing*. We define multiplexing as focusing our attention on the same intentional object using more than one medium.[12] Even in the pre-internet school system, many different multiplex strategies had been developed. For instance, teachers said things aloud as they wrote them on the blackboard; while students listened, looked at the blackboard and wrote things down in their notebooks.

The new media situation for our attention calls for both critical and creative (Bildung) perspectives on education and media; meaning that schools and teachers should support, encourage and challenge students to both *reflect* on their attention, the 'war of attention', their effect on others' attention, but also *experimenting* with developing new ways of being attentive in the new media environment. This new educational aim is required in the digital age.

New Teaching Practices

Now we turn to new possibilities for improved teaching practices and/or practices that are necessary in the new medium environment.[13] We are talking enhanced professionalism, media literacy and Bildung that teachers from around the world, have invented and which have been documented by researchers. By new teaching practices, we mean new teaching-orientated understandings and uses of media in digitalised society that are relevant in different ways in relation

---

[12] The concept literally means multi (many) plex (fold), like manifold. Fahey and Meaney (2011) only mention the concept *en passant*: 'It's not "multi-tasking" to take notes or have a conversation with your colleagues during a presentation—as long as you're talking about the topic at hand. Some call this "multiplexing" where overlapping tasks are closely related to each other and even complementary. Attention is not lost in muliplexing—in fact, it is multiplied.' The concept is also used in cross fields between neuroscience and computational mathematics in a comparable way with ours (Feng et al. 2014).

[13] The section about teaching practices is based on Paulsen and Tække (2018).

to the school's knowledge areas and, of course, to society and for the single human being in the digitalised society. We distinguish between four such new practices:

1. New participation practices (interaction).
2. New community practices (organisation).
3. New expression practices (production).
4. New impression practices (interpretation).

All four practices can, in principle, be actualised in one and the same teaching, meaning that, in such a teaching, there are both developed new ways of *participation* (in a class) and new ways of maintaining the *community* among students and staff through embedding digital media, but also new educational ways of working with impressions (e.g., finding and reading text) and expressions (e.g., making presentations). In the following, we review research literature that are relevant in relation to each of the four fields of practices. The aim is to discuss whether societies, schools and teachers, equipped with digital media, would be able – at least in principle – to develop new and different teaching practices that, on a general level, seem educationally relevant. For instance: if it is possible with digital media to expand educationally relevant ways of participating in teaching, almost everyone would agree that this might make it better, at least for those who otherwise would have weaker participation possibilities. Yet, we are aware that the same 'general possibilities' can be used for different purposes (both good and bad). We follow up this issue in Chapters 3 and 4. At present, our concern is only to discuss at a general level whether digital media opens up new teaching practices.

1. New Participation Practices (Interaction)

New participation practices build on an understanding and application of new possibilities for interaction and participation in the new media environment. We especially observe this in the form of written interaction especially through so-called 'social media'[14] that can be set up with private settings which either allow interaction or exclude it. Interaction media expands teaching possibilities as

---

[14] We define social media in line with Linaa-Jensen and Tække (2018: 42) as: 'a special type of Internet service where users can communicate (including, for example, sharing information, pictures and music). They operate through a digital infrastructure that enables, delimits and influences communication. Social media content is user-generated (produced, remixed, or at least copied). In principle, they allow for interaction (two-way communication). Last, they can almost always be accessed through different kinds of interfaces and different terminals.'

they change the environment in which we experience, think and communicate by adding a parallel virtual space for interaction to the visual and auditive face-to-face space (Tække 2002). Temporally, many can be actively participating in the interaction simultaneously, while spatially, participants may be physically separated, e.g. they participate from home or from abroad (Tække and Paulsen 2013; Crook 2008: 5).

International research into the use of digital media to promote interaction and participation has – so far – mostly been conducted at American universities. It shows positive results from both qualitative and quantitative experiments and studies with social media in education (Ebner et al., 2008, McNely 2009, Moody 2010, Junco et al., 2010, Atkinson 2010, Lowe and Laffey 2011, Shannon 2011, Elavsky et al., 2011, Elavsky 2012, Hosterman 2012, Yaros 2012), as well as in online courses where the use of social media is also proven to give students an improved social community with each other (Holotescu and Grosseck 2008, Dunlap and Lowenthal 2009). There are also studies that show that the media, if used properly, has a positive impact on the study environment (Ellison et al., 2007, Wright 2010, Elavsky et al., 2011, Reid 2011, Webb 2012). Here, we concentrate on the interactive aspect in regard to education and focus on the written interaction used in the SME project (see Chapter 3), primarily the use of Twitter for particular educational purposes.

The choice of Twitter in the SME class was particularly inspired by an American project in which researchers could report good results (Junco et al., 2010). The researchers describe a semester-long experimental study that investigated the use of Twitter in teaching. There were 70 participants in the study, with a control group of 55 first-year university students. The trial showed both significantly better engagement and grades in the Twitter group than in the control group. It also showed that both students and teachers became engaged in learning processes that transcended traditional classroom activities. The study shows that contact between teacher staff and students improved (2010: 10). The use of Twitter was also found to encourage students' cooperation both academically and socially. Twitter homework provided more educational activity and provided better feedback opportunities not only in homework, but in all sorts of other things. For example, there was a group that had problems accessing an online video that was on the syllabus; by using Twitter they immediately obtained help. The researchers, in comparison to the control group that used only Ning (a system similar to Lectio and Black Board), concluded that those using Twitter had more and better communication with their teachers. Similar results have been obtained by Menkhoff et al., (2015) and Kinsky and Bruce (2015) and good results have also been documented with Twitter in language teaching (Montero-Fleta et al., 2015). According to Menkhoff et al. (2015), Twitter is a good medium for creating academic engagement, where more people have the opportunity to express themselves and where the teacher is better positioned to observe whether students have understood the academic content. The use of Twitter is described as a new form of classroom teaching. Hattem and Lomicka (2016) discuss 18 studies where Twitter has been used in language teaching. Again, the results are predominantly positive and the only criticism, besides a number of tips for successful use, is that Twitter can seem overwhelming and can cause information overload.

Overall, in the new media environment, with Twitter and other social media, the possibilities to create educational interaction are expanded, thus creating more participation opportunities and forms that can not only be adapted to the different disciplines and educational areas in the school but can also redefine them. The latter, however, especially where third parties are invited into the interaction (what we define in Chapter 3 as 'third-wave teaching'), thus enable students to encounter a range of otherness that works conducive for Bildung, in living and engaging ways with content and form, which exceeds what a teacher in combination with a textbook can offer alone. Students connect to groups, other school classes, individuals (e.g., experts and databases, using the new medium environment as part of their education (Paulsen and Tække 2016). They take part in the convergence culture (Jenkins 2008) carrying out produsage (Bruns 2008), learning to navigate and take part in the new society and its forms of production, network, communication and culture. Where the teacher and textbook have previously been the primary 'otherness' through which students were to become good educated citizens, in school, this can now be expanded by meetings with other people and using content over the Internet; the teacher takes responsibility for these meetings as being academically and educationally relevant (Paulsen and Tække 2016c). Especially in the linguistic, cultural and humanistic educational spheres, there is research that indicates there is potential to strengthen the interaction and participation dimension of school subjects (Montero-Fleta et al., 2015; Hattem and Lomicka 2016).

According to Krutka (2015), this overall view appears to give a different picture to that of Postman's more pessimistic view. Admittedly, there is much about the Internet that fits with Postman's criticism in terms of technopolis: increased information overload, increased focus on speed and efficiency, individualisation and the like.

According to Postman (1993), education in Technopolis is quantified (e.g. grade systems and multiple-choice tests) and made into an economic relationship (e.g. taximeter systems and the like). In contrast, Postman argues that it is important to have meaning and coherence in education (an argument shared by Biesta 2006 and Klafki 2005). However, according to Postman (1993:186), modern education is characterised by the absence of meaning and coherence, since in a modern curriculum there is no central pervasive idea; on the other hand, modern education is simply a combination of subjects (see Klafki 2005 for similar criticism). Similarly, there is no vision of a person with Bildung other than a person with skills (i.e. a machine-human, only a technical ideal (thus the first of the two vulgar variants of Bildung that we criticised in Chapter 1)). Likewise, there is research that describes how new digital technologies are used for monitoring, behavioural control and testing (Livingstone 2014) that reinforce the features of the modern that Postman criticises. For example, Twitter has also been criticised for creating information overload, narcissism and having a mind-boggling format. Nevertheless, Krutka (2015) points to the potential these media have that point in a different direction. According to Krutka, media platforms like Twitter enable what he calls *affinity rooms* for professional exchange and development and emotional support from energetic colleagues.[15] The use of hashtags enables people to come together on topics to create dialogue and purposeful action (see also Poshka 2014 and the concept of public pedagogy). For example, educators (teachers, principals, educational researchers and others) have created these hashtags where substantial communication occurs. This allows teachers and others to connect with colleagues with similar interests and engage in social dialogue that was not possible when using individual personal computers. Krutka also mentions hour-long moderated chats on topics that address professional education challenges.

We conclude, in line with Krutka (2015), that the new media environment gives rise to both obstacles and possibilities and that it is, therefore, crucial to cultivate a critical and creative media usage that can go up against Technopolis and create a more humanistic, meaningful and context-based culture, through the new possibilities for participation.

2. New Community Practices (Organisation)

Community practices also relate to participation but at the organisational level. The new forms of participation require the development of norms and ethics

---

[15] See Mueller et al. (2014) for the similarity of online teacher collaboration based on Lave and Wenger's concept of practice communities.

that enable participation, as well as the acquisition of norms when connecting to communities, groups and networks outside the classroom. For example, many may be actively participating in the interaction at the same time. Spatially, for example, it must be organised so students can participate from home or from excursions and the class can connect with resource persons who are located elsewhere. All these opportunities require the development of community practices if they are to be actualised. There are a number of specialised media such as Wiki and YouTube that, in collaboration with interaction media like Twitter and Facebook and the digital board in the classroom, can provide fruitful media chains[16] (Paulsen and Tække 2013; 2015), as well as online supervision and feedback (Buus 2013). However, there are also a number of softer values where social media is important for a good teaching community and school environment (Ellison et al., 2007; Holotescu and Grosseck. 2008; Dunlap and Lowenthal 2009; Wright 2010; Elavsky et al., 2011; Reid 2011; Webb 2012; Avram 2014). With soft values we mean the potential to establish a better community. If the new media is used by students and teachers, there will be more opportunities to get to know each other, build trust, create things together, become friends, bond and maintain relationships, get to know each other's friends and form sub-communities, 'backchannel', network and plan parties and do homework together. In addition, general principled guidelines for the appropriate use of media such as Facebook may need to be decided for the entire school/institution (Wang et al., 2014; Menzies et al., 2017).

According to Ellison et al. (2007), a media platform like Facebook can help students accumulate, maintain and transfer social capital, help convert latent ties into weak ties by making visible information about one's-self and mutual friends, or friends of friends. Intensive use of social media provides a form of social capital that can be transferred so that one can exchange ideas and perspectives. However, Zeng et.al (2012) state that it is important that all institutions create a social media strategy. There are risks of defamation, bullying, copyright violation and, for example, false advertising. On the other hand, in the worst-case scenario, rules can violate freedom of expression and obstruct communication and participation. Thus, there are good reasons to establish guidelines for the use of a medium like Facebook (Wang et al., 2014; Menzies et al., 2017). There is no doubt that there are many positive experiences with the use of Facebook (e.g. in

---

[16] By media chain we understand the interaction between several media, for example the class is looking for relevant websites and tweet them to a common hashtag, where the pages are subjected to source criticism, again via Twitter, after which there are oral discussions about communication strategy in spite of rehearsal and finally the knowledge gained is entered into a wiki or a Google page – ready for retrieval in relation to the coming examination period.

first language teaching (Marciano 2015)). In addition, Leaver and Kent (2014) and Avram (2014) point out that the Facebook group function is good for teaching, as you can organise academic activities and content where you do not need to be friends with the students (one of the possible legal, personal or moral problems). You can ask students to contribute resources, annotate material online, make criticisms, review or just comment during the lessons. Facebook can provide an expanded space for interaction with other students and teachers, which can offset a lack of informal face-to-face discussions. At the same time, both Leaver and Kent (2014) and Zuboff (2019) point out that the teacher asks students to join a company that commercialises user data. In our opinion, this seems unacceptable in a democratic context, but in today's Denmark, Facebook is currently the number one social mainstream medium culturally, socially, commercially and politically.

In conclusion, social media can be a good platform through which to organise teaching, but it is not without its problems. On the one hand, there are poor and time-consuming systems such as Blackboard (the same conclusion reached by Mueller et al., 2014) and, on the other hand, there is Facebook's commercial monitoring of users.

3. New Expression Practices (Production)

Expression practice relates to the area of articulating oneself in the digitised community. It requires knowledge to write text for microblogging and blogging, as well as graphically setting up a blog, editing a video movie, recording a podcast, etc. One must be able to set who can watch and advertise the media product. You have to be able to handle different genres and aesthetics, as well as handle the programs that control the setup and execution of different media products. For this, there are soft skills such as being able to see social codes in the circles that one wants publish in. For example, might someone be offended? In addition, the discussion on whether students should learn to code, which can be both relevant in terms of expressing themselves through animations, games, etc., and in generating better reflexivity regarding the digital infrastructure regulated by algorithms and surveillance capitalism. It is important that instrumental skills are embedded in and never separated from humanistic, emancipatory and democratic educational aims (see Klafki 2005 and the critical Bildung tradition described in Chapter 1).

To take an example, we can look at weblogs: following the literature, blogs can be used for many things (e.g. language teaching) (Al-Qallaf et al., 2016, Karlsen 2015) and for professional immersion (Liburd et al., 2011, p. 23). According to

Karlsen 2015), a blog can function as both material and link collection and as supplement and variation in relation to written submissions. A study by Al-Qallaf et al. (2016) was teaching English as a foreign language. The results of the study showed that students came to write longer sentences with fewer errors in grammar and spelling. The students were more motivated and more positive about the subject than before. The teachers were also excited but were concerned about their own digital literacy skills. It was a closed class blog where one of the researchers acted as moderator and students and teachers could leave comments. The topics were based on curriculum, letters to friends, travel experiences and analyses of both educational films and other films (2016: 531). In the first two weeks of the 12-week project, the moderator (i.e. the researcher!) introduced some technical challenges; to create an account, post text, post photos, etc. In week four, a certificate was promised to those who showed more than a basic interest in blogging. In week five, the blog posts doubled. From week five, the moderator uploaded a video once a week to write about. All students were happy for feedback – preferably instant. Corrected errors were observed to have a positive impact on later blog texts (2016: 534). Thus, the experiment clearly shows that the students felt that they were motivated by writing blog posts and they learned the technical while working more with the English academic content than otherwise.

Another example is online shared documents such as Google.docs documented by Elavsky (2012) and Dall (2015), Mathisen (2015) and Løvschall (2015) from the BIT-project (that we followed as researchers). According to Dall (2015), shared documents can be used to strengthen writing in history and other subjects. However, the teacher must design the documents to suit specific academic needs and ideas. Initially, the teacher must work with the students so that they have a common understanding of the structure of the multi-modal texts, tables and pictures as they will all have different levels of media literacy.

The upshot is that many new educational relevant possibilities of expression – especially new and better possibilities of co-producing expressions in a class and/or together with others, as well as remixing former expressions and contributing to further remixing and culturation – come with the new media. New genres as fan culture, for instance, has also emerged and exploded in the last decades.

4. New Impression Practices (Interpretation)

There are myriads of specialised media that can be used in teaching. The textbook has been the primary reading medium in education since the acquisition of the print medium. Other media such as photocopies, the blackboard, films, overhead projectors and various authentic materials (e.g., newspaper articles) have been added as supplements over the years. With the advent of digital media, the old reading media have ben both re-mediated and re-functionalised (Finnemann 2005). In addition, information search and source criticism are now among the most important areas of impression practice. It is a common school practice (at least in Denmark) to search the Internet for facts and solutions to problems in all subjects. However, it is not an inherent feature to be able to find through the search engine's algorithmic structure and operation forms, as well as the use of the Boolean operators, how URLs are structured and how searches can be specified, etc. (Paulsen and Tække 2019). In addition, there is the whole field of source criticism, where students must, for example, orient themselves to various websites' own source references and/or the commentary track on Wikipedia. In an age of alternative news, mis- and disinformation, outdated school books and maps and access to large scientific databases, it is an educational problem in all academic fields, as well as an expression of critical Bildung, to be able to search information and to be able to relate critically to it, including being able to remix it in accordance with copyright and professional academic standards for originality and source references.

As we have already mentioned, notions of the great abilities of the digital native do not hold true (Echenique 2014; Cinque and Brown 2015), to which students look more for relevance than for credibility when searching (Kiili 2012) and can only poorly understand underlying business motives (Kiili et al., 2018). The use of Google and Wikipedia often takes place behind the back of teachers, which must also be seen as evidence for not (enough) teaching in information search and source criticism (Schreiber 2017: 221). If students are to be properly supported for the digitalised society, they must be encouraged to search for information and challenged to source criticism in school (Gretter and Yadav 2016).

Just as in relation to expression practices, there seem to be new, educationally valuable, ways of generating impressions in connection with the new media environment. Many new impressions can be established in teaching through the Internet and new ways of searching information and making interpretations can be created. At the same time, the enormous amounts of available information of dubious quality mean that it is important to encourage and support students to become better able to relate to sources critically.

Literacy and Digital Media Practices

Following Hutchison et al. (2016) who surveyed 1,262 students aged 9–12, the following applies: 'There is a need to support schools and teachers in understanding how to integrate digital technology into literacy instruction in a way that supports the development of the full range of literacy skills that students need, are able to do and prepares students to be literate in a digital world' (2016: 436). According to Hutchison et al. (2016), literacy today cannot simply consist of reading and writing printed texts; one must also learn to read and write digital texts. This dualistic idea means that the reader must not only be able to decode alphabetical texts but must be able to make sense of information based on images, sounds, videos, colours and combinations. To do this, one must be capable of locating information that is relevant in evaluating the validity and reliability of the information. Students must be able to navigate a digital device and understand a plurality of contexts, vocabularies and norms that are not normally associated with printed texts (e.g., understanding the use of URLs). To do this, they must also be able to communicate effectively digitally. Socio-culturally, literacy is about applying knowledge for specific purposes in specific use contexts. As the web is interchangeably, large and varied, it requires many forms of background knowledge and skills to make sense of it. The goal is not only to be consumers, but also to contribute to collective knowledge (2016: 436).

Digital Teaching Practices – Aims and Means

Marner and Örtegren (2013) and Marner (2013) discuss how the introduction of the new media in some subjects (where the media is part of the substance), transforms the subjects, which is consistent with the media-ecological perspective (see medium theory in Chapter 1). Marner (2013) reports on the use of IT in art education in upper school in Sweden and is based on observation and interview. The students find that the use of the computers is involved in everything in relation to the pictures. They make remix (e.g., the last supper with junk food). The students are inspired by each other and the older ones help the younger ones. This produces a multi-vocal teaching environment where everyone helps, inspires and instructs each other (Marner 2013: 365). A student expresses that it is not art teaching, but teaching in creativity, since they learn to use what they already have in their heads. Students are aware of the distinction between mastering and appropriation: 'This indicates that pupils are aware of the difference between what Wertsch (1998) calls mastery (learning to master the medium on the medium's terms) and appropriation (mastering the medium on one's own terms)' (Marner 2013: 366). The mastery became so good that students did not get good grades for the performance of the technical aspects (to paint a nice horse), but for the realisation of ideas (Marner 2013: 367). The teacher also supervises from home and in breaks. Some put their products online receive external comments from outside, others do not (2013: 368). This example shows that not only means but also goals have already been altered in some subjects.

The Struggle Between the New and the Old

Thus, in the new media environment, school subjects change – in the example above it is now not necessarily about drawing, but about remixing. Historically, according to Marner and Örtegren (2013) and Marner (2013), there is a variability in what is perceived as belonging to the subject and what does not. The new aspects of the subject will be seen as anomalies and will be neglected and placed at the periphery (Marner and Örtegren 2013: 677). Marner and Örtegren conducted 150 interviews at nine different schools to depict the discursive struggle with four different ways in which schools/subjects/teachers can relate to digitisation. The development of the subject (the transformation of what the subject is as result of the new media) is described using the concepts of the sacral and the profane, where the sacral is the spirit of the subject which cannot be avoided and the profane can be avoided, but which can later be incorporated in the sacral (but which can be seen as something imposed from the outside) (Marner and Örtegren 2013: 676). The results of the study show:

- **Resistance**: Especially observable in schools where the digital is perceived as irrelevant, which is why you stay with the paint brushes.
- **Adding**: (where activities are introduced only to do something digital) In schools where this occurs, it is concluded that adding digital is not enough if the digital is really to be integrated.
- **Embedding**: In schools where the digital is really embedded in the teaching, not just as an addition but as an integral part, the relationships between the sacral and the profane change by providing the communicative aspect at the expense of the aesthetic practical. It should be noted that right equipment is needed here for everyone.

- **Digital media as dominant**. Where this occurs, it implies unilateral instrumentalism that is not recommended.

Following these results, the point is that if subject matter teaching and Bildung in upper secondary school are to be changed qualitatively through the inclusion of digitisation (i.e., not just strengthened in terms of efficiency), then it requires that the digital be embedded as an integral part of the overall subject matter teaching. But not in a way where the digital media becomes dominant, nor in a way in which it is simply added, while most of the teaching and subject matter teaching remain unchanged (see also Cuban 2001).

Digital Teaching Practices and Bildung

From our perspective, teaching practices must always be applied in a Bildung context reflecting about knowledge, attitude and existence (see Chapter 1). Of course, much knowledge is at stake in both impression and expression practices, but in the unfolding of these practices, reflexivity can support their use in the service of the common good. Likewise, with community practice, where the skills of organising joint activities in social media call for reflexivity over attitude and existence. Participation practice in its innermost identity is always already reflexive, but the question is whether reflection is used in the public interest. The school must encourage and challenge students to develop existentially, to take care of each other and the community and to strive for the necessary knowledge to do so. Each small course within each particular subject must lift its small part of the overall Bildung of the students (see Figure 2.1, but also Chapter 4, in which we discuss this further).

In the research literature, the new digital community is characterised by the dissemination of knowledge, by participatory culture, convergence culture, appropriation, remix and produsage (Bruns 2008, Jenkins et al., 2013, Jenkins 2008, 2006).[17] Knowledge production now takes place through networking, where production involves a large degree of re-production, where already created media texts (text, film or, for example, programming code) are pieced together and remixed. In such a production context, one, as also pointed out by Hutchison et al. (2016), it is not enough to simply being able to consume media texts; a digital society – guided by critical Bildung – also requires that you actively participate critically in the production. Therefore, students must be

---

[17] We define *appropriation* as: 'The ability to meaningfully sample and remix media content' (Jenkins, 2006, p. xiv).

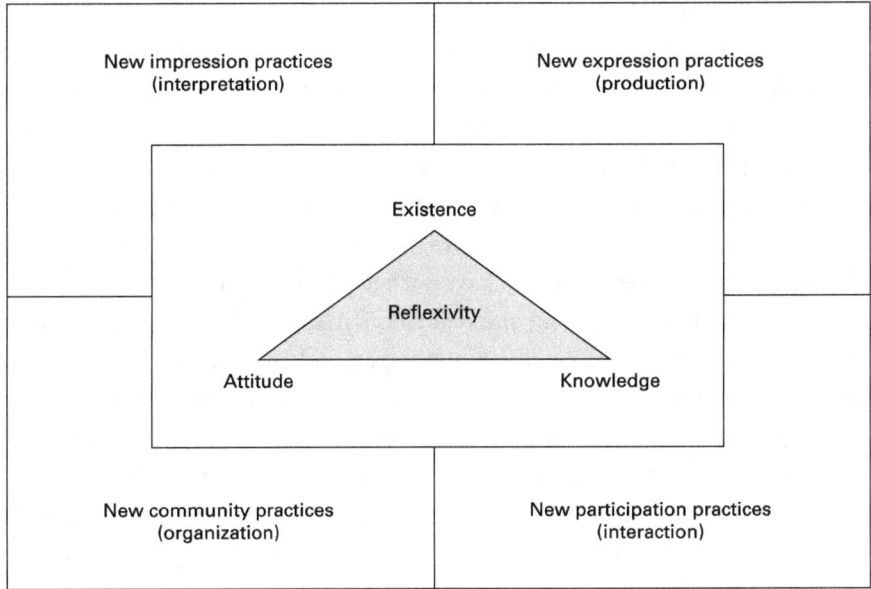

Figure 2.1 Teaching practices and critical Bildung.

challenged to enter into produsage contexts, become experimenting network participants and perform remix and appropriation. In this context, the teacher's role is to teach the students how to refer, applicate, paraphrase and remix in a legitimate and academically sound way.

Conclusion

In this chapter we have analysed obstacles and possibilities in relation to the understanding and use of digital media in the education system. We began with observations of the school in a historical medium perspective to provide a framework for our interpretations. Our basic argument was that teaching has been made possible and developed through successively actualisations of non-digital media, like oral language, writing and the print medium. All this resulted in closed classroom teaching which was the main structure of teaching before the advent of the Internet and digital media. Yet, with digital media (almost) everything changed; because the closed classroom became communicatively open and more contingent than ever. With the new radical openness both new obstacles and possibilities emerged, forming the initial digital situation, that now confront contemporary teachers and students. Also, we argued that present debate tends to focus on either obstacles or possibilities, but without sufficiently acknowledging the complexity of the new media environment. Instead, we called for critical, but nuanced stances towards digital media, acknowledging that impacts depend on how different actors understand, struggle and modify the media environment. Further, we observed students' competencies in the present situation and found not only that these have been overestimated, but teachers also lack skills and experience, that have not been developed because of prejudice, lack of time, tests, management and regulation. Also, we observed what the new medium environment means to attention span and concluded that we cannot multi-task, but also that this does not mean that we cannot use digital media in education – quite the contrary, we argued that digital media opens many new possibilities for teaching including new expanded forms of multiplexing. Finally, we followed up on this by arguing that schools and teachers equipped with digital media would be able to create new and better or at least expanded teaching practices; or more specifically: (1) new and expanded ways of participating in teaching, (2) new ways of maintaining and developing school communities, (3) new and expanded ways of finding, selecting and interpreting educational relevant impressions; and (4) many new exiting ways of creating, remixing and co-producing expressions in teaching. Thus, what is educationally new when it comes to the digital situation compared with 'before digital media' is, first of all, the radical openness, followed by both new obstacles and possibilities. Yet, this radical openness does not change education and teaching overall. The main educational problems and understandings might stay the same. It is 'only' the premises of teaching that have changed (even though some or all teaching subjects will change in content because of societal changes in the digital media environment). Also, classroom teaching has not disappeared. What really matters is, therefore, how societies, schools and teachers with different understandings begin to re-create classroom teaching, taking advantage of the new possibilities, but also working to overcome the obstacles.

3

The Three Waves

Until now we have outlined theoretical and research literature on the relationship between education and media. Especially we have outlined the concept of Bildung in Chapter 1 and the four didactical digital media practices in Chapter 2. In this chapter we briefly outline our own research from 2006 to 2019 and then present our theory – the theory of the three waves – about how the education system and actors within this system, like teachers and students, seem to develop their responses to digital media. We start by presenting these responses on a general level, but we also discuss different variants of these general responses, depending on the basic educational understandings that different educational actors rely on (see Chapter 1 for these).

Our Studies of Actor Responses 2006–2019

From 2006–2011 we carried out studies in different upper secondary schools in Denmark in the form of interviews and observations and small surveys about how digital media and wireless networks influenced the interaction between students and teachers (Paulsen and Tække 2009, 2010, 2010b). The findings were discouraging; they showed that these media have created many problems in relation to distraction, conflicts between pupils and teachers and a high dropout rate. The definition of the situation reported in interviews with both teachers and students was that the students were in a state of addiction! Our observations showed that the teachers either met the new media with prohibition or unconcern. The result was either control, surveillance, circumvention, mistrust, *or* ignorance of the new situation and the teachers either did not use the new media and the students was not supported to learn to use them, or teachers used them in a very limited and/or questionable way. Based on our theoretical analysis of the situation and reviews of the research in educational use of digital media (see Chapter 2) we have subsequently launched three action-based research projects.

The Socio Media Education Experiment

Our first action-based research project on education and digital media ran from 2011 to 2014 and was called the *Socio Media Education* (SME) project. Here we followed an experimental class (that ran from 2011–2014) in a Danish upper secondary school. Together with all the teachers of this class we tried to develop new and better ways of teaching in – and responding to – the new medium environment (Paulsen and Tække 2013; 2016). This enabled us to go into more detail and outline more concretely how educators could respond if they did not try to *prohibit* or *ignore* digital media, but instead tried to develop strategies for *initiating reflexivity* and also *teachingt through social media*. The theory of the three waves (that we explain in the next main section) was the result of the SME-project based on experiments, dialogue with teachers, design meetings. The results were documented using various online sources, not least 30,000 tweets from the class, but also interviews with teachers, school management, individual students and groups of students and observation in the classroom. The project was funded by the Region Midt (the administration level between government and municipality in Denmark).

IT for All

The second action-based research project we launched was situated at *Randers HF and VUC*[1] from 2012–2015. It was called the BIT project (standing for: IT for all). In this project we re-adjusted the teaching to meet the obstacles, possibilities and new perspectives opened up by the digital media environment, but we worked on creating benefits for *all* students, including those so-called "weaker students". The project was partly also a response to the technical changes we have seen all over the school world with major investments in wireless networks and interactive boards, among other things like iPads and smaller levels of investment in developing didactics to the new situation and further education of the teachers. To this end, the BIT project worked on the latter, integrating digital media into teaching by encouraging the teachers to experiment with knowledge sharing and discussion to help them reshape their teaching and thus develop more beneficial responses to the new media environment (Paulsen and Tække 2015). The project was documented through observations, online

---

[1] HF is an upper secondary school for adults and VUC is a general school for adults, but the classes we empirically followed and were in dialogue with, were mainly populated by 'almost young people', most of them only one or a few years older than those in 'normal' upper secondary schools.

sources and interviews and was funded by the school and Region Midt (see above).

Digital Supported Teaching and Bildung

In the action-based research project called DUFA (digitally supported disciplines and common Bildung) 2017–2019, we worked with two upper secondary schools (Rødkilde Gymnasium and Silkeborg Gymnasium) where, in both schools, we had a group of six teachers covering different subject matter. The task of the teachers in this project was to design teaching courses where they used digital media to support their disciplines *and* common Bildung (the latter being the general aim of all Danish upper secondary schools (Gymnasiums) specified by law. In DUFA book 1 (published in 2018) we provided the teachers with a research and theoretical overview, fleshing out a framework within which the teachers could design their courses. In book 2, published in 2019, we analysed 10 exemplary courses from the project, pointing out difficulties, shortcomings and providing the reader with four different and mutual supplemental scenarios for the future of the school (Paulsen and Tække 2018; 2019) (see Chapter 4 in this book for these four 'ways to go'). The project was documented using observations, online resources and interviews and was funded by the Danish Ministry of Education.

The Theory of the Three Waves

The theory of the three waves describes the general patterns of how schools seem to develop *responses* to the new digital media conditions compared to the media situation before the Internet. We propose that these responses imply a shift from *closed* classroom teaching (see Chapter 2) to teaching that takes the form of an *open* community between students, teachers and third parties. However, the shift does not happen at once. Rather, we suggest that it arises and develops through three *waves* containing different educational responses to the new situation. We have outlined our narrative theory in Figure 3.1. On the Y-axis we have *educationally relevant attention* and on the X-axis we have *time*. In our theory, we assume that before digital media there was a given level of educationally relevant attention. This assumption can be called into question insofar as attention towards the educationally relevant subject matter differed from student to student, class to class, time to time, etc. Yet, there is no doubt that what we can generally observe in *the first wave* of digital media and wireless networks is a huge drop in educationally relevant attention (Mathiasen et al., 2014). Also, we know that activity irrelevant to the educational purposes (e.g. responding to private messages) can significantly harm grade, recollection of information and note taking (Kuznekoff et al., 2016).

In our research we have observed that the first general response by teachers and schools to the new media situation is primarily either to *ignore* the new obstacles and possibilities or to *prohibit* the use of digital media for educationally irrelevant purposes Both strategies – ignoring and prohibiting – generally fail for several reasons (Paulsen and Tække 2009; 2010; 2010b; 2013). At the same time, the new possibilities for teaching are neither actualised nor invented. In the first wave, we consistently did not observe a realisation of new and improved teaching, but rather a destabilised teaching with students trying to multi-task between computer games, social media and the educational interaction.

The second wave occurs when schools, teachers and students begin to modify the new media situation and make use of new media to create new possibilities for better interaction between the students and the teachers. In this phase, teachers begin to use the new media to draw attention back to the classroom by using specially written, digitally-based interaction within the class and shared online documents where students collaborate, monitored and guided by the teacher. The result is an intensified educational interaction where the attention is re-captured and more and better possibilities for *participation* arise. For instance, it becomes possible for teachers to get answers from *all* their students *simultaneously* through the use of written interaction media like Twitter, instead of hearing one voice at a time. This – and similar uses – helps to get more students involved and engaged in the educational interaction (Paulsen and Tække 2013; 2015; 2016). Despite the positive impact of the second wave, it only consists of 'more' and 'better' interaction and does not radically alter the classroom setting or the educational form. Yet, *the third wave* – which is truly radical – is made possible by the digital media practices developed and facilitated during the second wave.

The third wave arises when people other than the students and teachers become integral parts of the educational interaction via the Internet. When this happens on a regular basis, it changes the educational form that has existed more or less since the printing press. Instead of a closed system of interaction between teachers and students, we now observe an open system of interaction in which other persons outside the classroom participate and contribute. Students now regularly meet people with other perspectives, views and responses and the teacher becomes a 'mediator of otherness and alterity'. In this wave, the teacher builds networks for educational purposes outside the classroom. Students connect to groups, other school classes, individuals and databases, using the new medium environment as part of their education. They take part in the *convergence culture* (Jenkins 2008) carrying out *produsage* (Bruns 2008), learning to navigate and take part in the new emerging society and its forms of production, network, communication and culture. The upshot is that teaching shifts from being a *closed factory* to an *open activity*, inviting different actors to participate. Instead of transmitting knowledge to the students, the role of the teacher is now to connect students with relevant otherness and make knowledge production possible across borders and differences.

The three waves correspond to some degree to Anderson and Dron's (2011) distinction between *three generations of distance education*. According to Anderson and Dron, first a *cognitive and behavioural generation*, next a *social-constructive* and finally a *connectivistic generation* have appeared successively. Even if it is possible to say to some degree that the responses we have observed fit in with these generations, we would argue that our theory and the distinction between the three waves works on a more fundamental level than the *scientific differences* identified by Anderson and Dron. Hence, we would argue that teachers and schools move through the three waves regardless of theoretical inclinations (but as we will also show at the end of the chapter, that there are *different variants* depending on theoretical inclinations or what we call their

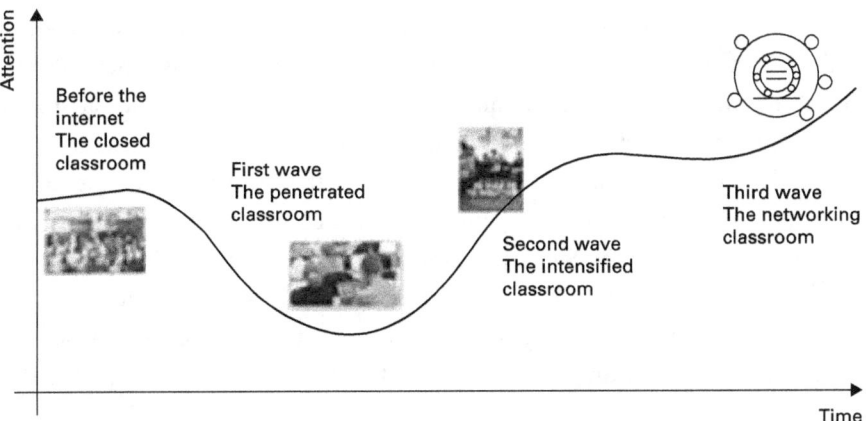

Figure 3.1 The three waves of responses to digital media in education.

basic educational understandings, cf. Chapter 1). In the first phase, all teachers and schools must find a middle way between extreme versions of prohibiting and ignoring. This leads to the second phase: the use of digital media for educational purposes and what we call the 'intensified classroom'. Yet, this does not completely solve nor repeal the distractions of the first wave but only deals with it more adequately. Further, the digital skills, experiences and competences achieved through the second phase (and the new developed media practices) *enable and motivate* the class to enter the final and third wave, where people other than the students and their teachers are contacted with the aim of contributing to the educational process. As Dede points out, schools are designed like custodial institutions, but we could have: 'In contrast, a "distributed" model of human and technical infrastructure encompassing a wider context of formal learning outside classrooms that includes parents, museum and library staff, community members and older peers as educators who collaborate with teachers in achieving equity and excellence' (2016: 106). As in the SME-project, we realised that these alterations are more practical and fundamental than shifts in learning theory. What we propose is not only a model of shifting learning theories, not just a theory of distance learning pedagogy, but rather a general educational theory of how the practice of education *as such* alters in the era of digital media, also accounting for the non-digital elements of education.

The First Wave – The Penetrated Classroom

With digital media and wireless networks, the classroom has opened up. This produces both a new space and a new time. Students can access educational communication from almost everywhere and at any time. Teachers can contact and interact with their students while they are at home or elsewhere. People 'from the whole world' can contact students and teachers in a classroom. The upshot is that communication in and out of the schoolroom has increased massively and attention is drawn away from the content of the teaching. Also, the homework culture is undermined because media platforms like Facebook, Instagram and Snapchat undermine concentration. When observing an upper secondary school class, you become witness to students trying to multi-task: they are trying to pay attention to the teacher and the educational interaction while they are surfing on the net and chatting on social media. This situation causes much frustration among the students, but still they cannot escape it:

> **Researcher** What about computers and IT and things like that, how much do you use it?
>
> **Student 1** Very much, I think. I also think, well, it can be difficult to administer sometimes (...) I'm being pulled slightly apart (...) then you could also just sit and play a little while something is being examined on the blackboard.
>
> **Student 2** You become addicted; you really do. If you find a funny game on the web, or it's Monday, and you just want to know what the others have been up to on the weekend, or something.
>
> **Student 2** You become addicted to it, because you know that you can always get hold of people and things like that, if you are bored.
>
> **Student 1** Yes, you take out your computer and switch it on and then it is switched on the rest of the day, and then you switch it off when you go home. And so, I think maybe it would be a better idea if the teachers just went in and said; okay, well, you may now switch on your computers because now we have to do something. (...) When it is right there, it's just so easy just to open it and then ...[2]

We found the statements about addiction surprising. When we started to analyse the situation, we came to the conclusion that addiction was an incorrect diagnosis, since only about 4% of the population struggle with addiction problems (Turan 1993, Young 1999) and more than half of the students felt disturbed by digital media (Mathiasen et al., 2014). Looking into medium theory we concluded that the problem was one of ambivalence because the old norm-system did not help the teachers, students, school management or the parents in the new situations (Paulsen and Tække 2010b; 2009). The students cannot help using the digital media for computer games and social interaction, even though they know that they do not learn as much when trying to multi-task.

The teachers have grave doubts about the use of digital media:

---

[2] This is from a student interview from 2007 (Paulsen and Tække 2013), before we launched the SME project in another upper secondary school in Denmark.

> **Teacher 1** I may well see on the students' faces what it is they're doing. Some are taking notes, while others are sitting with a broad grin – they are certainly not taking notes. But it is enormously difficult, and you cannot simultaneously teach and tell the students that they must be attentive or switch off their computers. If you try to go down and see what they are doing, they are quick to switch over to something else. And I think personally that it is frustrating. And now we've got wireless networks. Before, you could ask them to take out the network connector, but now they can sit and communicate with each other ...[3]

The teachers experience social ambivalence and do not know what to do in the new situation provided by digital media. In our observations, we found two different strategies used by the teachers and the schools: prohibition or indifference (Paulsen and Tække 2010; 2010b). In our analysis, we concluded that the problem could be explained as three kinds of ambivalence:

1. An *ambivalence of action*: This occurs when students do not know if it's okay to play a computer game, read a news article or look something up on Wikipedia: When the teacher explains for the third time something they already understand, or when they are waiting to get help because they cannot proceed.
2. An *ambivalence of interaction*: This occurs when students can interact with others inside or outside the classroom during lessons: When they receive an urgent message from home, or when they want to ask someone for help or feedback.
3. An *ambivalence of responsibility*: This questions who is responsible for the other two ambivalences: Students told us that they thought the teachers should take responsibility, but when teachers actually banned digital media and imposed control, the did not like the decision. Some teachers also tried to make their management or the students' parents take responsibility. In this way, the responsibility circulated among the players without anyone really taking it upon themselves. Our conclusion was that the new media environment had undermined what could be regulated through the old norm system (see Chapters 1 and 2).

---

[3] This is from a teacher interview from 2007 (see Tække and Paulsen 2013), before we launched the SME project in another upper secondary school in Denmark.

With the SME action-based research project, we tried to change this ambvilence by getting a school class, along with their teachers, to generate experiments and create new norms and didactics more adequate to the contemporary media environment. Since neither prohibition nor indifference is a particularly appropriate strategy to generate norms, we gave the teachers the double obstacle that they were neither allowed to prohibit nor to be indifferent to students' media use. In addition, they had to help students *reflect* on their media use and, in particular, to demonstrate that we cannot multi-task without very large attention and memory-related deficits (see Chapter 2). One cannot, for example, write and post a status update on Facebook and simultaneously listen carefully to a teacher's instructions. Moreover, the teachers themselves had to use social media, partly because international research shows that it offers many new opportunities for teaching (Chapter 2) and partly because it helps generate educational forms and norms that are more appropriate to the new media environment.

(1) Teachers may neither prohibit nor ignore media use in the class but must initiate reflectivity.
(2) Teachers must use social media to teach through.

Based on the teachers' and students' work following these guidelines (see Figure 3.2) they moved from the first wave to the second wave.

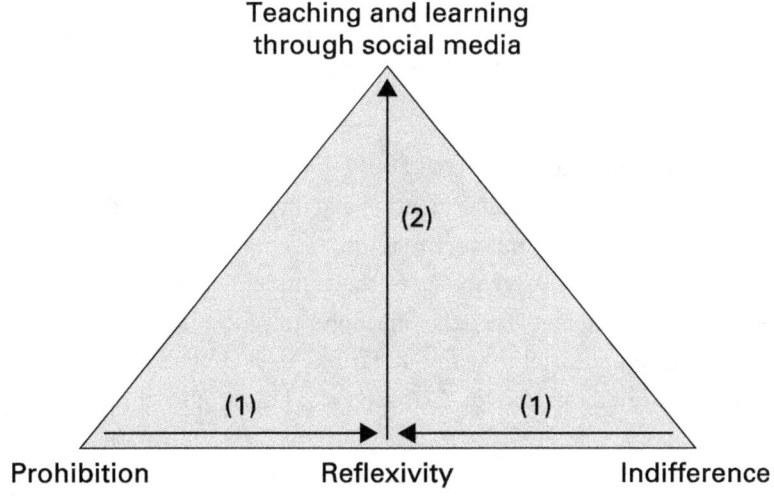

Figure 3.2 The SME second wave strategy model.

The Second Wave – The Intensified Classroom

The second wave arises when schools, teachers and students begin to make use of the possibilities of the new media to create a better interaction between students and teachers. In this second 'movement of the Internet', teachers begin to use the new media to draw attention back to the classroom.

As documented in Paulsen and Tække (2013), the teachers in the SME class temporarily succeeded in recapturing their students' attention when they simultaneously had to tweet about films they saw and presentations they attended. This was a re-colonisation of the communicative space which also has the advantage that because Twitter functions both as an interaction media and as a (temporary) storing and retrieving medium, the students' tweets after the lesson work as shared notes, for instance, about the film that they had discussed while they saw it.

> **Student 1**   When we saw a film, then the teacher questioned us on Twitter and we had to answer. I think it was really good.
>
> **Researcher**   And why was it good?
>
> **Student 1**   Because then you got it if it was something essential ... something that you did not get.
>
> **Student 2**   ... instead of remembering it all after the film. It can be relatively difficult to remember a whole film afterwards.
>
> **Researcher**   Wasn't it difficult?
>
> **Student 1**   No, not really, you only lose a few seconds because it is running at the same time. What you lose is just how the picture was.[4]

As evident in the interview, the parallel written interaction works as a support in relation to generating educational attention and understanding in the process and as production of notes and memory that the students can draw on later. The fact that the student has to actively relate to the comments and questions from the teachers and other students triggers reflections and focus. At the same time, the student can ask questions if they find it hard to keep up with the plot. However, the students do not look down at their screen to follow other things on the web.

---

[4]   Student interview 2, 2/11 – 2011 (Paulsen and Tække 2013) translated into English by the authors.

This is also helped by the fact that the teacher is sitting with the students, motivating them to take part in this collective analytical work. Not everybody can manage to write while watching (this also applies to writing notes on paper), but in a writing interaction medium one still gets the benefit of what others have written both during and after the film (Paulsen and Tække 2013). We have documented similar effects in relation to oral presentations, for example, brainstorming about a novel before the analytical work. The method falls short when the teachers give presentations because they cannot (sufficiently) keep their attention on the students' attention while speaking. On the other hand, if the teacher feels that the students do pay attention to other things, Twitter is helpful.

> I had some students today that did everything else than pay attention or were totally passive while we listened to a German song. Then I asked everybody to tweet all the German words that they picked up. That helped on the activity.[5]

Also, if all students are 'totally stoned', it is very effective to ask everybody to answer a question on Twitter. Using written interaction in this way, the educational community can *interpellate* students and thereby initialise involvement and maintain attention, activity, participation and work discipline. Also, according to both observations and interviews with teachers and students, more students are included in the educational interaction than if it just took place orally. Further, following our interviews, the quality is also better when written interaction is used and the students feel that the educational interaction better calls for attention when it also is on their screen. The use of written interaction demands practice; it is not easy to multiplex,[6] express yourself in 140 characters (now 280 characters) and be precise in an academic sense, using hashtags (#), links and tags (@). According to teacher interviews, they could not perform educational interaction in other classes with the same quality and participation as they did in the SME class, which were taught using this media practice.

Two of the teachers in the class became known as *Twitter teachers* because of how much they used the platform in their teaching. These two teachers obtained

---

[5] Teacher reflection 5:27 PM Mar 15, 2013 from the Google site (Paulsen and Tække 2013) translated into English by the authors. The Google site was one of the many ways we documented the SME-project. In this medium the teachers wrote field notes as a form of diary in regard to their SME teaching.
[6] Multiplexing is the situation in which the attention is pointed towards one intentional object but in more than one medium at the same time, such as listing and writing notes. It is not the same as multi-tasking, where you try to point your attention towards different things at the same time (see Chapter 2).

a better trust relationship with the students. They also acquired a greater knowledge about the students and the relationships between them, thus helping the teachers to perform better classroom management.

After the students and teachers during the first year acquired the sufficient competences in written interaction, the teachers began to provide homework help for one hour, five evenings a week.

> **Researcher** Do you think it's an advantage that you can get help when you are at home?
>
> **Student** Yes, I do, because you know it is not always that your parents can help with all subjects. So yes, it is great that you can write to your teacher and not have to wait until the next day.[7]

According to a teacher interview, the teacher felt that, because the community was also mediated through written interaction, she had the opportunity to catch up with students that she felt she had not had contact with during the school day.

A last experiment to be mentioned here was the use of the medium on a trip to Copenhagen, where the students and teachers organised many of their visits around the town with Twitter. They coordinated their moving around, their questions to guides, their documentation from conversations with guides, answers to teacher's questions, pictures etc. and become one big social organism moving around, sometimes splitting up in the physical space, but staying together in the virtual Twitter space.

Another medium that was used from the second year was shared online documents (they used Google.docs). These online documents were available to students working together using the same document on different computers while the teacher was able to monitor the groups' work. If it was homework, the students could work from different geographical places. The teacher could help them directly in their document if they, for instance, were on the wrong track. If it was group work at school, the teacher could go and talk with groups who were not working or who were having difficulties. This opens up advanced forms of process feedback instead of feedback being received after the work is done and the students are occupied with new topics.

The SME-class also worked with wiki spaces for all their subjects; this was a lot of effort yet, we concluded this to be critical:

---

[7] Student interview 17 14/3 2013 (Paulsen and Tække 2016) translated into English by the authors.

'On the whole, the potential for creating, sharing, gathering, evaluating and improving knowledge in the class via their wiki has only been activated to a limited extent. Only in a very few cases have students become active wiki users who use the medium to build and process knowledge related to online knowledge. The main rule has been that some individual teachers have used the medium to store and gather knowledge, while other teachers have not used it at all. Nevertheless, a number of uses have been attempted, which collectively activate all the potentials of the medium'.

Paulsen and Tække 2013

Yet, maybe this was a bit unfair because we placed many hard obligations on the teachers who, at the same time, had to live up to what they called the *upper secondary school reality*, with many academic requirements and exams.

During the second wave, the students acquired better digital competencies in regard to all four digital media practices. According to the teachers, as mentioned, the difference compared to other classes became huge, meaning that the other classes could not initiate the same educational methods as the SME class. The students also developed skills and experience with using Twitter as a backchannel, transforming the class into a new form of public, constantly discussing the educational content the teaching, and the presentation of it. Also, more students gained a voice and joined the educational interaction. Further, we found out that multiplexing is a form of single-tasking through which the students focus on the educational object with the advantages of the digital media for interacting, storing and retrieving. Also, the border between school and home was surpassed with the virtual homework help that the teachers provided. This also gave rise to a more trusting relationship between teachers and students, based on the fact that teachers were no longer perceived as a threat who would prohibit media use or, for instance, confiscate smartphones etc. Also, the teachers now had more and better knowledge about their students, which resulted in better group work and cooperation.

As an overall observation, the re-stabilisation and restructuring of the educational interaction by means of the new media intensify attention on educational content and reduce social ambivalence and, to a high degree, the students' self-distraction. The students are then supported, challenged and encouraged to acquire a culture that takes educational advantage of the new media environment. Yet, in the second wave, we also noticed more surveillance and control. Somehow, the class turned into a teaching machine leaving out the surrounding world. Also, as we will return to, the teacher's attention was only on the class community, which permitted only small glimpses of the students as individuals, but not on the networks that thrived in the class.

The Third Wave – The Contact-Seeking Classroom

The third wave focused on the possibilities for interaction outside the classroom. In the SME class, Twitter was the primary medium for this purpose, but Facebook, Google+, Google Sites and Skype have also been used.

From the second year, the teachers had to work on cultivating the contact between the class and the surrounding world to establish dialogue with network relations. The re-stabilised educational community of the class should, in this way, achieve that the otherwise disturbing contact with the surrounding world would become an educational asset and hereby turn the situation for the better so the contact, instead of drawing attention away from the educational interaction, would qualify it. Moreover, our thesis was that this contact would enrich and inspire the information situation with angles and perspectives going beyond what the teacher could offer. Generally seen, this move would cultivate the class to take a more educational advantage of the contemporary media environment.[8]

One example was when the literature teacher initiated contact with the Danish poet Kasper Anthoni. The class read one of his collections of poems and through two sessions asked him questions on Twitter. According to the teacher, the students usually have little or no interest in poetry, but this contact really got them interested. Also, according to the students, the experience was 'very motivating' and 'mind-blowing'.

> **Student 1**   I think it was a totally different way to analyse poems. A much better way I think.
>
> **Student 2**   Yes, when we have the author [on Twitter] we can question him if there is something we cannot understand in the poem and ask him what he meant and then he can come with a tweet about it.[9]
>
> **Student 1**   It helps with the interpretation. If I ask him how he got the idea, then he says that he had a feeling, and then it is easier to interpret the poem. I think it was good.[10]

---

[8] Following Jenkins (2013; 2008; 2006), we now see a participation culture characterised by shaping, sharing, re-framing, re-mixing and appropriation, and with Bruns' (2008) produsage and inter-creativity.
[9] Group interview 1, 31/10 2012 (Paulsen and Tække 2016) translated into English by the authors.
[10] Group interview 5, 31/10 2012 (Paulsen and Tække 2016) translated into English by the authors.

The interaction with the poet is exemplary for the concept of the third wave. The teacher takes a back seat but still takes the responsibility, letting the students get to the source and letting it be the centre of their attention and reflection. The teacher has made the connection to and appointment with the poet, has helped the students to read the book and to find good questions and has divided them into groups for the sessions. These efforts were good investments because the students' motivation and involvement were triggered by direct contact with a real author through Twitter.

In another example, a teacher gave the class an assignment to contact local companies using predefined types of media that the teacher knew the companies used, such as Twitter and Facebook but also websites with embedded chat. This also had a very positive result in regard to motivation, involvement and the information situation. The students, including some who were not usually motivated, explained in interviews that it felt very relevant and authentic to communicate with local businesspeople and that it helped them to apply theory to their cases.

Another example is where other school classes were contacted (one in Denmark and one in Germany, both with very positive results). Again, we see that the students were very involved and motivated by communicating with others outside the class, here with other students of the same age. According to the teachers, more students were drawn into the schoolwork than usual. It felt more important to the students to contribute and the quality was higher than normal because they felt they were being observed by others of the same age and representing their own class. Both classes also acquired new angles on their subjects, and information from angles other than those represented by their own teacher. In relation to the German class, it also became important to write correctly and the students felt that the language written by the German students was a more real German than that used in books and spoken by their teacher.

> **Student** I feel that I learn better by communication instead of reading a book. Also, the lingual, not just the grammatical. If you communicate with someone from Germany, then you learn better German than if you sit in the class talking German. That's the way it is.[11]

---

[11] Student interview 13, 14/3 2013 (Paulsen and Tække 2016) translated into English by the authors.

Moreover, the students also felt that they themselves had something to contribute to the other classes.

Gradually, the students built up networks, for example the poet, and they could ask questions both when they were at home and in class. An example was when a student asked her sister who studied economics in Copenhagen:

> **Student 2** We were to do a presentation about the American presidential election and then the presenter said something I did not understand – and we had to use Twitter during the presentation so I wrote to my sister on Twitter about it. Then she answered and I could catch up and understand the presentation again.[12]

After the presentation, the student explained the difficult part of the presentation to the rest of the class. Again, we see new and useful knowledge come from the surroundings of the class through the new media.

The last example we want to mention here was an activity where some of the students and teachers from the class, according to an appointment, sat at home one evening watching a TV documentary about the financial crisis, using Twitter to interact about it. After some time, one of the students observed other Danes watching the documentary while on Twitter were using a global hashtag to interact about it.

> **Researcher** So, you were discussing the documentary with the others from the class and then it was extended. What do you think of that?
>
> **Student** You also got other people's opinion [...] and there were really many opinions and tweets and it was going on log after the programme ended. It was really exciting.
>
> **Researcher** Was it good for the discussion that it was not just the class and your teachers?
>
> **Student** Yes, I believe so. Because we maybe have a little bit the same opinion in the class, because we have the same teacher, and it is the same things we do. And then there were other people's opinions, people that are another place in their life, and have another perspective on society.[13]

---

[12] Group interview 6, autumn 2012 (Paulsen and Tække 2016) translated into English by the authors.
[13] Student interview 9, 9/1-2 (Paulsen and Tække 2016) translated into English by the authors.

Here, an educationally relevant hole is knocked in the class' re-stabilised educational interaction and perspectives pour in from the outside. As we saw with the poet, the cultivated opening pushes the teacher into a new position. Not necessarily weakened, but more in line with the new media environment as organiser of otherness that helps the students understand the different opinions in society. We asked the student what it would be like if the SME class had not had the contact to the external world:

> **Student** Yes then I believe, then it would be biased, the teacher's opinion would shine through very much. Now we get others' opinions, others' view on the things. This means that what the teacher says is not just right, but that you then also can find information about: can this really be true? Why does she say that? And such things. So, it makes us think in another way.[14]

In the third wave, we see that the students become more involved and motivated in relation to the schoolwork. Our interpretation is that this has to do with the fact that they are real and authentic cases. In contemporary culture we cannot expect that anybody, not even students, can muster real involvement and motivation if they have to work with pseudo cases or outdated texts. The world is full of real authentic cases and every mediated communication of mass media content is selected with high relevance criteria, also counting actuality. The fact that the students worked and interacted with real people in real situations with real consequences cannot be overestimated. Such setups with real people in real situations interpellate the students to the academic work and educational interaction. An old man talking from an old book about an old outdated case simply does not appeal to most students in Danish upper secondary schools. Also, the methods presented and documented by the SME project have shown that students feel that they represent themselves and their school class and want to make a good impression. This has to do with social identity and the personal history of self-presentation, which is important not least for young people. *You are what you tweet*. During the work with third wave methods, students are encouraged to form networks and are also supported to handle social codes on the web. This means that during their education, they actually learn something about the external world. Yet, this does not mean that they are not going to learn subjects like Ancient Greece or Rome or world literature history, but that the

---

[14] Student interview 9, 9/1-2013 (Paulsen and Tække 2016) translated into English by the authors.

teacher must find setups that feed into the way young people can be attracted and interpellated in our present time. Lots of other school classes work with the same topics as lots of specialists and would love to answer questions about history and literature. In addition, there are lots of opportunities to go to virtual museums etc. We have also documented a strengthening of the educational community because the third wave methods cultivate cooperation with differentiated roles. Students now learn from people outside the classroom, with help from each other and their teachers.

The Upshot of the Three Waves

During the first wave, the old classroom is opened up by the access to the Internet that wireless networks and digital devices make possible. Students are distracted and teachers do not know what to do. Hence, the first wave undermines the old organisation of the classroom and traditional teaching methods. The Internet becomes a *challenge* to teaching. Initially, the teachers and schools react by either prohibiting or ignoring this new technology, giving rise to a huge drop in educational attention in the classroom. They enter the second wave when they succeed in drawing attention back to the educational interaction between teachers and students through the use of social media. In this phase, social media platforms are used to re-stabilise and intensify the educational situation. A new, strong echo room[15] is produced by combining the old and the new. The third wave arises when teachers and students go a step further, succeeding in establishing educationally relevant interaction (through the Internet) with third parties outside the class (authors, researchers, foreigners, etc.). Only in this third phase does the Internet become a way of new *perspectives* that thoroughly alter the old educational setting. In this phase, the teachers become mediators of otherness and students learn not only from their teachers and textbooks, but also from *many* others. Here, we see resources from and cooperation with the whole world included in the teaching, in similar ways to current knowledge work described in research literature (Jenkins 2013, 2008, 2006; Bruns 2008).

Yet, it is also possible to understand the three waves, not so much as developmental stages, but as *important dimensions* that can and should be addressed educationally in the new emerging media ecology that includes digital media. Thus, students and teachers in classroom teaching can activate, foreground

---

[15] See Chapter 2 for *the echo room* concept.

and choose to respond to (in different ways) to one of the three dimensions, depending on their specific situation and interests. Yet, our point is, that such responses are not simply chosen like ready-made products on the shelf in a supermarket; rather they must be *developed* through experimentation. Further, our point is, that such developments quasi-logically 'move' from wave one to wave three; yet in a way, one returns again and again to waves one and two; the third wave is therefore not understood "as a final destination" ruling out the two others. Rather, moving towards the third, again and again, tends to develop a complex teaching culture, in which all three dimensions are addressed, building up a style of teaching, in which students and teachers develop (more or less unique) ways of (1) protecting and dealing with their limited awareness in the new open media environment, (2) integrating new media to support the internal communication and activities in the class and (3) making contact through the internet with educationally relevant otherness outside the classroom; perhaps all at once, after a while of experimentation. Yet, as we also show and argue, in the final main section of this chapter, this general pattern can be formed very differently, transforming teaching into totally different spaces.

Finally, it must be added, that we have built this theory on our empirical findings from our studies of the Danish upper secondary school from 2006–2019, especially the SME experiment from 2011–2014, where teachers worked with the use of – and reflection on –digital media together with their students within the educational practice. What we have observed other places and read about (e.g., Mathiasen et al., 2014; Kuznekoff et al., 2016) mostly shows signs of the first wave. In other words, in the perspective of the theory of the three waves, the biggest attractor of the first wave is *distraction*, while the main attractor of the second wave is *concentration* but under the conditions of a technically reclosed classroom (the educational machine). In the third wave, the main attractor is *involvement* in the world, levelling out distraction and utilising genuine new learning and Bildung possibilities of digital media. The SME experiment shows us the contour of how things might develop if schools and teachers take a few steps further.

Obstacles in the SME-Experiment

What we have depicted from the SME in this chapter until now seems very positive when viewed from the perspective of the theory of the three waves but in the practical world there were many problems. The teachers had great difficulty producing new norms and didactics adequate to the SME-philosophy where they were not allowed to prohibit or ignore media use and had to initiate reflexivity and use social media in their teaching. They also had problems with the technical dimension which meant that their own media literacy was more or less flawed. Some of the teachers (the Twitter teachers) took greater advantage of the new situation while others more or less gave up. A group of other teachers at the school even formed a counterculture and tried to put pressure on the Twitter teachers to slow down their efforts. A problem with the model of the three waves, or an extension of it, is that the X-axis, representing the time dimension in the practical world, was shown not only be linear but also to contain oscillations so that teachers and students constantly jumped between the different waves. Here our conclusion is that students cannot maintain 100 percent focus at all times and it takes time for the new norms and didactics to become developed and fully embedded in the school culture.

Even though the 'Twitter teachers' and the school management were very positive about the project there was a general exception to the philosophy of avoiding prohibition and indifference: in practice, in all three years, there was a ban on sharing assignments, which meant that this practice took place in closed networks between students. The teachers were well aware that the students had a closed Facebook group for the whole class and that assignments and results were shared, but they felt able to stop cheating by comparing assignments. But there were many closed Facebook groups and many network exchanges took place via messages between students within different class networks. The teachers could not prove that students had cheated – they could only reveal the weakest students who had directly copied and were unable to reformulate, reversing sentences, restructures, etc. What the teachers achieved was to prevent knowledge sharing among students, strengthen class networks and weaken community and authority. They did not teach in produsage, appropriation and remix and, in that regard to refer, applicate or paraphrase in a legitimate, academically sound, way. The students did not learn to search for the best assignments, to review them, learn from them and remix them correctly (Paulsen and Tække 2016; 2016d).

These problems follow the research put forward in Chapter 2 under the heading 'The debate' and by Marner and Örtegren (2013) in 'The struggle between the new and the old'. We see a struggle between the sacral and the profane, between old culture, habits and teaching forms and new digitally supported ways that are vulnerable in practice, but seem powerful, frightening and alienating because of the power and momentum the digital is gaining, not least because there is political pressure to use digitalisation to streamline and instrumentalise.

The Three Waves and Bildung

Even though we have documented good results in regard to Bildung in many of the SEM-experiments (Paulsen and Tække 2016b; 2017), there is no tight coupling between 'digital Bildung' and third-wave teaching. Third-wave teaching (as well as first- and second-wave teaching) can be carried out in different directions (i.e. as very different variants) depending on the basic educational values and understandings that societies, schools and teachers rely on. In Chapter 1 we distinguished between four such basic educational understandings. The first two, which we called the vulgar, common or mainstream outlook, are not in line with genuine and reflective kinds of Bildung. These imply respectively a teacher and a teaching that seeks to (a) control the output of teaching or (b) facilitate student's self-development. Let us like in chapter one call the first the *engineer* teacher/teaching and the other the *gardener* teacher/teaching. In opposition to this we conceptualise genuine Bildung-orientated teaching as a combination of (a) one that seeks to challenge students to work critically with how they are in the world (their knowledge, attitude and existence); and (b) one that experiments creatively with developing new ways of being in the world (i.e., trying to create new ways of perceiving, acting and producing). In Chapter 1 we called a teacher/teaching relying on the first of these two reflective kinds of Bildung a *challenger* and the second, a *creator*. Yet, we also argued, that these could be understood as 'two sides of one coin', which is exactly what we are going to do here in Chapter 3. To simplify matters, in the following text we use the term challenger to understand a kind of teacher and teaching that relies on *both* views (i.e., both are *questioning* students' way of being in the world and *through experiments* encourage students to *develop* new ways of being in the world).

Thus, we can compare how actors – identified respectively as *the engineer, the gardener and the challenger* – with different basic educational understandings are likely to respond differently to the three waves; giving rises to different variants of the general patterns we have described above (see Figure 3.3).

The three actors are reconstructed based on Bildung and educational theory (Beck et al., 2014; Biesta, 2017; Dewey, 1997; Hansen et al., 2019). Whether actual teachers can identify themselves with – and eo ipso act more or less in accordance with – one of the actor-types or a particular combination of them is another question, only possible to answer ex post the distinction being made. Yet it is our own experience that actual teachers easily can

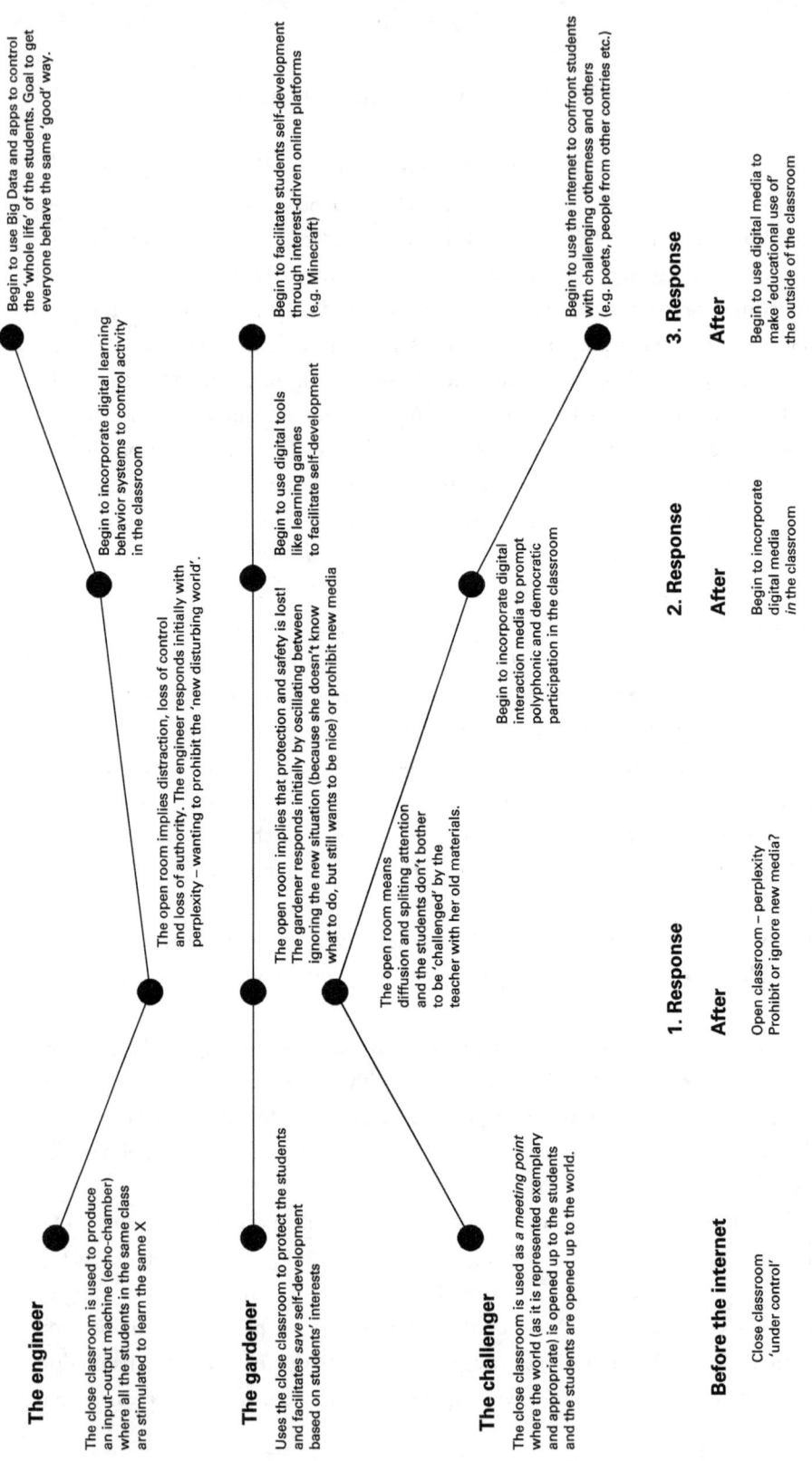

Figure 3.3 Different variants of responses to digital media.

identify themselves with the actor types and discuss how much, when and why they act like engineers, gardeners or challengers – the three types we operate with here. This is similar to Habermas' approach in his magnum opus *The Theory of Communicative Action* (Habermas, 1992) where, based on different positions within sociology, he reconstructs the concepts systems and lifeworld. In a similar manner, we want to reconstruct three trans-epochal and trans-individual teacher-actor-types – each understanding teaching in a certain way and wanting something definite in relation to students. They are trans-epochal because they aspire to validity both before and after the arise of digital media. Thus, it should be possible to identify all three both before and after the coming of digital age (in educational theory but also in practice). This trans-epochal feature is crucial if we want to understand how the three actors begin to act, with the advent of social media. We hereby also assume that digital media, as such, has not been invented by teachers. They can only say yes or no and shape digitalisation of education differently. That they are trans-individual means that they can more or less identify with all three actor types, depending on context, time, situation, educational setting, subject matter, personal values, outlook and so on. Yet it is perhaps likely that many individuals and school traditions will identify mostly with only one of the three. Yet we acknowledge that, in reality, it might be muddier. Conceiving theory as a dramatisation of thought (Biesta, 2010; Deleuze and Guattari 1995; Dewey, 1997), the model with three kinds of teachers might exaggerate things but also make the real drama – how teachers are likely to shape digitalisation – much clearer.

The Engineer Variant

Let's start with the *engineers*. When digital media appeared – and opened up the classroom, as described above – the engineer's first response can be seen as a function of what the new digital media situation did to their closed classroom: it made it open and (to begin with) uncontrollable. At first, this new open room implied distraction, loss of control and loss of authority. The first response of engineer teachers was frustration: 'Shut down the Internet,' they cried. While students' attention was drawn away from teaching to other things, the functioning of the teaching machine declined. Media platforms like Facebook were apparently better able to catch students' attention than the teaching machines of the engineer teachers (Paulsen and Tække 2016).

Eventually, more and more engineers realised that it was impossible to shut down the Internet or make prohibition effective. This led to their second response: 'If you can't beat the new media, then join them.' The engineers began to use and incorporate digital learning behaviour systems to control activity in the classroom. Or more generally, they reconstructed their teaching machine using digital means, thus making it more powerful. However, they also took a further step, thus forming a third response. Using new digital technology, some engineer teachers and schools also started to use big data to control the whole life of their students (Paulsen and Tække 2019b). Before the advent of digital media, it was only possible for teachers to control the behaviour in their classroom, but it is now possible to monitor, control and affect students regardless of where they are.

Together, these three responses – frustration, incorporation of digital media for better control in the classroom and taking control of students' lives outside of the classroom – form the plotline of the engineer teachers. To begin with, control is taken away from them, but in the second and third responses, they regain control and become even more powerful. This plotline is produced by the engineer teachers themselves. First, they feel threatened, but they then develop a new kind of control, realising that this can be made even more efficient by the new media ecology. Yet this is only made possible by making alliances with new digital control systems, called for by the engineer teachers and developed by companies that realise this new market. Also, political systems, wanting more control, support the plotline.

An example of the engineer plotline appears in a study at an English school (Livingstone, 2014). The study was completed during the school year 2011–2012. The students were aged between 13 and 14 and it was a regular English school class in a suburb of London. According to the study, teachers at the school used a so-called 'school information management system'. According to the researchers, this created a control system in which the digital technology was made part of an instrumental learning culture. The teachers used the system to monitor, record and control students' learning behaviour, attention and performance. The technology thereby functioned as a panopticon, associated with sanctions. Among other things, the teachers recorded students who did not perform sufficient learning behaviour in relation to learning goals. Thus, teachers spent a lot of time entering data and executing output from the system. The data entered by the teachers into the system were also stored and made available to optimise the system and were used alongside other data, such as the socio-economic background of the students.

The Gardener Variant

The plotline of the *gardeners* is quite different. With the arrival of the Internet and digital media, the classroom has opened up, meaning that safety and protection is lost. Companies now have direct access to students' mental processes, 24 hours a day, both when students are in the classroom and when they are at home. Thus, actors with non-educational goals interrupt and influence the students with temptations and glamourous content, commercials, games, and so on – undermining the educationally framed self-developments that the gardeners pursue. The first response to all this by the gardener teachers is ambivalence. On the one hand, they want to protect the students by trying to shut down the Internet or prohibiting the use of smartphones and/or other new media during teaching hours. On the other hand, they also want to be nice and respect the students as being able to make their own choices. Thus, the gardener teachers oscillate between protecting the students (by trying to prohibit use of new media in school time) and ignoring the new situation (being too kind to prohibit media use). The result is ambivalence, frustration, and conflict.

Yet, after a while, realising that neither prohibition nor ignorance is adequate as a general strategy and by acknowledging that new media has learning potential, more and more gardener teachers switched to a second response. This is to use new media to draw attention back to teaching again and to facilitate students' self-development. This is realised in the form of digital learning games and the like but also through the use of smartphones, tablets, to support students' creative activities, (e.g making small films and other things with new media). By doing this, the gardeners extend the good old analog palette of creative productions – poster and so on – with new multi-modal digital production possibilities. This also makes it possible for teachers to link their teaching to contemporary digital children and youth culture. Doing this, they move in the direction of a third response, where they begin to incorporate interest-driven digital online platforms, like Minecraft, to support the self-development of their students.

In Denmark, we have seen many examples of the gardener plotline (See Paulsen and Elf 2020; Paulsen and Tække 2015; 2019a). It has been a common argument that teachers and schools need to use the new media to meet the students where they are (on Facebook, Instagram, etc.). Using new digital media for learning can make teaching both more interesting for students and exploit new digital possibilities. Yet it has also been the case, as researchers have documented, that new potentials of creativity, production, interaction, connectivity, and so on have not at all been actualised in reality (Paulsen and Elf, 2020). Technology naïve strategies, such as buying tablets for every student without developing new kinds of teaching with tablets, have been especially damaging (Paulsen and Tække, 2018). Also, digital media has not always in practice been as flexible as that postulated in theory. Yet all this can be seen as a kind of teething process. In a Swedish study (Marner, 2013), it is argued that digital media should neither be implemented as dominating nor as just an add-on; instead, it should be embedded as an integral part of the overall subject matter teaching (see also Chapter 2).

The Challenger Variant

Finally, the plotline of the *challengers* is different from both engineers and gardeners. On entering digital age and opening up their classrooms, the challengers saw that the attention of their students went to other things that were more appealing but with less educational value, making it harder to challenge the students with good old materials. The analogue material looked outdated, and community and dialogue within the class was undermined. The first response to the new media was mostly resignation and despair. To really challenge students and encourage them to think deeply and perhaps also develop new alternative ways of being the world seemed to be mission impossible in the digital age; many challengers might have thought that Ancient Greek art, master novels, classical music, difficult mathematical proofs, philosophy, and books such as Das Kapital appeared to be impossible to bring within the reach of most students' attention and interest. The frustrating thing for the challengers was that, more than ever, challenges to prevailing thought and practice were required, but at the same time these were unlikely to become meaningful to most students.

Yet, after a while challengers began to realise that new digital media also carried opportunities for working with participation and emancipation anew. Thus, the challengers' second response was to begin to incorporate digital interaction media to prompt experimental and polyphonic participation in the classroom. Through media platforms like Twitter, the challengers started to let more students' voices come to play, creating a more democratic infrastructure where different voices could be articulated (Paulsen and Tække 2018; Poshka 2014). Also, the challengers began to confront students using up-to-date digital materials, such as online discussions, digital films, websites and streaming from political forums. But they also began to work critically with key digital problems, such as fake news, the power of algorithms, big data, and digital surveillance (Paulsen and Tække 2019a). All this led to the third response, where the challengers began to use the Internet to confront students with challenging otherness, unfamiliar persons (e.g., poets, politicians, researchers, people from other countries with other backgrounds and worldviews) but also tried to make new resonances, partnerships, networks and encounters through creative experiments in the new radically open media ecology. The teacher then becomes (more than ever possible in the closed classroom) a mediator of otherness and potentially genuine innovation. On an everyday basis, teachers can now confront students with educationally relevant others and different kinds of alterity in real online meetings. Teaching then shifts from being *about* the world/others to *being* with *others* and experimenting *with* the world. The students are challenged by greater plurality of perspectives and engaged in real encounters and involved in the real creative world.

It is no secret that our sympathy with the challenger plotline is high. As we see it, the digital age, despite all its problems and calamities, is a wonderland for critical challengers who want to confront their students with appropriate, relevant, and difficult otherness. Also, the new media makes it easier to confront and mix different expressions produced by the students, their teachers, and others with one another. Real polyphonic teaching can then be realised.

Combining Strategies – Media Reflection as an Example

Yet, it can be sensical to combine all three kinds of teachers/teaching. That we endorse the challenger, does not imply a total rejection of the other strategies. Let us therefore, based on our SME project, exemplify a combined strategy, one in which teachers work to support, facilitate and challenge the student to obtain improved media reflection.

One of the most important elements in the SME-experiment was the work with reflexivity. The teachers had to help students to develop a reflected use of media and they themselves had to develop a reflected and understanding way of being concerned with the students' use of media. This included helping the students to be attentive in relation to their attention. In all probability, this double task can only be maintained adequately through interaction between the students and the teacher. Neither the students nor the teacher has a priori knowledge of the right way to handle this new complexity (see Chapter 2 in relation to multi-tasking). Depending on how good one's short-term memory and how strong one's will and situational involvement is in a learning activity, one can switch between different activities. Also, reading, writing and IT-skills have a strong effect on how good the single student is at switching back and forth between the teaching and other interactions such as gaming, surfing the net or reading the news. Each individual student must be aware of their own attention span and strengths and weaknesses; the teacher must help them understand and take action based on a reflected point of view. One's standard in the different school subjects also has influence on whether the student can afford this diversion of attention. This means that it can differ, not only from student to student, but also from subject to subject (e.g., from English to Maths). The work on attention and self-reflection in the first year of the SME-experiment was an important step for the students on their journey towards thinking for themselves and developing social responsibility. Together with educational interaction using the social platform Twitter it provided them with the skills required for their later contact in and out of the class. Here we are on the level of the engineer wanting to help the student with competencies not to try to multi-task, competencies to use, for instance, Twitter for educational interaction (but also wanting to facilitating student's own self-development of reflexivity, thus pertaining to the gardener plotline). The level of the challenger is reached when students are confronted by 'real practitioners from the surrounding world' who present their texts, methods, experiences and meanings. Thus, the challenging teacher becomes a guide who helps make the connections, provides relevant material to prepare the meeting and helps the student to reflect on how they have performed. Over time the students might learn how to interact within the new media environment and to take full responsibility for the whole arrangement and situation and its organisation. They might also – at least they are encouraged to – learn to think for themselves and make decisions in new social situations in a professional context. In the beginning guided by the teacher and in groups, but over time the students happen to be alone in such situations only guided by themselves. This means that the students are not only performing the language games developed in class between teachers and students with almost no other consequences than the marks and reactions from other students familiar with this form of surrogate learning. Rather, the students are in real situations with real consequences with real people.

Similarities and Differences

If we compare the three plotlines, some shared features can be detected. Before the arrival of the Internet, all three actors[16] benefited from the closed classroom, despite their different ways of dealing with this educational architecture (see Chapter 2). In their different ways, they learned to master this room. However, engineer teaching was very different from gardener and challenger teaching. If we imagine students entering a school and a classroom (in, let's say, 1989) inhabited only by engineer teachers, it would probably have been a very different experience than if they had entered a school with only gardeners or challengers. Yet, in reality, it might be the case that many students in Western post-World War II societies experienced a mixture of all three.

What is important here, regardless of how big the differences were before, is that with the advent of the Internet, wireless networks, and digital media, all three types of actor were perplexed. This is because they all relied on the double-chamber system (see Chapter 2). Therefore, the first responses to the digital age were equally confused: Should we ignore new media, or should we prohibit them? Thus, they all responded initially to the open classroom with perplexity – oscillating between prohibition and ignoring strategies. On the other hand, it also shows that when the three kinds of actors really begin to act after a while, and thus form their plotlines, they also begin to distinguish themselves more and more from one another, perhaps so much that when it comes to the 'third response', there were greater differences among them than before the digital age. Nevertheless, it is also possible to *abstract* some common features. Thus, all actors – abstractly seen – start by being perplexed (in many different ways) by the new initial openness. This is their shared first response in all its infinite diversity. Then, after a while, they begin to incorporate and imbed digital media in the classroom teaching. This is their shared second response – which comes in many forms that continuously transform the reconfiguration of classroom teaching and its capacitates (including closing the classroom once again). Finally – and still abstractly – they all begin to use digital media to make educational use of the outside world, by using the Internet and digital interaction media. This is their shared third response, which also comes in many different forms and transforms classroom teaching even further. These abstracted cross-plot-similarities point to a common way of responding to the new, despite their

---

[16] *Actors*, the three constructs of ways to perform Bildung, is maybe best understood as attractors where we in the real world would find no pure (e.g. engineers) but definitely some teachers who is mainly like the engineer.

differences. It shows a general cultural pattern in which they all integrate digital media educationally. Yet, this pattern is continually rewritten, because each new response transforms the educational media ecology, meaning that, in reality, the three main response outlined are activated, modified, further developed, transformed, multiplied, combined and altered sequentially. When for instance external people are introduced into the classroom by the use of digital media and the internet (thus activating and modifying the third response), it might foster new problems of awareness (the analytically 'first' response) or new ways of using social media to carry internal communication in the class (the analytically 'second' response). Thus: the three responses can be seen as theoretical constructs that make it possible to analyse and abstract to some degree a general evolving pattern, with affinity to what Peirce called 'the first, second and third' in his thinking about signs. That being said, it may be that we are only describing the initial phase of a digital revolution; it cannot be excluded that the future might bring forward different and also more rejective responses which would transform this into a totally different pattern.

Conclusion

In this chapter we have outlined our research from 2006 up to the present day. We have focused mostly on the SME-experiment and presented our theory of the 'three waves'. We have examined this theory, explaining examples and drawing a picture of moving from distraction in the first wave to concentration in the second to connection outside the classroom in the third. We also have presented critical remarks to the praxis in the SME-class to show that the integration of digital media is neither an easy nor unproblematic task – rather a micro revolution challenging the sacral spirit of what is acknowledged as teaching. Finally, we have pointed out that even though a class runs through the three waves it is possible to do that without really aiming for Bildung, that is encouraging and challenging the students to work creatively and critically with their otherwise taken-for-granted ways of being in the world, perceiving, acting and creating. This means that digitalisation does not directly have a certain effect (or impact that positivist/deterministic research talks about) but instead opens/expands a new (im)possibility space that politicians/schools/teachers (and other actors) can respond to differently, modify and change by responding to the new situation, rather than viewing it in terms of causality, impact and determinism. In Chapter 4, we outline a connected model for digitally supported subject-matter teaching and Bildung.

4

Bildung in the Digital Age

This chapter explore how educators, teachers and students can work with Bildung-orientated teaching in the digital age. That is how they, from a Bildung perspective (see Chapter 1), can understand, apply and modify digital media (with the aim of supporting Bildung processes). We have investigated this question in depth in an action-based research project called DUFA (literately meaning *digitally supported disciplines and common Bildung)* (see Chapter 3) in dialogue with teachers, teaching in ten different subjects within science, social science and the arts. The chapter is divided into two major parts. In part one we outline the DUFA project and our theoretical framework to analyse and discuss 'Bildung potentials' in the ten courses that the teachers in the DUFA project developed. This framework is based on the theories put forward in the former chapters. We use it to analyse and discuss the ten DUFA courses, but it can also be used to design, analyse and discuss other courses, thus dealing with the question of how educators on a concrete level can work with Bildung in the digital age. In the second major part of the chapter, we elaborate on four different ways of working with Bildung, extrapolated from the DUFA project. The proposal of these four paths of designing and carrying out Bildung oriented teaching in the digital age, is the main focus of the chapter.[1]

The DUFA Project

The DUFA project worked on how to strengthen subject-matter-specific Bildung contributions by relating to digitalisation in specific ways. In the project we initiated and analysed exemplary courses in ten different subjects. The fact that the courses are exemplary does not mean that they are perfect or comprehensive, but that they possess a Bildung potential that we then analyse and discuss.

---

[1] This chapter is mainly based on Paulsen and Tække (2019).

The ten courses were developed during the 2017–2018 school year at Rødkilde and Silkeborg Gymnasium in Denmark and have covered mathematics, physics, biology, chemistry, social studies, history, Danish, Chinese, design and visual arts.

The subject matter contributes to three major school areas: (1) *science* which includes maths; (2) *social science* which includes history; and (3) *the arts* which include Danish as first (literature) and second language subjects, but also subjects such as design and visual arts. We agree that the three areas are not fully comprehensive for all school education and that some subjects will fit better into the categories than others. Nevertheless, we will argue that by discussing examples in all three areas, we will deal with something that has exemplary value for much of the teaching that takes place in both primary school, secondary school and in higher education.

What we are trying to identify is how to support the main areas – the sciences, social sciences and the arts – in a broad sense, by ways of understanding and applying digital media (IT). More specifically, our concern is to identify what kind of educational Bildung engagements can be strengthened or reinvented through specific ways of using and understanding digital media (IT) in the main academic areas. This examines the most important dimensions of Bildung, namely *knowledge*, *attitude* and *existence*, but also the general development of a world relationship where one can (1) *master* oneself and the world (e.g., master grammatical rules), (2) *understand* oneself and the world as far as possible, for example, understand people who think differently than oneself, and finally (3) *create* a different and better world (e.g., act creatively, innovatively and critically).

The question we want to answer in this chapter is whether and how in the main academic areas (i.e., by perceiving man and the world as respectively nature, society and culture) one can understand and use digital media to support the Bildung engagements which is the point of having a school. An important and underlying challenge lies in the fact that digital media is both part of (1) the process, that is, in the teaching itself, which must take into account and apply digital media in an adequate way and (2) the result, namely in the formative idea that an educated citizen must be able to master, understand and improve the digital society.

An Analytical Model

In this subsection, we will briefly present an analytical model (see Figure 4.1), which is based on the theoretical framework outlined in the former chapters, but also works as framework for the design of the exemplary digitally supported courses in the DUFA project. The model integrates (1) the three dimensions of Bildung – knowledge, attitude and existence (see Chapter 1), (2) the four different media practices (see Chapter 2), and (3) the three different waves (see Chapter 3). We will present the model here, but for interpretations of historical, philosophical and media theoretical backgrounds and assumptions we refer primarily to these former chapters and secondarily to our earlier books from the SME, BIT and DUFA projects (Paulsen and Tekke 2013; 2015; 2016; 2018; 2019). The aim of the model is to be able to analyse and discuss how one can work with (the three dimensions) of Bildung in the four different media practices, moving over time from wave 1 to wave 2 to wave 3.

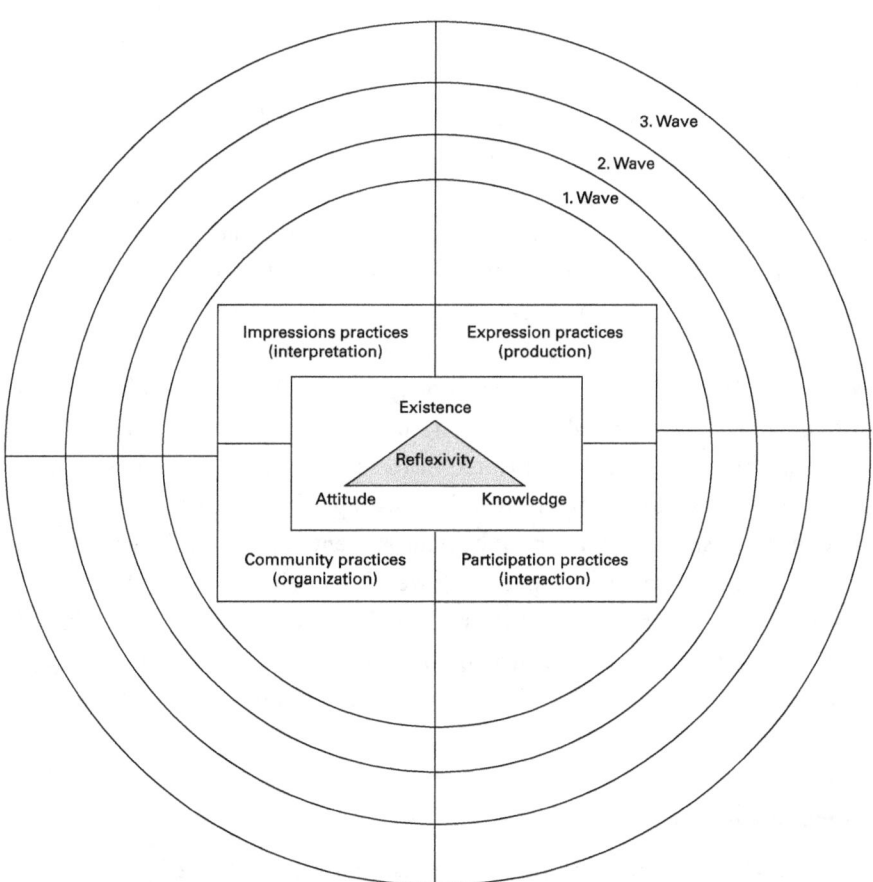

Figure 4.1 An analytical model of how to work with Bildung in the digital age.

Bildung Analytics

Analytically, we see Bildung as the union of three inseparable elements namely knowledge, attitude and existence. *Knowledge* denotes *the question* of *what* students need to know about themselves, society and the world in order to create a better world than the one we have today. *Attitude* denotes the *questions* of *how* students should relate to themselves, others and the world, in concrete matters of concern. Thus, it reflects the fact that even if one has knowledge, one can still behave like a dictator. Against this background, one must be able to balance between taking good care of oneself, others and the public good. *Existence* denotes the *question* of *who* the students can or ought to be; encouraging and challenging them to raise, develop and qualify their individual voices and ways of responding to others.

Bildung is also the basic aim of Danish upper secondary education and all subject matter should therefore contribute to general Bildung. From this perspective, the various subjects can be seen as social and historical constructions that contingently contain different selections of what Bildung should be about. In our categorisation we are gathering the subjects in three different areas and distinguishing between: a scientific, a social scientific and a cultural and humanistic contribution to Bildung.

From a Bildung perspective, a successful course in a specific subject matter must always be analysed in the light of its contribution to Bildung. This, of course, also applies to digitally supported teaching, but in the phase of digitalisation that we are now in (the initial phase) it is important to discuss how the digital contributes to (or undermines) Bildung. The question thus becomes partly whether and how the use of digital technology can contribute to working critically with the questions of knowledge, attitude and existence. Also, a distinction must be drawn between process and result, in the sense that the digital, on the one hand (process) can help or not help by creating a better teaching and, on the other hand (result) can help or not help the student to act critically with shaping a digital society in better directions. However, the relationship is complex. For example, it may not necessarily help students to reflect critically on what they do with technology, that they learn to program (result). As another example, students may not achieve better learning because the teacher uses PowerPoint (process).

Media Analytics

In the analytical model we also distinguish between four media practices as explained in Chapter 2.

1. *Participation practices* (interaction) relates to the educational understanding and application of new possibilities for interaction and participation in the new media environment.
2. *Community practices* (organisation) also relates to participation, but at the organisational level. New forms of participation require the development of organisational forms, norms and ethics that enable participation, as well as the acquisition of norms when connecting to communities, groups and networks outside the classroom (third wave).
3. *Expression practices* (production) relates to the area of articulating oneself in digitalised communities. It requires knowledge and skills to express oneself in new media both socially and professionally.
4. *Impression practices* (interpretation) relate to skills to search information and conduct source criticism. With regard to all four, there is a commitment to reflexivity in relation to Bildung.

The digital media practices are educational in the sense that they can support education – and Bildung – through digitally supported teaching. However, digital media practices must be developed by teachers and students and learned by students through the various subjects to support Bildung. On the surface, they are the same in all subjects, but if we examine them closely, we see differences in the different subjects. Each subject matter must therefore contribute both to Bildung and to establishing media practices that enlarge the possibility and capacity for such Bildung contributions (see Chapter 2).

Wave Analytics

In the analytical model, the wave theory (see Chapter 3) is seen as three levels of development through which teaching transforms to new modes of communication and organisation that becomes possible with digital media. So, here it is a measurement for what kinds of obstacles and/or possibilities the teaching is working with, at each stage (wave). Yet, as we also noted in Chapter 3, it is also possible to understand the three waves, not so much as developmental stages, but as *important dimensions that can be addressed* educationally in the new emerging media ecology that includes digital media.

In the first wave, it applies to the most basic steps of Bildung, namely those relating to attention, media choices and security (including privacy and security settings, as well as network etiquette). Another aspect is that the students, who are (wrongly) regarded by many teachers as competent media users, must learn almost everything from scratch, so that they need to learn how to use word processing programs, spreadsheets etc. The first wave is therefore analytically seen as a phase in which the school begins to work with Bildung in relation to the digital. This must be practiced without prohibition and indifference (see Chapter 3). To this end, it is a particularly important first-wave obstacle to work with attention in the new media environment. For example, work on becoming aware of and resisting the temptation to multi-task and of external commercial powers that through the web try to draw one's attention away from classroom-relevant activities. In addition, it must also be observed and considered whether the media most suitable for teaching are included and whether they are appropriately adjusted (regarding notifications and private settings). Wave one lies beneath the other waves and is a prerequisite for moving the teaching into them. At the same time, wave two and, in particular, the following wave three, are reinforcing awareness and concentration by motivating and engaging students – and thereby counteracting multi-tasking, that is often seen as the biggest wave one obstacle.

In the second wave, students must be encouraged, challenged and supported to handle media that enables written interaction and collaboration in the classroom, as well as entering into such virtual class intra-community and network. Work is being done on building norms regarding the new interaction situations and the transparency and registration that comes with digitalisation. For example, shared documents allow the teacher to provide process feedback. The new information situations regarding information search and source criticism are also formed at a basic level, in addition to work on processing, selection, storage, categorisation and retrieval in media chains including media platforms like Twitter, smartboard and Wiki.

In the third wave, Bildung relates to the contact with the outside world, where the confidence with 'internal interaction' in the first two waves is put at risk in authentic transactions with otherness from the surrounding community. Be it professionals, politicians, representatives from sport or the arts, people with a particular occupation who are professionally relevant or, for example, friendship classes. In this phase, students practice networking and forming relationships with others from outside the class.

While activities in a class can theoretically and empirically oscillate between the waves, there is a fluid transition between the three. Our studies show that a student can go from a full on 'third wave encounter' to a first wave distraction involving multi-tasking in the next lesson. On the other hand, when we observe the waves analytically, we observe whether a course has Bildung potentials in relation to one or more of the first, second and third wave obstacles and possibilities.

Four Ways of Working with Bildung

The analysis of the ten exemplary courses from the DUFA-project extends to more than 150 pages in Paulsen and Tække (2019). What we want to do here is to briefly outline four different scenarios based on our findings. Even a very brief summary of the courses would take up the rest of the book. Therefore, we jump directly to sketching out the four different, but overlapping and coexisting, paths of working with Bildung in digital age that was our conclusion of the analysis of the ten courses (an analysis made possible by using the analytic model above).

The big question that the DUFA project was put into the world to answer was whether certain understandings and applications of digital technologies and media can support and enhance subject matters and Bildung in school. The ten courses analysed showed that it is possible to support and strengthen subject matters and Bildung through certain ways of dealing with digitalisation. However, this does not mean that the answer is thus unconditional and unambiguous. Several factors are worth mentioning in this context. Understanding and using digital technologies and media in specific ways (which in DUFA seem to support and enhance subject matters and Bildung) does not mean that one should or can do the same in other classes. There are several reasons for this.

First, all classes are different, which means that doing the same thing in two different classrooms can give different results (all students do not have the same needs) (Dewey 2000; Biesta 2011; Hansen et al., 2019; Luhmann 2006).

Secondly, we have only examined whether certain understandings and applications of digital technology and media can support and enhance subject matters and Bildung in relation to a digital society. However, there may be other and better ways of doing this that we have not explored, including analogue means, and there may be more important problems in other contexts to focus on than those the DUFA teachers have had in mind and where the use of digital technology may not be as helpful (Postman 1993).

Third, the world is always changing. This means that the consequences of using digital technologies are changing as the overall media environment is changing. For example, using a commercial media platform such as Facebook in 2020 is not the same as using Facebook in 2010, just as in 2030 it will probably be something else (if it will even exist). The new media is radically changing the technical, commercial, social, cultural and political landscape Thus, there may well be good reasons for using a medium in Year X that is outdated in Year Y.

Thus, simple lines should not be drawn between digitisation and teaching (see also the introduction to this book). We cannot in any way say from the DUFA studies that digitalisation of teaching supports and strengthens subject matters and Bildung. What we can say is that we have uncovered a few experiments that point to how subject matters and Bildung in specific and unique contexts could be strengthened and supported through certain ways of understanding and using digital media and technology. That said, however, in the following we will venture into a cautious extrapolation. As we evaluate it, the ten DUFA experiments, in conjunction with the research we reviewed earlier in the book (see Chapter 2), indicate that the school with advantage can take on at least four non-mutually exclusive approaches in regard to being critically-constructive about how to understand and use digital media and technologies in education:

- *Path 1*: is to develop new transdisciplinary teaching practices that embed digital media as part of a larger pallet of media and technologies.
- *Path 2*: is to develop new special educational practices to the single subject matters that, through embedding digital media and technology and by reciting subject matters and teaching to a digital society, can reconfigure what the subject matter in question is.
- *Path 3*: is working with the digital in teaching as an 'epoch-typical key problem' (see Klafki 2005).
- *Path 4*: is to further develop what we have called third wave activities, thus contributing to the transformation of what is meant by classroom teaching.

In the following, we elaborate on the four paths, and exemplify, based on the ten experiments, how to move along these paths and discuss what obstacles and possibilities we see in relation to each path. It should be noted that we know that it is important to be aware of other paths. These four paths are just our best estimate.

Path 1: New Transdisciplinary Bildung Practices

The first path is to develop new transdisciplinary Bildung practices that embed digital media as part of a larger pallet of media and technologies. Some of the DUFA experiments provide examples of how to support Bildung commitment in general in upper secondary school. However, the examples are by no means exhaustive. In particular, we would like to highlight the following three experiments:

- An experiment on process feedback and dialogue developed in social studies.
- An experiment on peer feedback and mutual correction work developed in biology and chemistry.
- An experiment on assignments, assessments and teacher feedback are made transparent developed in mathematics.

All three experiments are about how to use *online sharing documents* and *written interaction* to strengthen and support the following options:

- peer feedback, teacher feedback, especially process feedback, and feedback from the outside;
- academic collaboration and group work;
- cross-inspiration; and
- institutionalising independent work by drawing on the work of others.

These examples of digital support do not relate to specific subjects or disciplines, although the specific designs may differ in different subjects. It thus points to a transdisciplinary potential for education which, in particular, has to do with strengthening the way in which one can create an academically fruitful and formative expression practice in school. This is based on some of the new opportunities for participation (interaction) and community (organisation) that digital media such as online documents and online groups affords and teachers in these years develop.

What unites all four options is that they rely on the *digitalisation of writing*.[2] Peer feedback, academic collaboration, teacher-process feedback and transverse inspiration are not new inventions that new technology has brought us. Even feedback from the outside is not new, albeit has been an exception. Thus, it is primarily about optimisation (and support) of existing practices, with digital tools. However, in relation to the fourth option (which relates to the relationship between one's own expression and another's expression, which is included in one's own expression), there are, however, a number of additional principles that we will discuss here. In a sense, it can be said that in the digital medium, the difference between original and copy disappears. This is, for example, the thing that has disrupted the music industry, since in digital media you can copy music tracks infinitely many times for free (if you have the equipment). This is a basic

---

[2] Even pictures, audio and video exist in dynamic writing qua the computer's functional architecture – everything in digital media is, so to speak, text files written in different programming languages (Finnemann 2005).

condition that applies in principle to all digital and digitalised products.³ In principle, one can see, share and store a filmed teacher instruction as many times as necessary. In addition, we see shifts in time and space, where digital objects have a different materiality than non-digital ones. In time, one can consult, edit and produce digital objects synchronously, near-synchronously and asynchronously and even super-synchronously.⁴ In space, you can access anywhere in the parallel digital space (cyberspace) from anywhere (Tække 2002). In addition, several persons can, in principle, view and access the same digital objects with these object properties and displacements in time and space.

This opens up unlimited general possibilities for all subject matter insofar as teachers and students can master the necessary media practices. Here, however, the DUFA courses show us a number of obstacles, consisting of a lack of digital consciousness and digital competencies when it comes to teachers and students and in an undeveloped social structure. Like in the DUFA experiments (and, for example, the SME experiments in Chapter 3) the first thing is to develop social norms and a teaching practice which support the digital remediation of collaboration and feedback before the schools can go 'all in'.

Yet, we also have concerns about the current actualisation of digital support potentials. As it is now, one can choose between poorly functioning and secluded learning systems, designed for the sake of commercial interests that pull data out and seek to automate teaching into a form of learning based on profiling, big data and machine learning algorithms (Williamson 2017). Alternatively, one can choose the commercially well-known actors like Facebook, Google, YouTube and Twitter (who also use data etc.). We will not discuss this here but will stick to the fundamental possibilities that digital media opens up (however, we return to the big data issues in Chapter 5). In the DUFA courses, free, open and well-functioning digital media were used.

In the social science course with process feedback in Google docs and peer feedback in a Facebook group, it turned out that it was not bad with norms. However, one can have reservations, especially from a Bildung angle. The success criterion was to design exactly the assignment that the teacher had in mind: The students had to learn exactly this, X and sharing documents and written

---

[3] Digitalisation is the term for the conversion of analogue objects into digital objects. Thus, many books, films and recordings have been digitised. All previous communication media can be remedied through digital media (Finnemann 2005).

[4] Supersynchronous means that, for example, if you have temporarily been away from an online conference, you can catch up by playing back what has been going on while you were away at a fast pace, thereby catching up on what you have missed.

interaction were used for that purpose. Yet, the general possibility of digitally supported feedback and mutual inspiration can be dealt with in different ways. The unfolding of these potentials will also help to develop norms and culture for when not to use digital media (e.g., keeping external logic and values out of the education system which should be aimed at Bildung; see Tække 2019). However, two intra-educational issues need to be addressed: originality and transparency.

The issue of original/copy is affecting society for good and evil today and is most 'evil' because we live and think in the old media environment. The structures that society is built on, and which the adult generation has internalised through their own upbringing and education, are undermined by digitalisation. You can't make a living selling copies of something that is free to produce. A school is not affected in the same way, since the production or subjectivation of students into educated citizens, is not directly affected; man is not a digital object. Yet, the problem is that many of the products that students need to help them become educated are digital and can be copied, edited, etc. in time and space. Structures and rules are not geared to this new situation, which is why control systems are being built to maintain old rules and forms of teaching instead of trying to create something new.

In the DUFA courses we can see how the digitally supported scaffolding of help to self-help presumably minimises the problem of so-called plagiarism. However, over time, the educational system may react quite differently to the problem , which is really only a problem from the perspective of the old media environment. It is a basic condition that digital objects can be copied, but also edited, etc. in time and space. We already live in a participatory culture characterised by sharing, spreading, remixing, reformulation and appropriation,[5] produsage and intercreativity; this culture is characterised by the fact that, together with others, differentiated products are produced in networks where the producer, distributor and consumer are not as clearly separated as before (Bruns 2008). Against this background, it might seem appropriate to modify teaching practice to legitimise that assignments consist of clipping together paraphrases, summaries and quotes, but with close reference to sources and explanations of the student's contribution, as well as justifications as to why they selected the materials on which the assignments are based. This would be an academicisation of the way we have actually always worked! Tasks

---

[5] Jenkins (2006, xiv) defines Appropriation as: 'The ability to meaningfully sample and remix media content.'

have always had to be based on other's materials, such as a short story and previous interpretations of it, as well as texts about authorship, time and the environment, about other works that are similar or inspiring, etc. In the digital writing process it is, on the one hand, easy to find something and to cut it together, and/or to rephrase some of another person's assignment. On the other hand, the student not only has the sources selected by the teacher, or in larger tasks, also by the librarian, for the assignment, but is also required to find sources herself. In other words, the school must focus on digital teaching objects and find out through experiments how best to teach in the new media situation. This is where the last issue that we will look at in this section, transparency, comes into play.

Digital media provides opportunities for transparency that can easily get out of hand in a negative sense and transform into surveillance. In relation to the original/copy problem, legitimisation of appropriation and remix creates a basis for students to willingly provide transparency in relation to their work process. This will make possible to teach how to legitimately and academically piece together an assignment using other student's work, how to find and apply primary texts, refer and quote. In the DUFA-project we observed how already the scaffolding through shared documents and written interaction, with peer feedback and teacher process feedback, reduced headless plagiarism. In the course of mathematics, the teacher chooses not to just lay out all the completed assignments in the Padlet, but to let the students upload their completed assignments and then correct them. This allowed the weakest students to look for and use others' expressions to improve their own. However, they were fully aware that it would not help them when they were later given a test if they had simply plagiarised blindly without further consideration. In turn, it helped them to see the other's assignments and paved the way for a culture in which they gradually laid out their assignments and, by the teacher pointing out their mistakes, could gain insight into how they could have done better. Here, however, the password is culture. Culture for transparency is poorly matched to performance culture and mark tyranny where, as a student, you are judged by what mark you get. The method of using Padlet to submit assignments asynchronically creates a situation where, if the students are told to share their work with each other, they tend to wait to share until the end of the allocated period because they are also encouraged by the school system to think of themselves as competitors. Weaker student thus risk failing the exam without Padlet assistance.

If we look at the transdisciplinary practices (with shared documents etc.) from the perspective of the three dimensions of Bildung, there are ways to use the new digital media to challenge the students both according to their *knowledge*, *attitude* and *existence*.

Knowledge of mastering and handling digital objects can be promoted, encouraged and challenged in all subject matters. You will be able to sit in different places and times and work on the same document or coordinate other teaching activities through written interaction. If you are at home and have a problem with a math piece, you can, for example get help via written interaction, for example in a media with the same functionality as in a closed Facebook group. Student's understanding of themselves, media and the world is likewise helped along as one can interact with otherness elsewhere in the geographical space. Finally, creative forms of knowledge (i.e. creation and innovation) can be promoted and challenged because students either from the classroom or from their home (or elsewhere) can now be encouraged to take part in productions and appropriation communities and networks.

Attitude is a crucial educational prerequisite for knowledge to flourish sensibly and not result in antagonism and a world that is worse. Attitude turns out to be crucial in all four forms of media practices (see Chapter 2), but let's just mention 'community practice' here. In all three of the transdisciplinary experiments highlighted above, good and appropriate forms of community were developed. One example was that, in all three courses, we saw that students were willing to share their knowledge, interim calculations and results. This is not a matter of course but is 'culture dependent'. The experiments indicate that with the right cultural work in the classroom as well as the right organisation of the activities within digital media, the students are encouraged and supported to be helpful and generous towards each other. Also, the new transdisciplinary media practices seem to offer more possibilities to understand how others understand and thus more opportunities to relate to how you understand yourself. In the above experiments, we see, for example, how students partly gain insight into how the teacher understands a task, and partly how the other students in the class understand the task and how the students work with their own understanding. One could say: they practice *an understanding-seeking attitude*, where one diligently and consciously pivots between the understandings of others and their own understanding. The result seems to be that the students succeed in creating a community where they have a 'good attitude' to each other in class.

When it comes to *existence*, it is obvious that in the era of social media, one must write oneself into existence (Sundén 2003, Tække 2007). With Facebook, the distinction between one's online self and offline self has disappeared. This means that we will have to co-create our social self in both speech and written interaction. In the digital age, we make traces as communication takes place in a storage and retrieval medium. In this situation the school must help students to write their way into existence. If this is successful, the students (all else being equal) can build up their self-relationship critically and find the voices that harmonises with who they are becoming in conversation with the otherness they meet digitally and analogously. This self-work that is scaffolded in the school through good community practice will provide the prerequisites for mastering oneself and the world (e.g., one's insecurity) and help one to find one's own voice in various situations. Initially, this will only be by meeting with the teacher and the other students, but eventually through encounters with external alterity as well. This also helps to support the understanding of oneself and the world that develops over the school years in the encounter with otherness and the greater experience of who one is, what abilities one has and who one wants to be; and perhaps also lays the foundation for creating a better world of coexistence.

Path 2: New Special Subject Matter Bildung Practices

The second path is to develop new special subject matter Bildung practices which, through embedding digital media and technology, reconfigure what the subject matter in question is and thereby redefine it. This transformation involves a clear shift in the teaching and, to some extent, also a shift in educational aims. In particular, five of the DUFA experiments point in this direction and thus provide inspiration for reflection on how it can happen and whether it should happen. Since all technology has a faustic aspect, in this context one should not only look at what new possibilities a media offers, but also on the obstacles; what is lost, neglected or impossible (Postman 1993). The five DUFA experiments that exemplify the redefinition of subject matters through digital embedding are:

- A course in designing an allotment hut, in design and visual arts.
- A course about social media and political elections, in social studies.
- A course in embedding digital timelines, in history.
- A course in programming physics learning games, in mathematics and physics.
- A course about social media in China, in Chinese.

In the design and visual arts course, the technological development of 3D mathematical drawing programs caused a shift in both means and aims. Besides the use of media in general, the use of SketchUp[6] was central. As a means, part of the practical work in the subject has now shifted to the acquisition and use of this program. Manual work with pencil, calculator and ruler has been replaced with a program that has all the features needed to make 3D models of physical objects that can be virtualised in geographical contexts. This, in the first place, allows the educational aim of the subject matter to be reinterpreted to the acquisition of higher and more realistic standards when it comes to the 3D product. Second, the aim can be shifted to actual design, aesthetic, and social assessment criteria such as we saw in the Swedish research in Chapter 2 (Marner 2013; Marner and Örtegren 2013). It is not a part of a house designed with a pencil and ruler that is assessed, but the actual location of the house in the landscape, its socio-cultural characteristics in relation to the target group, etc. Third, students now work in a mode comparable to that architects and engineers work in, which is why students gain a more realistic insight into the design work. They gain insight into the virtual work and are assessed on design criteria and not on fine motor control in ruler use. The Faustian aspect here is whether the students who have shifted to virtual work lose touch with the physical world: working with a ruler, or, for example, a two-metre ceiling height. This is a risk, but it is taken into account in the exemplary course, as students have to make a total physical measurement of their rooms at home, which should be modelled in the 3D program as in the first exercise. During the observations, a student forgot to measure the door height in her room. It gave rise to many attempts to remember the height, e.g her own body in relation to the ceiling height, and in relation to the height of the doors in other rooms. In addition, there were measurements of the classroom's basic areas, physical LEGO exercises, etc. The design of the allotment hut 3D models was not only a phantasmagorical simulacrum, but also a greater opportunity to form a realistic model of a finished product that could be put into context.

In relation to *knowledge*, the reconfigured design and visual arts course challenged the students to master themselves and the world on a higher and more up to date real-world level. The students now do something that mimics what professionals do outside school, to which teaching now transgress what was possible before. Knowledge ambitions thus might get further, as education can set the aim of teaching higher, when less time is given to the old manual work, while the new manual work with 3D brings the student to a higher level of

---

[6] SketchUp is a 3D modelling computer program for a wide range of drawing applications such as architectural and interior design, landscape architecture, civil and mechanical engineering and film and video game design.

knowledge and a greater understanding of herself and the world. Students can now use more energy to get into the context and design more purposefully and adequately. This also includes encouragement to be more creative and innovative. When it comes to attitude and existence, the experiment does not seem to actualise new possibilities for challenging the students in those two Bildung dimensions. This may be due to a lack of third-wave teaching in the documented DUFA course (the students did not interact with people from the outside (people from the target group)).

The course about social media and political elections in social sciences also has brought a shift in both educational goals and aims. The means changed because the students in the experiment interacted virtually with politicians and met them in the new media environment. The aims changed because the students followed politics into the new media environment as a new topic with its own ontology (e.g. its own agenda-setting influence). The alternative would be to go to voters' meetings, analyse electoral advertisements and articles in newspapers. These are still important parts of politics studies along with reading electoral programs, etc., but they can no longer stand alone as social media has become an important political platform. The aim has thus shifted to include empirical work *in* the new media arena. Here, the Faustian aspect will be the loss of the physical electorate, which is not, however, a necessity. There is no doubt that the analysis of what is happening on social media and the new possibilities this has created (i.e. interviewing local politicians on social media) is now an important part of the teaching. In addition, in the future, the use of microtargeting and dark posts should also be included.

When we look at the process as potential Bildung engagements and focus on knowledge, the students are challenged to get a better understanding of the world, here in the form of election campaigns on social media, through the interactions between the students and the interviewed politicians and, most importantly, through interpretations and discussions of the findings in groups and in the class together with the teacher. Regarding attitude, students are challenged to develop a better understanding of how action is taken on social media. The results of the experiment showed that a lot of the students – self-confessedly – were initially very naïve about social media and political elections, but the course allowed them to become more critical. When it comes to existence, the process challenged the students to contact and interact with strangers (i.e., politicians) and also to develop their own critical voice in that situation and subsequently reflect on the incident. In the DUFA experiment this led some students to create a new and more independent attitude to politics.

The course about timelines in history worked by embedding digital timelines. This does not really change the aims of the subject matter, but it improves the means. With digital timelines the students are supported to get a better overview of historical time, but also to work more creatively to create an overview of long-lasting and extensive historical events and periods from the internet (e.g., pictures, text etc). In the experiment, this also included work with critical attitude and source criticism in relation to digital sources. Perhaps this can be interpreted as some kind of change in the aim of the subject, to some smaller degree similar to that in the design course. The students were challenged to be more aware of the 'construction' and contingency of historical overviews. This can be seen as a kind of incremental innovation that helps students to gain a better overview of the short and long lines of history. As a faustic aspect, it can be mentioned that timeline automation for overview may weaken our mental overview, in line with Plato's argument that writing weakens our memory (see Chapter 1).

When we look at the course as Bildung engagements, it challenges the student's *knowledge* in terms of understanding; they are are now encouraged to 'with better means' acknowledge and create short and long lines in history which, in turn, provides a better basis for creating a critical *attitude* to history and maybe for understanding oneself in an historical context (existence).

The course in programming physics offered a change in terms of both means and aims. The point is that the upper secondary students are programming digital games, which are tested and used by students in an elementary school. The mathematics is transformed into knowledge of the equations of physics and then into a multimodal mathematical simulation in the program *Scratch*.[7] This operationalisation of mathematics was not possible before. The product is a digital object. In addition, the various media for written interaction, as well as Padlet, etc. were used to scaffold the programming in Scratch. The students are challenged to become familiar with programming and obtain technical insights into how algorithms are adapted and work. The course raises mathematics from calculating something to implementing the calculation in a game where it is executed so that an object, for example, moves in a certain way. To be realised, the cause required a complex organisation with multiple teachers and consultants, virtual interaction, class hours and a confrontation with a user group. The faustic aspect may be that you become good at *using* mathematics, but do not necessarily

---

[7] Scratch is a free programming language, developed by MIT, that makes it easy to create interactive stories, animations, games, music, and art and share your creations on the web.

obtain a deep understanding of mathematics as something important in itself. In interviews, it is suggested that, despite the many hours of the course, the students have not really learned anything new about mathematics. On the other hand, their mathematics skills might have become more robust and they might have learned to operationalise their knowledge. Including programming in mathematics and physics, including interaction with an online programming community associated with Scratch (third wave), transforms what science education in an upper secondary school can do. Students are introduced to programming and gain insight into a digitalised and algorithmic world, including remix culture, in an online programming community. The focus is on expression practice – to create and produce digital learning games.

The course challenges and supports both mastering, understanding and, especially, a creative science Bildung engagement. It challenges the students' knowledge, their ability to collaborate and relate to programming, science and primary school students (attitude) and also encourages unique and individual choices, considerations and expression (existence). By producing games for primary school students and through interaction with an online community, students are involved scientifically in the world. By including programming, subject matters in science are updated to a digital world. When we look at the course as Bildung engagements, it challenges the students to better master, understand and create digital media. This also encourages the students to form a reflected attitude to a world governed by algorithms, which could, however in the DUFA course, be more worked on more obviously by linking a social or humanistic subject to the process. Attitude and existence are perhaps traditionally weak in the sciences which, more than other fields are subject to a rationalist paradigm.

The course about social media in China in Chinese is an example of how digital media is revolutionising education. The fact that pupils in Denmark can interact with pupils in China is, if not revolutionary, a qualitative change compared to writing paper letters to each other. Students sit in the present, feel the mutual presence, want to make themselves understandable and get the language alive. The teaching resources have changed, both technically, organisationally and didactically, but the aim is still mastery of a foreign language and an understanding of China and its rich cultural heritage. The process can also be said to teach about the new media and the media situation in China and these are new aims. In this way, the process is similar to that in social science and politics. Social media is now widely used in China and is changing what China is. If the subject matter is to remain adequate, the media must enter the curriculum not just as a tool, but as an integrated part of the subject – otherwise you will not learn about China and Chinese, as it is now. The course could have made more effort to provide a critical attitude with regard to digital media and surveillance in a dictatorship state. However, this can be included in the future. This course is a good example of why the third wave is important in teaching. As the world is now interconnected, the diversity it offers – or perhaps the knowledge and cultural respect we have developed for differences – cannot be recreated in a closed classroom. Perhaps before digital media, it was enough to read a book about China? It seems almost absurd now.

Looking at the course as Bildung engagements the students are encouraged to improve their knowledge of the Chinese language so that they became better at mastering it. Also, they are challenged to strengthening their understanding of the Chinese people and China as a country. However, as with the course about learning games, the current design does not seem to contribute much to the development of a critical attitude. From the outside, it seems more astonishing, since language subjects are precisely within the cultural field, but perhaps the teaching of languages is under such pressure that there was no surplus capacity to focus on technological surveillance and suppression. In addition, language can almost resemble mathematics when the assessment is not focusing on the foreign culture but on the code of language. That being said, the course has, of course, contributed to both attitude and existence since the students first imagined interacting with Chinese students and then did so. They have thus had to imagine and identify with cultural politeness and find their own voice in relation to this. The course also exemplifies how the use of social media and digital media in linguistic and cultural subjects can make a transformative difference, as teaching can change from simply being communication about (e.g., Chinese) to becoming communication with both Chinese (friendship class) and outside experts (professionals). Embedding interaction with Chinese students seems to bring students closer to a better understanding of Chinese culture as well as their own culture, society and everyday life. In addition, it allows the possibility of maintaining further voluntary contact with Chinese students. Both expression and impression practices appear to be strengthened. Interaction possibilities in teaching are increased and improved and more students can develop their own voices. It gives rise to new ways to organise community activities. The experiment both enhances the internal interaction in the class (second wave) and opens up more interaction with the outside world than was previously possible (third wave). Since the experiment takes place in Chinese, where the language skills being worked on are relatively elementary, the internal interaction aims at mastering linguistic skills. However, the interaction with the outside world provides ample possibilities to support an understanding-orientated and creative Bildung engagement that addresses both attitude (e.g., being open and critical) and existence (e.g., gaining personal relationships and contacts around the world).

In general, the introduction of digital media into individual subjects paints a transformational picture of the way they are being taught, both in terms of means and aims. This is summarised in the following table:

Table 4.1 New aims and means in the single subject matters

	Mathematics and Physics	Social studies	History	Design and Visual Arts	Chinese
New aims	Programming, computer games and algorithms	Politics and social media	Search criticism in relation to Internet sources	Digital 3D design solutions	China and social media
New means	Online community, online group, programming language	Social media, online sharing documents, websites, online group	Digital timeline tool, digital remix of materials for overview	Digital drawing program	WeChat, and digital language tools

As shown in the table, all five examples involve both new specific aims – or perhaps, more precisely, new kinds of academic content – and are embedding new means. In relation to aims (or content), the courses mainly take up subjects that they have already been in touch with, but which are now emerging in new ways. For example, political elections in social studies, where the object (politics) has changed with the advent of social media. This means that we have a new aim within the subject matter which is to challenge the students to become wiser in relation to what social media means for political elections. This is an *update of the subject matter*. Similarly, digital means are being used to meet these new aims, which are, in most cases, closely related to the subject (e.g., a digital drawing program in design). This is unlike path 1, where we saw that the media could be used in almost any subject. Prevalent to the five examples is that digital media does not completely replace analogue media but instead *extends* a media chain so that the teaching involves both analogue *and* digital media in a way where the latter are embedded in an otherwise predominantly analogue teaching. We would therefore say that they all provide examples of a digital renewal of the different subject matters, understood as a modification of the existing subjects rather than the emergence of completely new subjects.

Path 3: Digitalisation as a Bildung-Relevant, Epoch-Typical, Key Issue

The third path is to work with the digital in teaching as what Klafki (2005) calls an *epoch-typical key problem*. This is especially important in relation to challenging a student's reflexivity, so that the use of media does not happen blindly, but through critical understanding, dialogue and genuine participation. Only one of the DUFA experiments primarily pursued this path, but there are several courses that contain elements that go in a similar direction.

- Course on the Internet's structure, information search, source criticism and correction of misinformation, in English.

According to Klafki, students in school – seen from a critical Bildung perspective – should not only be adapting to an existing society but should also be able and willing to improve society. Therefore, if students are to work with information search and source criticism in teaching, it must be done in a way that encourages them to co-decide on the development and use of the Internet with special regard to information search and source criticism. Klafki's answer to how this can happen is the idea of an epoch-typical key problem.

Instead of the idea of cannons as a substantial core, for what one should work with in school, Bildung, according to Klafki, should be understood as historically conveyed awareness of an epoch-typical key problem both in the present and in the supposed future; including the understanding that everyone is co-responsible. Back in the 1980's Klafki proposed five such problems: (1) the issue of peace, (2) the environment, (3) societal inequality, (4) the dangers and opportunities of new technical governance, information – and communication media, and (5) experiences of love, human sexuality and gender. Yet, this list is not fixed; in Klafki's view, the question of what the most important epoch-typical key problems are should always be open to discussion by schools, teachers and students.

The criterion for such key problems is that they are time-specific structural problems of societal and worldwide importance which, at the same time, relate to each individual in a central way. The course on information search and source criticism relates precisely to a worldwide problem with fake news, alternative truths, misinformation, echo chambers, etc. With the insurmountable complexity of the Internet, searching for and finding relevant and valid information has become a problem for everyone. This, on the one hand, has given many a more reflected relationship with truth, since, we do not necessarily believe what is written in the newspaper or what has been said by the President of the United States. On the other hand, our best way to find truth might also include digital media, even though they offer much false information, as well as machine learning algorithms that, based on big data and profiling, allow us to receive different 'truths' about the same objects (see more about this in Chapter 5). According to Klafki, it must be possible to agree on the seriousness of such a problem, and to recognise that there are different answers to the problem, and that these answers may depend on interests and attitudes. By working with such a problem, it becomes possible to create teaching that is both relevant and interesting to the students and which deals with something that is world relevant.

Information retrieval and source criticism relate, in particular, to what Klafki calls 'dangers and opportunities of new technical governance, information – and communication media'. However, as Klafki also points out, the key problems are interrelated and therefore must not be worked on separately (so as not to miss the possibility of developing coherence in thinking). Information search and source criticism exemplify this, as the Internet offers various information on both the peace issue, the environmental issue, societal inequality and experiences with love, human sexuality and gender relations (e.g., different information about the state of the climate, or whether gender is determined by nature or society). Thus, information search and source criticism raises questions that relate to all the key issues.

All this puts huge demands on a single, defined course like the one in the DUFA project. Still, the process of searching information in English goes far along the paths Klafki points out. The first part of the course teaches how to google, URL understanding, the anatomy of search results and the structure of the Internet (www.), advanced search functions, all of this in combination with information search exercises. The next part is about consuming web content and looked at topics such as clickbait, alternative truth, going viral, fake news and source criticism. The big question was how to evaluate a website's validity. Before the final part of the course, the students are presented with target group analysis and it ends with a dissemination section where group work is done on a dissemination project, organised as a competition to get the best possible engagement on one's information product, which can be in the form of an Infographic or an Explainer that exposes and corrects untruths from existing websites.

The clear general aim of the process is to empower students to be both critical and competent in information search and source criticism. The course created some specific opportunities (or possibilities) for the students to improve their knowledge, achieve valuable experiences and act 'on it'.

According to Klafki (2005) not only must we work intellectually with the epochal problems, but also with their 'importance to us' and 'demands on us'. If you only deal with information search and source criticism intellectually, you will simply turn it into a 'school subject', which is something you talk about, but do not connect with life. Through projects, studies and practical processes, information search and source criticism must be sought out and discussed. As far as possible, the school should help students to gain experience and to share their solutions. By the end of the DUFA course, students not only acted by conducting and learning information search and source criticism, they also were capable of disseminating and then correcting misinformation on the internet.

However, such a course must not stand alone, since it will slip into the background and therefore not affect either the students' general being in the world or their study activity. Also, within the general epochal key issue of 'the dangers and opportunities of new technical governance, information – and communication media', information search and source criticism are central, but other issues are also compelling, such as those related to the field of machine learning algorithms, big data and profiling, as we see in the Anglo-American school world (Williamson 2017). It is important that the education system takes this trend very seriously because it discourages Bildung and is a relapse into behavioural pedagogy (see Chapter 5).

From the perspective of the three Bildung dimensions – knowledge, attitude and existence – students on the course are challenged to improve on search information and practice source criticism at such a high level that they can actually review the structure and logic of the web both in theory and in practice. When it comes to attitude and existence, the course encourages the students to develop a more critical attitude, and become existentially involved in the 'fight against misinformation' on the Internet.

Path 4: Third Wave Activities that Transform Classroom Teaching and Bildung

The fourth path is to develop what we have called third wave activities (i.e. activities that include digital mediated interaction by challenging others), thus helping to transform what is meant by classroom teaching. As we have pointed out in the analyses, in the third wave activities there is a very large untapped Bildung potential. Some of the DUFA experiments contain actual third wave experiments and can therefore provide inspiration for further development along this path.

- The course on social media and political elections, in social studies. Interaction with subject relevant people (politicians) and professionals (expert in elections).
- The course on social media in China, in Chinese. Interaction with subject-relevant people (students in Chinese friendship class) and professionals (expert in China).

Increasing interaction in the classroom using digital media does not, in itself, lead to the development of a new style of teaching and Bildung that takes full advantage of the new interaction and representation possibilities between the class and the outside world. If the school wants to act more extensively and innovatively, it can create a new hybrid form of teaching, involving not only teachers and students, but also other actors, via the Internet. In this new form of teaching, the school must try to cultivate relationships whereby the teacher intervenes both in the educational community and in the individual student's learning network. This approach, which has been actualised to some extent in some of the DUFA courses and which is a potential extension of others, provides a classroom, which we call, the contact-seeking classroom. Only with this form of teaching can the closed echo-chamber classroom be broken and the focus on how pupils can be engaged and involved in the world through teaching be realised.

The contact-seeking classroom occurs when people other than students and teachers are integrated into the teaching via interaction on the Internet. When it happens on a daily basis, it changes the classroom that has existed since the school began in the media society that preceded the present. Instead of closed classroom teaching between teachers and students, we can now begin to observe an open interaction system. This gives the education system new perspectives on what teaching is and how teaching can proceed. Students can now meet people with other perspectives, viewpoints, experiences, knowledge, languages and reactions. The teacher and textbook become decentralised. From being the ultimate other through which students are to be formed, the teacher becomes a mediator of otherness. Students meet their contemporaries, with other views and perspectives, which they, with the teacher's help, critically relate to and process before, during and after the meeting itself. The increased engagement that can be documented in the contact-seeking classroom (Chapter 3), we interpret as, among other things, a consequence of the authenticity that students experience in their schoolwork when it involves outside contact.

The course in social studies invites the students to involve themselves with the world by interacting with local politicians. In this we see an example of actualisation of the third wave. This knowledge and information gained from the outside eased the problem of the textbooks having almost nothing to say about the importance of social media in elections and in the political system. The students found it both interesting and instructive that they themselves had to study how the parties used social media. The contact with the politicians was an eye-opener for the students because they had not imagined that it was possible. To this end, it gave rise to reflections on the importance of social media, both in their own lives, and in relation to current political processes. Thus, the course encourages the students to relate to and participate in the democratic debate, which is done on a qualifying basis in teaching. Students are then challenged to critically make up their mind and understand that politicians can use social media to manipulate and acquire voters who may not agree with their values. This gives students the opportunity to consider how political culture and participation can be improved for the benefit of the public and not just to consider how a politician can optimise effective communication. Since politics and ideology are at the core of social science and since politics today is also largely carried out on social media, it is almost impossible to meet the subject matter's requirements without third-wave activities.

If we generalise from this course, third-wave teaching is a way for the schools to involve their students in the societal development. Borders change, the focal point of the media shifts, perspectives change, history is rewritten, new markets emerge, old species die out, pandemics spread in record time, ice melts, and how much has the water level risen today? The world is accelerated in dynamic and unsteadiness, and the schools should probably stand a little on the sidelines and observe and reflect. However, the school must have updated and nuanced information for its Bildung processes which address the epochal key issues of the time.

The course in Chinese also had third-wave activities, partly with an expert and partly with a friendship class. Again, we saw high level of commitment. In the SME-experiment there was also great success with friendship classes, which often form the lowest hanging fruit when it comes to third-wave activities. The classes have a slightly different curriculum and a teacher who explains things that are a bit different, for example, lives somewhere else may have different socio-economic background, etc. They represent an otherness. The activity induces engagement and diligence beyond what one sees otherwise. Authentic third-wave candidates may also be practitioners (e.g., a politician), or experts (e.g., a university election expert), or someone who is just authentic in their role (e.g., a refugee), or condition (e.g. pregnant). Thus, there are many ways that each can provide educational input from the current world. During programming learning games, we saw other teachers associated with the course as professional experts who assisted with the academic processes; this is another category associated with third-wave teaching.

In general, from the experience of the SME-experiment, and the DUFA-project it is important to work thoroughly with the issues that belong to the first and second wave, both in relation to Bildung and in relation to media practices, before establishing contact out of the class. Thus, one must be able to organise (community practice), participate appropriately and professionally (participation practice), be confident in information search and source criticism (impression practice) and be able to express oneself in and handle the necessary media (expression practice). The knowledge, attitude and existential development must be matured for the contact in question so that the teacher believes that both the students and the person from the outside do not suffer harm.

To summarise the third wave-path based on Bildung engagements, we see improved opportunities for challenging students' knowledge in individual subjects, partly in terms of the adequate information that can be extracted in the contact and partly in terms of better mastering, understanding and creating of the world. Attitude is also challenged both in terms of mastery and understanding of otherness, as these are authentic situations that are prepared, executed and reflected upon, which also strengthen the creation of oneself and the world. The same goes for existence: through the interactions with real challenging, and different others, chances for better understanding of oneself and development of one's own voice are improved.

Conclusion

In this chapter we have elaborated on four different ways of designing and carrying out Bildung orientated teaching in the digital age.

The first path takes digitalisation into consideration on a general transdisciplinary level. With digital media it is possible to create and develop new transdisciplinary teaching practices, in which digital media are embedded and integrated with analogue media, that can be applied in all subjects, in different variations. We point to the digital *mediacy* (see Brügger 2002) as consisting in a resolution of the distinction between original and copy played out in a new space-time that disrupts the current mode of society, including the education system. The perspective indicates that the new information and interaction situations calls for a restructuring and new norm-building adequate with the new media environment. Such attention to the new spatial and temporal possibilities could move the school as a whole (i.e., all subjects) towards a new mode with new criteria for what an assignment is and how it is produced. It requires changes to rules, practices and culture. However, there is no ready-made solution that can be implemented, which is why the school must start an experimental and innovative movement through which the new material basis for the social is generally developed in all subjects as a basic condition.

The second path follows the individual subjects, where the development deals with how the individual subjects re-configure both means and aims in the virtual space. There are major differences here, namely that all subjects can advantageously change means, but where only a few, as it seems now, will change aims. That is not to say that the qualitative leaps provided by the new means, for example, to make systematic searches of databases and use sensors and webcams all over the world, will eventually result in pushing the aims of all subjects. In the DUFA history subject, only an incremental change was seen that gives little advantage in historical overview. Subjects that can more easily simulate their teaching object digitally will be better able to change both means and aims. If the teaching object can be remediated digitally or, if it is simply born digitally, it should easily be transformed. Yet, it is not a goal in itself that teaching must change. It is only a requirement if the digitalisation of society (or something else) calls for it. When it comes to means, all subjects will be able to change, as they all rely on communication to a greater or lesser degree and therefore will be able to undergo shifts like those we looked at in 'the first path'. For instance, subjects such as sports and biology undergo changes with regard to means (everything that is included in the subjects can now be tracked, measured and calculated), while the aims, for the time being, seem almost the same. In visual art and design, we see a more profound change because the subject's object in the outside world has changed as has the object for assessment, from work with a ruler to the product's fit in the landscape and cultural context.

The third path dealt with epoch-typical key problems. It linked the media revolution with a fundamentally critical, democratic, humanistic and emancipatory foundation. We exemplified one of the media practices from the DUFA model and illustrated how searching valid information is crucial to the human being in today's society. It is important for Bildung (knowledge, attitude and existence) that each epochal key issue is linked to the other epochal problems. In order to understand, for instance, the climate crisis, one must be able to search and thereby build valid knowledge that will enable the students to master and recreate themselves and the world. This path is important because it anchors the shifts in communication patterns in the world society (political, economic, military, in relation to gender, etc.), that is made possible by digital media, in a humanistic Bildung tradition. This can, through criticism as a societal feedback loop, prevent society from distancing itself from a society based on human rights, sustainable nature and peace (one can think of the UN goals in this context). In this way, the school must take responsibility and encourage the next generation to be able maintain that responsibility.

The fourth path is concerned with third-wave teaching. This points to the fact that the school can keep up to date with the rapid and dynamic developments in the school's environment. It is not useful to teach outdated content in an outdated way. Third-wave teaching solves both problems at once, with contact outside the classroom. This, in turn, is not easy, as our previous research shows that one must first work with first- and second-wave issues, and practice media skills. On the other hand, this form of teaching seems to engage and involve students both in school subjects and the world because of its intensity and being updated with media use and the organisational practices and social encounters with alterity and challenging otherness it entails.

If we try to put together the four paths, the school seems to be at a crossroads. The paths are not mutually exclusive but complementary. Turning to the first path, we generally see the school as a system that, in all subjects and in its foundations, must seek to find itself in a world where digital media offers new possibilities to structure teaching and schooling. Looking down path 2, we see the individual subjects that must find their reconfigured way into the digital world. They must keep themselves informed about the course created some specific opportunities (or possibilities) for the students to improve their knowledge, achieve valuable experiences and act 'on it'. Looking down the third path, we are reminded of our responsibility to work out what digitalisation itself means – as a main problem of our epoch – and to seek to influence this development based on a Bildung ambition. Looking down the fourth and final path, we see a mode where the other three roads can meet and begin a spiral. The school in general, each of the subjects and our responsibility for digitalisation as an epochal key problem can be part of the process of teaching. The development of the school becomes an objective that is continually revised and developed using processes that reproduce and modify the school's mode through each and every school hour executed with the other three paths in mind in third-wave actions.

5

Big Data

As was the conclusion in Chapter 3, digitalisation, even as third wave activity, does not necessary mean that teaching is really Bildung orientated. In this chapter, we discuss the mediatisation of education in relation to *Big Data* as an exemplary Bildung issue. We address the question of how schools and teachers can and should deal with digitalisation – here exemplified by Big Data – seen from a Bildung perspective (see Chapter 1). Yet, we do not put forward definitive answers but only discuss how one could and should understand and respond educationally to Big Data. Before we can begin to elaborate on different educational responses, we must clarify our understanding of Big Data. This means asking: What *is* Big Data? How can one understand this new phenomenon? We suggest that Big Data should be understood as a new type of machine (and medium), referred to as a 'Big Data Machine', that has technical, social and cultural components and that other machines (big organisations) like states and companies can develop and use to optimise and automate their activities. Based on Levi Bryant's onto-cartography (Bryant 2014, see Chapter 1) and the literature on Big Data (Boyd and Crawford 2012, Chen et al., 2016, Han 2016, Sivarajah et al., 2017, Williamson 2017, Hansen 2018), we try to identify how Big Data machines operate and transform input into output. In doing so, we show that Big Data machines can function with different inputs and generate different kinds of output. We are particularly interested in the citizen aspect both on the input side (e.g., tracking, collecting, calculating data) and in the output side in regard to nudging and manipulating citizen behaviour. When we highlight this human aspect of the machine, we call it the 'Citizen Big Data Machine' and it is primarily this type of machine that forms our focus.

After defining our concept of Big Data, we discuss how different political systems on a world societal level might respond to Citizen Big Data Machines. We will focus on educational policies and ask the question: Does it matter educationally how political systems respond to Citizen Big Data Machines? When discussing responses, we will ask: Do states like China, the US and the EU try to make use of the new machines and/or impose restrictions on them and/or try to educate (new) citizens to relate to them in certain ways? More precisely, China is used to exemplify Big Data for state control and surveillance; the US is used to exemplify Big Data for marked business; and the EU is used to exemplify Big Data for democracy. Yet, the point is *not* to give a full description of how Big Data is treated in each of these three contexts. What is at stake is more basically to point out three different ways of dealing with Big Data. This also implies that when we, for instance, analyse 'state control and surveillance', we primarily refer to examples from China, ignoring, for instance, the National Security Agency (NSA, US) or the many surveillance cameras throughout the UK.

Thus, what we suggest is that at least three different responses to Citizen Big Data Machines can be identified. The first response is to begin to develop and use Citizen Big Data Machines to optimise the state's activities directed towards its citizens (and perhaps also foreign citizens), including state educational activities. This is perhaps the response mostly adopted by China (though also, in part, by other stats). The second response is to allow big companies to buy, develop and make use of Citizen Big Data Machines to optimise their market positions and/or sell Citizen Big Data Machines, or products generated by such machines, to their customers, including 'the educational sector'. This is perhaps the response mostly adopted by the US (though also, in part, by many other states). Both the 'state' and 'the market' response strategy fits with the educational outlook we, in previous chapters, have called the 'engineer' and the *technical and causal understanding* of teaching and media, constraining education as a pure techno-bureaucratic space. This means that, equipped with new Big Data technology, the technical mainstream view of education seems to be reinforced globally. Yet, there might also be a third response and thus an alternative to mainstream education which is to protect civil society from states and companies that use Citizen Big Data Machines to monitor, control, manipulate and affect citizens. This protection can be established through laws but also via educational policies that aim to teach people to be critical and on guard. This is perhaps the response adopted, at least in part, by the EU (representing a minority in the world society). This response fits with the educational outlook we in previous chapters have called (a) the *voluntaristic* and *facilitating* understanding of teaching and media, constraining education as a totally free and safe space for pure individual self-development, but also with (b) the *critical* and *explorative* – understanding of teaching and media. Yet, the latter view would also suggest that students are not only protected against the new Big Data machines but also develop both a critical understanding of them and power to use them, if possible, to take over the machines and modify them for good reason. Further, the even more creative and experimental understanding of Bildung (see again Chapter 1) would suggest, that teachers and students, if possible, should make creative experiments in teaching with Big Data machines. We return to these suggestions in the end of the chapter.[1]

What is Big Data?

According to John Caputo (2018), Big Data is the 'Great Other' of our age and is typically viewed as the mythical non-human algorithm able to understand us better than we can understand ourselves and, as such, decide everything for us. Thus, today, there are business owners, politicians, educators, researchers and others who dream and work on developing Big Data that can replace human thinking. As Chris Anderson (2008:1) describes:

> *This is a world where massive amounts of data and applied mathematics replace every other tool that might be brought to bear. Out with every theory of human behaviour, from linguistics to sociology. Forget taxonomy, ontology, and psychology. Who knows why people do what they do? The point is they do it, and we can track and measure it with unprecedented fidelity. With enough data, the numbers speak for themselves.*

As we later elaborate, however, numbers do not speak for themselves. The myth of the big algorithm contains problematic assumptions and consequences. First, however, we must clarify what Big Data is. The phrase 'Big Data' originated in the 1990s and referred to large amounts of data stored, processed and analysed by supercomputers. However, the datasets that were considered enormous in the 1990s can today be processed on ordinary computers using ordinary software. Furthermore, today, the term 'Big Data' also applies to data sets that are not necessarily large but complex. Thus, as a *technical phenomenon,* Big Data is about developing computing power and algorithmic precision to gather, analyse and compare complex data sets. *Socially,* however, Big Data is about developing and using data analysis for social purposes (e.g., to target companies' advertisements, to optimise politicians' election campaigns, to control learning in school and much more). *Culturally,* Big Data emerges as a mythology in which the new data sets are ascribed validity and objectivity (Boyd and Crawford 2012).

---

[1] This chapter is based on Paulsen and Tække (2020).

On the technical level, Big Data presents engineering challenges, such as designing computer systems that can store, assemble, analyse and visualise complex data sets (see, e.g., Sivarajah et al., 2017 about the main challenges of Big Data). At the social level, however, the challenge is how to collect, analyse and use Big Data to monitor, predict and make social decisions in areas such as law, health, economics and journalism. For instance, in a split second, the AI Watson can review millions of patient records, research articles and clinical studies (Chen et al., 2016), yet Big Data is also used to decide who should receive certain news, how long prisoners should spend in jail and what constitutes appropriate assignments and student behaviour in school. Such challenges regarding the application of Big Data are of a social nature and are connected to our view of what society should be. They also relate to the cultural level, which concerns how Big Data is understood and evaluated (i.e., what understandings and norms evolve around its use?). For example, does it become a norm that it is legitimate for states and companies to monitor, record, analyse and try to influence human activities down to the smallest detail (e.g., our heart rates, moods, political views, shopping habits, sexual inclinations and knowledge)?

Big Data Machines

To get a clearer understanding of how Big Data works, we will now try to build a theoretical model by drawing on the *onto-cartography*, developed by Levi Bryant (2014). The aim of onto-cartography is to understand machines and media and thus make it possible to map relations between machines and media *and* address political, social and ethical issues. We will attempt to understand Big Data as a new machine/media type and analyse how it works, what it can do, where it can be applied and with what political and educational consequences and dilemmas.

First, Big Data can be understood as a machine that operates using only one thing: Big Data. Ever since Aristotle, we have struggled to understand the causes of everything. But that is changing. In the Big Data age, we can process unimaginable amounts of data that give us insight into how things are *connected* – but not why they are related as they are. An increasing number of decisions are based on knowledge of statistical correlation – the way things are statistically related – rather than on knowledge of causality (Han 2016). The machine – able to use Big Data – is built to collect, analyse and structure complex data sets and, through its operations, transform data into new informative data products – revealing something valuable about the data set collected; for instance, identifying patterns in the data set, predicting future states or actions in the world from which the data set is derived, or suggesting different kinds of actions (given certain rules).

Yet it is important to note that all machines, as Bryant argues, are pluripotent, meaning that they can be used not only for one thing but for many things. Where a vacuum cleaner has a rigid coupling to its function (it can be used to vacuum), a computer has a loose coupling to its function and can be used for almost any purpose, which is also true for Big Data Machines. They can be structurally coupled to different machines and purposes, fulfilling different tasks.

Furthermore, the Big Data Machines can be good or bad at these things and their operational structures can be rigid or more or less flexible depending on their programming. However, the important point here is that all Big Data Machines essentially transform collected, stored and analysed Big Data into output data that differs from the input. In other words, they function as input-output-machines, selectively open to only certain inputs and only able to produce certain outputs through their internal capacity and operations. In this way, the Big Data Machine is preconfigured or programmed; even machine learning algorithms and neural networks follow a programmed grammar (with incorporated values and logics). This is illustrated in Figure 5.1.

An example of a Big Data Machine is that used to calculate the weather forecast. Such machines may appear to objectify how nature works, but we should remember that machine learning algorithms will always be biased, since there is always programming involved (e.g., what is registered in the first place, how the data is processed and what output is requested). Big Data Machines play an active, but not neutral, role in the construction of reality, since they are constructed and operated by the scientific communities and, perhaps through these communities, also influenced in their design by the interests of commercial and political actors. In the next section, we examine Big Data Machines that not only involve such actors but also involve the users they serve (monitor and

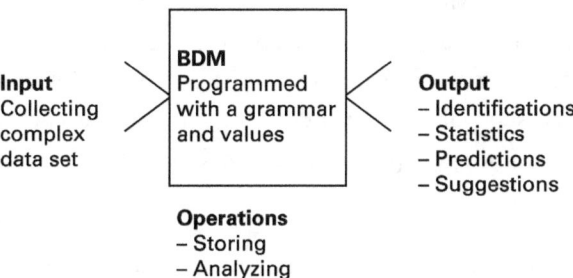

Figure 5.1 A Big Data Machine.

potentially manipulate) as components of the machine: in other words, as a set of sub-machines.[2]

Citizen Big Data Machines

Let us know look at the type of Big Data Machines we call Citizen Big Data Machines (CBDMs). The special thing about this type of machine is that it collects data about citizens. These data are transformed by the machine into new kinds of information about citizens: information that identifies patterns (correlations) in citizens' behaviour (including expressed values), that predicts future behaviour and actions and that suggests certain content to send to certain individuals, based on these predictions in order to influence their behaviour. In principle, this machine works in the same way that Cambridge Analytica, who called their method psychographic segmentation, was alleged to have worked. The method combines Big Data with theory of persuasion and personality tests (Hansen 2018, 24). Between 2007 and 2012, a research team at Cambridge Analytica found a connection between personality tests and Facebook profiles (especially what people 'Like' on Facebook) (Hansen 2018). They did this by asking millions of Facebook users to complete personality tests, which they then crossed with t social media behaviour (Hansen 2018). This project revealed that, by using this technology, it is possible to predict with some accuracy people's preferences, orientations, emotional states, financial circumstances and much more.

The CBDM trawls the internet and digital media and collects digital data produced by citizens, including data about what websites people visit, what they write, whom they befriend, what they do online and economic transactions – in principle, if relevant to the specific machine, all their digital activities and footprints (it also gathers offline data such as geotagging and credit card use). Furthermore, the machine can predict (with different degrees of success) what a citizen's 'next move' will be and what they will most probably like, agree with, or vote for. Using this information, a state, for instance, can either order a citizen to do what it wants, or to nudge them in its preferred direction. With regard to the latter possibility, a state theoretically can nudge a person to think or buy something that they otherwise would not have done, or for instance, could manipulate a person to not vote if they are predicted to vote for the 'wrong' candidate.

---

[2] We here followed Bryant's (2014) suggestion that a new big machine emerges when new powers emerge from combining machines and where these new powers cannot be found in each of the machines combined.

Such a machine is likely to be in high demand by big organisations who wish to keep track of citizens and influence their behaviour. Furthermore, it is only such big organisations that will have the required financial and/or political power to make claims on the CBDMs. It can also be assumed that the complex CBMs can only function efficiently if they are operated by big social organisations. To obtain socially relevant output, many human users must interact with the machines in a coordinated manner. We therefore predict that the new CBDMs will mainly be developed into media that can be used to improve, optimise and automate the powers and capacities of states and big companies to keep track of and influence citizens – their behaviour, choices, attitudes, learning and desires. This is illustrated in Figure 5.2.

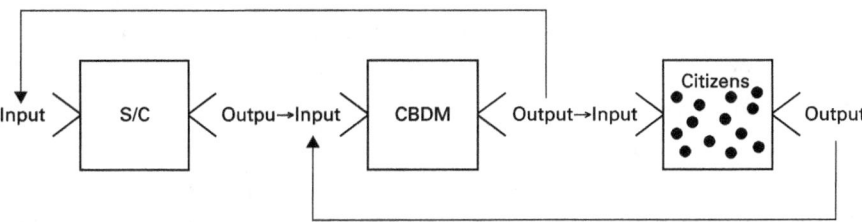

Figure 5.2 Citizen Big Data Machine as state or corporate medium.

As illustrated in Figure 5.2, the CBDM mediates between states (S) and/or companies (C) and citizens. States and companies control the programming of the machine (how the machine learning algorithms works) and they can use the CBDM to keep track of citizens' behaviour and activities as well as try to influence the citizens based on analyses of the data collected through this tracking.

Big Cyborgs

We can speculate that a new type of socio-technical-political machine will emerge from the combination of states and/or companies and CBDMs: a new Big Cyborg. Just as water (H_2O) emerges with unique properties when two hydrogen atoms and one oxygen atom are combined, it is likely that combining states/companies with CBDMs will give rise to new big powers and capacities that neither the state/company nor the CBDM possess separately. Will these powers be (a) a structural power to keep track of citizens; or (b) an operational power to form, select and relate political or commercial messages (in the widest sense) to specific segments/groups and individuals?

Concerning the tracking of citizens' behaviour, one could perhaps object that the CBDM can do this alone – because it is this machine alone that is structurally open to complex digital data input and that makes the tracking possible. However, strictly speaking, the CBDM does not track citizens' behaviour and values. What it does is collect digital data and digitalised analogue data. A social machine like a state or a company must (a) work out and maintain criteria for selections and (b) form strategies for intervening (e.g., sending special messages or killer drones). This is complex and needs to be worked out by different combinations of decision makers, engineers and computer programs. In other words, to obtain the power to really track citizens' behaviour, values and desires, the political/commercial, social and technical apparatus must be stitched together. The same is true for the operational power to form, select and relate political or commercial messages to specific segments/groups and individuals.

Perhaps one can best describe the relationship between the state/company and the CBDM as the relation between a knight and his armour or a gunslinger and his gun. The point would then be that the media we use contributes to the type of being we become. A man using a gun becomes a gunman to use Latour's (1999) famous example. And, in the same manner, a social machine like a state or company that uses Big Data, becomes a new creature – the Big Data State or the Big Data Company. Yet it is not only gunmen who arise from the combination of men and guns. In a certain way, the gun also uses and modifies the man – it encourages the man to become a certain person (the gunslinger) with somehow modified motives, powers and capabilities. One could perhaps argue that the gunslinger is not only a gunman but also a man-gun; that is, an extension and activation of the gun-creature who becomes alive through being incarnated 'in human hands', urging man to develop the gun's manifest being by picking it up and using it. In the same manner, the CBDM could be expected to modify both the powers and motives of states and companies and thus rule the social machines. From this point of view, the new CBDM needs states and companies to become alive. Thus, the Big Data State or the Big Data Company could also be

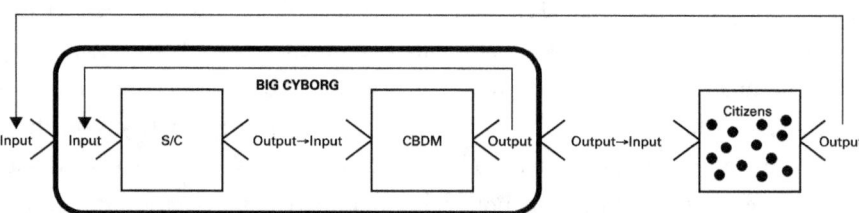

Figure 5.3 The new emerging Big Cyborgs.

understood as two modalities of the Big Data Monster – the State Big Data mutation and the Company Big Data mutation. In Figure 5.3 illustrates the situation where states/companies (S/C) and CBDMs have become parts of one bigger emerging machine type – the new Big Cyborgs.

If we are right here, it means that we are today confronted by the rise of Big Cyborgs – implying that states and companies are becoming stronger and different creatures than we have seen in the past. Before, companies had to advertise and perhaps prove the value of their products and politicians had to 'sell' and prove their political programmes. Now we are subliminally measured and nudged and spoken to in individualised ways (through dark posts).[3] Before, a politician would have an opinion that everyone could discuss and, for example, the mass media could analyse and confront. Now the politicians can 'whisper' to us all differently. The public and the press (the democratic institutions) have now become disconnected unless transparency is re-introduced in the CBDM through democratic co-involvement.

The relevant democratic and educational question then becomes: is it possible/desirable to educate individual citizens to be able to cope with these new mega powerful creatures? If we assume that it is not possible for the individual to merge with a CBDM (because it is too 'big' and only suited to big social machines), what should the citizen strategically do or be encouraged and supported to do educationally? Should they act with or against the new Big Cyborgs? Could/should they join each other and form NGOs that can also take on new Big Data powers? Should/could they refuse to uphold companies and states that use Big Data, or should/could they co-manage the new cyborgs in good ways? To be even more frank: how can democracy – that is, 'the rule of the people' or, even more etymologically correct, 'the strength of the people' – be possible if Big Cyborgs monitor, control and steer the citizens? Or the other way around: How can citizens control and modify the Big Cyborgs – either directly or indirectly – through social organs like parliaments?

The core of these questions concerns the relationship between the new Big Cyborgs and the citizens. If this relationship resembles that between the sun and the flower, that is a one-way structural coupling, democracy is ruled out (in favour of a big cyborg dictatorship or oligarchy). If, on the other hand, there is a

---

[3] Dark posts are targeted ads on social media. Unlike normal posts they do not appear on user's timeline. They also do not show up in the feeds of the user's followers. Because they are not 'published' the same way as organic posts (unpaid posts), dark posts are more formally known on Facebook as unpublished posts. They are not formally on the user's page. Effectively, they only exist for the targeted users that see them.

two-way structural coupling between the Big Cyborgs and the citizens, some kind of democracy is possible. A two-way structural coupling means that both parts – the Big Cyborgs and the citizens – can respond to each other and modify each other. In this case, the cyborgs will be media for the citizens and the citizens media for the cyborgs. Both parts will extend their powers through the other.

Yet none of the machines are cable of directly modifying each other. The Big Cyborgs can only access the citizens and their doings and preferences in the form of digital data. Moreover, they can only (as cyborgs) generate digital output. To modify citizens, the Big Cyborgs can do one of two things. Firstly, they can generate digital changes – sending digital content to citizens and making digital restrictions. In this case, they use digital media and the internet as contact media. Secondly, they can be structurally coupled to human/social beings or other digital or analogue machines that respond to the output of Big Cyborgs by, for instance, carrying out 'orders' that affect citizens (e.g., preventing the citizen from obtaining a loan or traveling abroad). In other words, to manifest their powers, the Big Cyborgs need human beings, digital media and/or other machines – by themselves, they cannot actualize their powers. It therefore matters which media ecology they are part of. It is similar for citizens. Citizens cannot directly modify the Big Cyborgs (being all too big). To modify Big Cyborgs, citizens must organise themselves (i.e., build stronger social machines, NGOs, unions, networks, democratic assemblies, public media, democratic research institutions and other democratic social formations and movements) or somehow gain democratic representation on the boards of Big Cyborgs.

Assemblage of Machines

It is worth adding that all machines are composed of networks on different scales. That means that they are constituted by endo-relations between machines that generate an emergent whole with unique powers – a bigger machine. This bigger machine is thus an assemblage of machines that can be in conflict with each other, since they each possess their own powers, selectivity, operations and dynamics. This is evident when it comes to the Big Cyborgs. These consist of states or companies combined with CBDMs. But states and companies are extremely complex machines that consist of many social machines (e.g., departments) that, in turn, consist of people with different goals (that, in turn, also consist of many things, e.g., brains). States and companies also consist of other machines – such as technology, buildings, rules, myths – that are required for the state and company to function. The same is true for CBDMs, which are

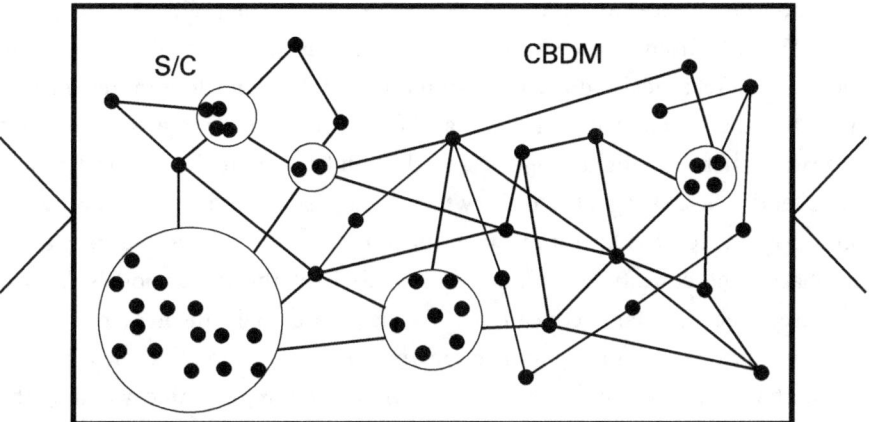

Figure 5.4 The inside of the new Big Cyborgs.

not only technical machines but are also constituted by a mix of different machines. No CBDM can run without having social and human machines as essential components – e.g., big engineering departments that maintain, develop and adjust the machine 'from the inside' but also big lobbies who generate and maintain myths about the CBDMs (often by using them). Without all this, the machine would be less powerful (if powerful at all). In Figure 5.4, we have tried to illustrate this internal complexity of the new Big Cyborgs.

The implication of this internal complexity is that the new Cyborgs consist of heterogeneous elements that make them more or less stable and place them in a constant state of disintegration. If observed only from the outside, they might appear as powerful, 'unbeatable' and impossible for citizens to catch up with – and, in a sense, they are. Yet if observed from the inside, that is, if we open up the black box, it becomes clear that they are shaky in their internal order. It might not be possible for citizens to affect the Big Cyborgs from outside, but some citizens – for example, those who work in the social departments of the machines and can become whistle blowers, saboteurs, hackers or ethical subjects – can, on different levels, affect many of the smaller machines that operate inside the cyborgs.

How to Respond to Big Data?

Until now, we have treated states and companies abstractly as being cable of using and merging with CBDMs. However, it is possible to observe different contemporary strategies for and views on Big Data at the political and societal level. We will discuss three such different 'models' (media ecologies): a state model, a market model and a democratic model. Our aim is not to comprehensively describe what is happening in China, the US, the EU or anywhere else. We instead wish to highlight *tendencies* and speculate about the implications of these tendencies. Our goal is to show that the way societies respond to Big Data on a political level is also important educationally. We therefore also wish to emphasise the educational implications of each of the three models. This is because education (and educational policies) essentially involves modifying citizens and/or encouraging and supporting citizens to modify themselves for the better (whatever this may be). We will, therefore, examine whether the respective models imply that Big Data is used to modify citizens educationally (in a certain way) and/or citizens with or without Big Data are encouraged and supported educationally so that they can use and/or modify/restrict Big Data powers. We conclude by raising the democratic question: How can democracy – that is 'the rule of the people' – be possible in a world with Big Cyborgs and Big Data machines?

The State Model and Media Ecology: The State Rules

Let us start with what we call 'the state model', which is understood as a certain political way of responding to Big Data. The core premise of the state model is that the state (i.e. the most powerful organisation) should collect, own, control and use Big Data about citizens to control their behaviour and thus maintain order. This includes controlling students, thereby the shaping of citizens with Big Data. An analogy is Tolkien's famous lines: 'One Ring to rule them all, One Ring to find them, One Ring to bring them all and in the darkness bind them.'[4] In this media ecology, the state's power is reinforced and the people's power (i.e., their democratic potential) is weakened by the partnership between state and technology.

We will now highlight some of the tendencies that China is displaying towards such a state model (Liang 2018; Backer 2018, Helbing 2019). In China, the totalitarian regime is rolling out a kind of digitalisation that makes it possible to monitor the population in ways that were unthinkable a few years ago. One example is the use of GPS in school uniforms. The so-called intelligent uniforms record when students arrive and leave school – and pass this information on to

---

[4] Tolkien, J. R. R. (2012). *The Lord of the Rings: One Volume*. Boston: Houghton Mifflin Harcourt.

the state (and perhaps also to parents and teachers). Cameras with facial recognition technology at school entrances help detect cheating and set off an alarm when necessary. Likewise, there are schools that have software and cameras installed in the classrooms to monitor children's facial expressions and assess whether they are concentrating (Reed 2018). Another example is WeChat, which, aside from being a chatting and writing tool, has (among other things) a built-in card service, video conferencing service, payment service and taxi booking service. Both the company behind WeChat (Tencent) and the Chinese government can thus keep track of what their 700 million users are doing. In addition, China is developing a 'social credit system' that awards each person a number of points based on their observed behaviour. As a result, citizens can be rewarded, punished or prevented from taking part in various activities (Zuboff 2019: 455). For example, parents with a poor credit score might be prevented from enrolling students in certain schools (Liang 2018, Backer 2019). Also, the Chinese authorities are setting up a lot of surveillance cameras in China (Wong and Dobson 2019). These cameras will, among other things, send information to the national 'social credit system'. This system ensures that people comply with political requirements and can thus be viewed as the implementation of the world's first digital totalitarian state (Wong and Dobson 2019).

Figure 5.5 illustrates how the state model works. The big state cyborg tracks the behaviour of students and citizens by being structurally coupled to surveillance cameras, sensors, digital media and devices (e.g., smartphones, GPS uniforms and chips). Thus, schools (and other social institutions and areas), citizens and students are made into *small* cyborgs, enabling the 'big state cyborg

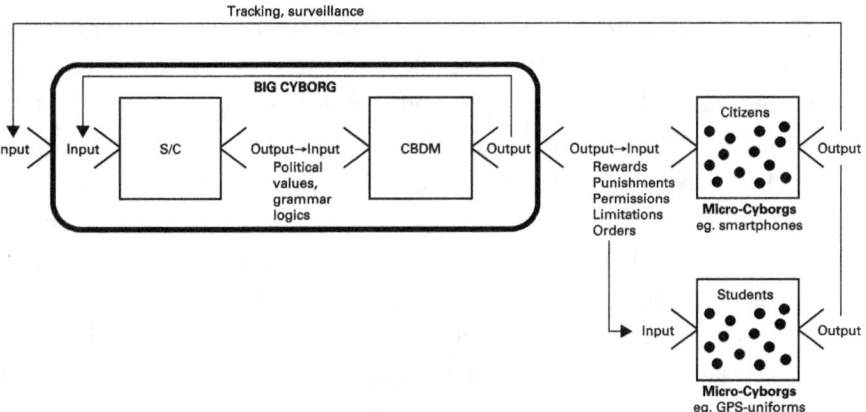

Figure 5.5 The totalitarian state Big Data Cyborg.

machine' to track them. The big cyborg can also analyse the obtained data and produce citizen predictions, rewards, punishments and permissions. By being structurally coupled to digital systems, social systems (like the school) and state employees (like teachers), the big cyborg can *affect* citizens with these rewards, punishments and orders. However, it can only function internally if the government/state feeds the Big Data machine with political values, that is definitions of preferred behaviour and order that the system should maintain, which functions as necessary input for the Big Data Machine. This means that the big cyborg is not only a technical machine but also a big social, cultural and bureaucratic system, with many different elements and interests as well as potential conflicts, bribery, corruption and other social-cultural phenomena. The machine is officially designed to maintain order in the interests of everybody, but, in reality, the inside of the machine is perhaps better characterised by social power conflicts and economic, political and technical inequalities.

The Market Model and Media Ecology: The Market Rules

Another way of responding politically to Big Data, which can complement or be combined with the state model, is what we call the 'market model'. The core of this model is that companies are politically non-regulated and thus free to develop and use Big Data to monitor, manipulate and nudge citizens and students as well as to sell and buy collected data about citizens and students. To illustrate this model, we will highlight some of the tendencies that Anglo-American societies are displaying towards it. According to Shoshana Zuboff (2019), the use of Big Data by companies in western societies is just as – if not more – shocking than the use of Big Data by the Chinese state: citizens in the West are profiled, categorised and their behaviour is anticipated; this not only leads to nudging but also to assessments on whether people are deemed creditworthy, can get insurance, or are able to rent an apartment. All these things are at risk of being decided by algorithms in Silicon Valley.

Although Edward Snowden demonstrated that the American state is highly active in its surveillance, the USA is dominated by private actors. A commercial company like Facebook can collect, own, control, use and sell personal data about citizens. Facebook is one among other Big Data company cyborgs based in the US that has a tremendous impact on citizens' desires, views and behaviours. In this media ecology, the market's power is increased, though new media people become enslaved to acting only as consumers, optimising their consumer lives. In the Anglo-American world, this also applies to the education system, which is seen as best driven as a CBDM by the big company cyborgs under the influence of the shared myth of Big Data.

In his book *Big Data in Education*, Ben Williamson describes how the development of Big Data takes place within the education system in the Anglo-American world. This development is driven by cooperation between scientists, Silicon Valley companies, venture capitalists and politicians (Williamson 2017: 12–15). These systems have gathered around the myth of Big Data. Williamson describes this as a *sociotechnical imaginary* defined as 'collectively held, institutionally stabilized, and publicly performed visions of desirable futures, animated by shared understandings of forms of social life and social order attainable through, and supportive of, advances in science and technology' (Williamson 2017: 16). This imaginary is instantiated as computer-based functional specifications that determine the social and educational life of the school system, forcing its norms and logics onto the teachers and students.

According to Williamson, algorithmic machine learning makes it possible to predict students' possible future progression through predictive analytical processes and to control the knowledge students acquire and the tasks they are assigned through prescriptive analyses (Williamson 2017: 111). The selection of tasks for the individual student is matched by the machine learning algorithm not only in relation to all the data on the individual student but also against all the students' progression curves, which determine their next specific task (Williamson 2017: 112). It is, of course, smart that students are assigned tasks that correspond to their closest learning zone but, in the larger context, the way one is measured and circulated through the system, also dictates how one is treated. This means that people will live a predictable life that they will adapt to. In addition, even machine learning algorithms must have feedback to learn, which means that they can never do anything really new or experimental in terms of teaching (Williamson 2017: 113).

However, it is not only cognitive learning and the technical part of science that are important when it comes to Big Data and machine learning within the teaching area. Psychology is also important. This is a school of thought called *growth mindset* central. This behaviouristic theory suggests that, since students have been able to contribute to the socio-technical imaginary, they can develop their intelligence and become better decision makers through self-optimisation and hard work (Williamson 2017: 141). The CBDM then becomes a Student Big Data Machine (SBDM). This machine is not neutral in the sense that it merely helps students (e.g., to develop their own unique personality to become a self-regulating critical citizen); it is a citizen system that conforms with the imagined CBDM society.

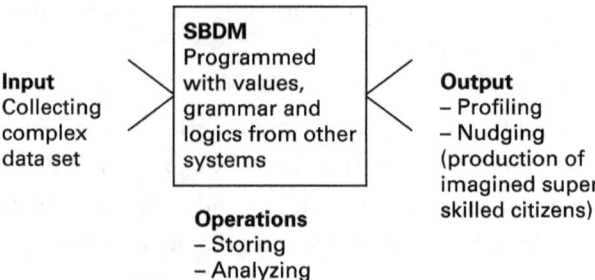

Figure 5.6 Student Big Data machine as a medium for producing the desired citizen.

As illustrated in Figure 5.6, the Big Corporation and State Cyborgs colonise the education system by forming the SBDM, which monitors, calculates and nudges students in an attempt to produce a desirable citizen. According to Williamson, the SBDM normalises surveillance and, because the reward is based on visible behaviour, such a practice constitutes raw behaviourist nudging, designed to make students conform with specific behavioural norms. Williamson refers to this as *psychological governmentality*. The model is reinforced by persuasive computing including hyper-nudging and online intervention through social media platforms (Williamson 2017: 144). According to Williamson, we are approaching an actual *nudgeocracy* (Williamson 2017: 145) and *governmental psycho-policy* (Williamson 2017: 147; Han, 2016). Like in the private sector, where companies quantify emotions in the CBDMs, we can now see psychometric methods for measuring and managing mood and behaviour within the SBDM.

The datafication of the student's non-cognitive learning is part of a biopolitical strategy designed to shape the citizens into pathology-secured individuals. Up to 100 emotions have been identified (Williamson 2017: 137) to help 'improve' student performance (including academic persistence, self-regulation, engagement and motivation) through appropriate practices (Williamson 2017: 135). Various techniques to measure things such as facial expressions, eye tracking, skin temperature and conductivity can reveal the learner's emotional attitude. Treating students in this way is edging towards a quantified self, which, based on behaviourist rationales, must align with an individual who is encouraged to enter the capitalist system with an emotionally appropriate mindset and the correct cognitive settings.

In this scenario, we find a classroom which is monitored and in which the teachers and students must follow the grammar predetermined by other systems and executed by algorithms (Tække 2019). However, according to Williamson, such a politically initiated and automated performance culture leads to an increase in stress and anxiety (Williamson 2017: 146). Such a culture features a dystopic (first order) cybernetic system in which students are treated as trivial machines and expected to adapt to a commercialised society in which freedom is limited to the few rich individuals who control the Big Cyborg.

The Democratic Model and Media Ecology: Protecting and Empowering Citizens

Both the state model and the market model – and combinations of these two – increase the power of Big Cyborgs and decrease the power of citizens. They therefore undermine and weaken 'the power of the people' (i.e., democracy). Also, they both, in different ways rely on the educational outlook we, in previous chapters, have called the 'engineer' and the *technical and causal understanding* of teaching and media, constraining education as a pure techno-bureaucratic space. This means that equipped with new Big Data technology, the technical mainstream view of education has become globally hegemonic. Thus, it has become mainstream norm – among politicians, companies, researchers and educators – to accept, that education is about shaping, nudging and producing conforming citizens with technological means (including programme for international student assessment (PISA) and the like), both in schools and elsewhere (e.g., on the market, producing desirable consumer behaviour and nudging people to buy certain products etc.). In Chapter 1 we called this a vulgar idea about education, which we criticised as being based on problematic assumptions and aims, seen from a more reflective Bildung point of view.

Against this background, we will now discuss a third way of responding to Big Data, which we can call a 'democratic model'. The core of this model is that citizens and students are protected against Big Cyborgs and empowered to be on guard and act collectively both with and against Big Data Machines. To illustrate this model, we will highlight some of the potential tendencies that the EU is displaying towards it. We will not attempt to describe the relevant situation in the 27 EU countries but will consider how citizens within the European *Bildung* tradition could be empowered to 'counter' Big Cyborgs and act both with and against Big Data in a democratic way.

On the societal level, in the EU, we have seen the introduction of GDPR (General Data Protection Regulation) and other initiatives, among them the will to protect the privacy of EU citizens. However, since the EU also contains liberal capitalist systems and this freedom is used by Big Companies to monitor and restrict the freedom of citizens, the Anglo-American Big Data tendencies described above have also been seen within the EU. This is also because American Big Companies also wish to play the same game in Europe (as described above). But what about teaching in the EU? What are the chances of safeguarding teaching from the Big Cyborgs?

As the research we have put forward until this chapter suggests, it is possible to perform teaching in the digital medium environment that is in line with the *Bildung* tradition (Klafki 2005). This research describes an empowering of the students and a view of the classroom as a cooperating education community that is free to update old forms of literacy and curriculum in line with the development of contemporary society in *contact* with surrounding society. In line with the Bildung tradition, this research puts forward critical thinking, democracy, emancipation and humanism and defines Bildung pedagogically as the task of critically working with and challenging a combination of three overlapping components: a student's *knowledge, attitude* and *existence*. For instance, when students upload photos to Instagram, the *knowledge* component involves working with and challenging *what* the students takes as a good photo, but also knowledge about whether it is desirable to use Instagram. The *attitude* component involves working with and challenging *how* students approach social media – e.g., naïve or critically, egoistically or altruistic – but is also concerned about what it means to others and what body ideals are reinforced when they are portrayed in uploaded photos in one way and not in another. The *existence* component involves challenging *who* the students are – or who they want to be – but is also concerned with what kind of a person a student becomes if they upload a photo with a specific way of portraying a body/person. This way of working critically with knowledge, attitude and existence must – according to the Bildung tradition – penetrate every social and educational activity from coding algorithms to writing essays.

It seems logical and in line with the development until now in the continental European tradition of Bildung that teaching should encourage and challenge students to understand Big Data and algorithms, helping them to become critical of the CBDMs and the Big Cyborgs. But will this be enough to safeguard the independence of the school? And what about the potential to use BDMs in school for good proposes? Is it also possible to educate students to use BDMs themselves?

Technology in this book is viewed as pluripotent and can take on different purposes/values according to which other machines/media they are structurally connected to. Furthermore, social systems (for example) can expand their capacity and power through such couplings (Bryant 2014). In this way, digital media, not least the algorithms steering the CBDM, can be programmed to perform certain functions, which will have a built-in motive. Big Data involves statistical calculations and finding correlations. Yet the technology has the inherent problem that it therefore, in a time-dimension, only ever 'looks back'. You are your history, or the history of those with whom you are matched in the profiling.

If a SBDM is to be used in schools, there must still be a teacher with an holistic perspective on an individual student when cognitive help is received from the SBDM (e.g. what the next math problem should be). Behaviourism (e.g. reading emotions in students' facial expressions through the use of webcams) seems far away from the Bildung tradition. Yet perhaps, in a better world, such behaviourism could be used to detect students' anxiety, loneliness or stress so that they could be offered help? And perhaps the psychologist could also use BDMs to identify different forms of assistance that have previously helped students correlated with those in question? In our view, the BDM or the SBDM can never stand alone. However, with the right modification, critical sense and knowledge, we propose that the BDM and CBDM and some sort of open and transparent SBDM under democratic control could perhaps find its way into schools. But, to include the Big Cyborgs, the CBDM and the SBDM and create a school that strives for *Bildung* in terms of democracy, emancipation and humanism and work critically with knowledge, attitude and existence in all aspects, a high degree of transparency and democratic control is required.

Within the model displayed in Figure 5.7, it is the teacher and the students that decide on the use of the different BDM and this demands critical thinking, extended forms of media practices (BDM literacies) – and a continual work

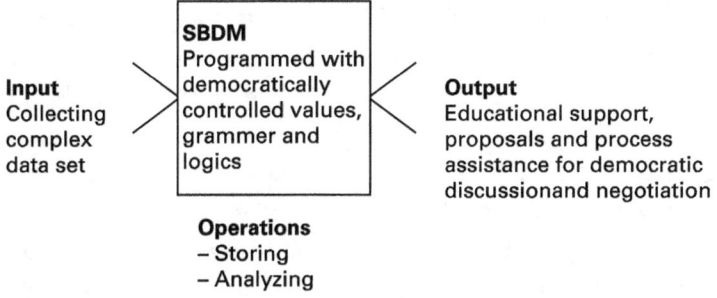

Figure 5.7 Democratically controlled SBDM.

with *Bildung*. The students must be encouraged to learn the principles that the different BDM employs, including not only the correlative nature of Big Data and how the maths works but also the values and logics of commercial companies and governments built into the CBDM and SBDM. This involves continual analysis of how the different machines work in all the special cases where the BDMs are involved in relation to both cognitive and behavioural aspects. This might require the use of open-source software to remain free from the influence of the Big Companies' CBDM and SBDM, but perhaps an EU regulation about transparency and school democracy would force the Big Companies to design systems that can be trusted. New social structures must also be created with regard to designing school councils that can be trusted to hold the Big Data correlations of individual students and the roles and level of authority for the individual actors, such as parents, psychologists, students, school management and teachers, must be decided. It is important that it is not just the school management and functionalists and/or representatives of Big Companies and governments that have a say. Perhaps they should have no say at all, other than in reference to hearings and specialist statements. In relation to the voices and *Bildung* of the students, the students must be supported and encouraged to gain *knowledge* in relation to how a BDM works, how it is built and programmed, how the neural network functions and with what bias. Some maths students can most likely also learn how to design machine-learning algorithms and train neural networks, but the important thing is that all students are challenged and supported to learn the relevant principles so they can voice their opinion at school and become critical citizens. The students must also be challenged to reflect on their *attitude* and be encouraged to assume the perspective of others subjected to the correlative dictatorship of the CBDM and SBDM. They must be encouraged to become citizens who can recognise how others are influenced by the implemented norms, values and logics of systems regulated by Big Data. This concerns not only the healthcare system and the cord system but also fake news, commercials and echo chambers. The students must also be *existentially* challenged in relation to who they become and what it means for them as people if they construct, use or participate in processes that use BDM. Finally, if one wants to take up the track of more creative and experimental kind of Bildung (see Chapter 1), it might also be possible and desirable to let students experiment with using, modifying and re-building Big Data Machines in different school subjects, but also reflect critically on this and work to generate 'benign effects' through assembling social, cultural, technological and physical elements.

Conclusion

Inspired by Levi Bryant, we have developed a conceptual framework to discuss Big Data as an exemplary Bildung issue. This has enabled us to distinguish between (1) Big Data Machines ((BDM), a machine that collects, stores and analyses big and/or complicated data sets), (2) Citizen Big Data Machines (CBDM), a BDM that monitors, stores and analyses data about the citizen and perhaps also treats them according to its preprogramed values depending on statistical correlations, (3) Student Big Data Machines (SBDM), which is the same as a CBDM but designed to control the learning and behaviour of students, (4) Big Cyborgs, Big States and Companies who empower CBDMs/SBDMs *and* control their grammar (but are not mentioned explicitly) and (5) Small Cyborgs (citizens who use digital technology to modify and strengthen their power but who risk being monitored, manipulated and controlled by Big Cyborgs).

Through our analysis and considerations, we have also described three ways of responding politically and educationally to Big Data: (1) a state model where the state develops and uses CBDMs and becomes a dominating Big Cyborg which rules and manipulates its citizens and students; and (2) a market model where companies are free to develop and use CBDMs and become dominating Big Cyborgs who rule and manipulate citizens and students. In these scenarios, we see a development or at least a tendency towards controlling, nudging and even suppressing citizens, which works against the creation of a critical and autonomous people who can participate in a democratic society. The tendency in the first model is towards total lifelong control and suppression while the tendency in the second model is a nudgeocratic shaping of the citizen to behave, feel and think in accordance with capitalistic structures. Both models rely on and reinforce a *technical and causal understanding* of teaching and media, constraining education as a pure techno-bureaucratic space. As an alternative third response to Big Data, we have outlined a democratic model which, based on the continental *Bildung* tradition, tries to find an answer to how one could respond democratically and critically to Big Data. In this model, students and citizens are educationally and democratically encouraged to become critical Big Data users, securing democratic control over the new technological powers and being protected against the new Big Cyborgs. We have suggested that one could supplement this with creative experimentation, letting the students experiment with using, modifying and re-building Big Data Machines, but also reflecting critically on this and working to generate 'benign effects'. Thus, in this model, students and citizens are protected against Big Cyborgs, but are also supported to become empowered small cyborgs that can be on guard and act both with and against Big Data machines. Only this third model seems to secure democracy understood as 'the rule of the people'. However, this is highly unlikely to be successful in a world dominated by Big Cyborgs creating 'super humans' in the image of their values and logic. Think, for example, of super workers or soldiers controlled by and subjected to the Big Cyborgs. The big question of Big Data therefore becomes: What should we do if we wish to sustain democracy?

6

Filter Bubbles and Lockdowns

In this final chapter we analyse two current challenges: (1) filter bubbles – the polarisation of society related to social media and (2) teaching during the lockdowns due to COVID-19. These two analyses – together with the arguments and analyses put forward in former chapters – lead us to the final conclusion of the book, namely that a critical-constructive Bildung approach to teaching, in our view is both possible and desirable, in the digital age, in which we are now living. This in contrast to purely technical views on education or in opposition to purely voluntaristic views see chapter 1). Thus, we argue that the new media situation that includes digital media must be taken seriously, in school teaching, with the aim of supporting and challenging students to explore, evaluate and improve their knowledge, attitude and existence, critically and constructively in the new media reality, encouraging them to work for the wellbeing of all people and life on this planet in the digital age.

Polarisation can be seen most evidently in relation to so-called 'Trumpism' and we discuss the tendency in relation to Bildung and social cohesion in the first section of this chapter. This concerns the polarisation problem of what can be seen as the post-factual society, with low confidence in the fact-producing institutions, with consequences for, e.g., the climate debate and the struggle with the Corona pandemic.

In the second section of this chapter, we use the COVID-19 pandemic lockdown of the education system with Denmark as an example to try to give a snapshot, or diagnosis, of the contemporary education system's ability to use digital media for teaching and Bildung purposes. We discuss the physical lockdown of the school system in spring 2020 in relation to education and Bildung, to 'take the temperature' of the current state of development in digital mediated teaching. This can be looked at as a stress test of the education system, which is therefore also related to Bildung, if society is not to end up as a pure instrumental system.

Yet, we want to stress, that the lockdown created a peculiar situation where only distance teaching was possible, together with other peculiar and extraordinary circumstances (e.g., the lack of many normal physical-social contact and activities). In former chapters we have advocated that, in line with the critical-constructive Bildung tradition, it is actually possible to develop 'good teaching' in the new digital media environment. But we do not argue that full online distance teaching (or learning!) could or should *substitute* for teaching, where students and teachers are physically present to each other. And no critical and serious research on media and education that we have relied on in this book supports, as desirable, full online teaching. What we have argued, is only that some kind of hybrid – combination – teaching, which includes *both* digital and analogue media, teaching with and without physically present teachers, students and third parties is possible and – in certain forms – desirable and necessary. Thus, nowhere in this book do we suggest that teaching should be carried out as pure online teaching. Instead, we suggest that it could and should be developed through experiments, using combinations of different media, including physical presence. In the meantime, the situation in spring 2020 suddenly became a huge experiment where all teachers at every level of the education system were forced to do their best under lockdown conditions; this has allowed us to examine the current capability of the educational system regarding digital media and teaching.

Both challenges (i.e., the polarisation of society related to social media and the lockdowns due to COVID-19) show the need to develop teaching that aims for critical-constructive Bildung activities situated in the new media environment that includes digital media. Thus, we conclude this chapter – and the book– by highlighting the advantages of a critical-constructive Bildung approach to teaching in the digital age but also by summarising some of the most important ways this can be pursued; in doing so, we argue that this will also make society better off with regard to populism and further pandemics.

The Polarisation Problem and Social Media

In our critical-constructive concept of Bildung we distinguish between three important dimensions: *knowledge, attitude* and *existence* (see Chapter 1). The first of the three dimensions concern facts and, more broadly, are about what knowledge is and what knowledge a citizen requires to participate in good and adequate ways in the society. Yet, it is important to restress that the task, seen from a critical-constructive Bildung perspective, is not to transfer or infuse a certain amount of knowledge into the students; this will instrumentalise education and is an all-too-simple model of how knowledge and learning function. In previous chapters we have called this a technical view of education. From a critical-constructive Bildung perspective, knowledge should rather be *addressed*, meaning that teachers should encourage, support and challenge their students (and themselves!) to explore and improve their knowledge, which is a totally different thing than trying to transfer or infuse a certain amount of knowledge to the students.

Bildung, Critical Knowledge and its Institutions

Thus, students should, for instance, seen from a critical-constructive Bildung perspective, work critically with newspaper articles, confront different sources and perspectives with each other and try to find out, as part of their teaching, what can be argued to be more valid, sound, supported by evidence and/or good arguments etc. than other, less-convincing, statements. Also, it must take into account, that in a functionally differentiated society, which is as complex as ours, many facts are impossible to fact check.[1] What can be done is source criticism: seeing things from different perspectives and media, using libraries and public institutions and consulting different experts, but also being aware that all this depends on trust in institutions, which again depends on both developments of trustworthy institutions and the people who secure, support and trust them.

If the civilian independent democratic institutions lose the trust of the people, we are in a situation where humanity will not be able to deal with huge and essential problems like climate change or a global pandemic. With the digital media revolution and social media, we have seen polarisations between institutions like the mass media and healthcare and, for instance, election authorities on the one hand and populist politicians and groups on social media on the other (Jurkowitz et al., 2020; Li and Su 2020). In the new media environment, communication is taking place more directly between politicians and citizens (groups or filter bubbles of interconnected citizens, respectively), which disrupts the habitual connection between citizens and politicians filtered by the mass media's critical intervention. Also, the cultivated elite of the public sphere has been bypassed by webloggers, microbloggers and youtubers. Some of these bloggers provide fake news and earn big money through clickbait activities

---

[1] Following Luhmann (2000b) what we know we know from the mass media – and now we also got the Internet and social media.

in the form of news links with conspiratorial headings (Allcott and Gentzkow 2016; Edson et al., 2018).

The Creation of Filter Bubbles

In the meantime, most bloggers probably do try to be honest, but the complexity is enormous and hard to navigate. This problem has increased because our new communicative infrastructure has been commercialised. One consequence is the risk of filter bubbles where, for instance, people only get search results when, e.g, Facebook updates their feed only with views that confirm their own convictions. Humans seem to have a tendency to consider information to be true if it confirms what they already believe and this effect is increased in online communities, creating the risk of mutual confirmation of fake news (Giglietto et al., 2016, 4).

The algorithms of social media platforms increase this tendency but do not create it in the first place. Within the population, individual choice seems to limit exposure to attitude-challenging content in the context of Facebook (Bakshy et al., 2015). Thus, most people share false and misleading content because social media focuses their attention on factors other than accuracy (e.g., partisan alignment) (Pennycook et al., 2020). Social media platforms, or rather the companies providing them to us, with their enormous possibilities for democratic debate and connectivity, are, paradoxically, responsible for some of this bias in *connectivity,* in disconnecting society as a whole and separating it into subsystems with different connections and views (Tække 2019b).[2] They[3] divide users into different filter bubbles or enhance the tendency instead of trying to balance the situation with their algorithms. The filter bubbles are like separated worlds of knowledge with different conceptions of what is true, providing society with huge disconnectivity between them (Li and Su 2020).

On the one hand, this seems like a retrogression to the era of the party press, but on the other hand, it is something that is new and has not fully been explored. In the time of the party press, the form was simple transmission; now there are many possibilities for fact checking, feedback and discussion in various groups. The commercialisation of our communicative infrastructure with algorithms only aimed at making companies rich might be a problem if it means that the

---

[2] A survey carried out in the United States found that 44 per cent of the population get their news from Facebook (Gottfried and Shearer 2016).
[3] In the terminology from Chapter 5 'they' are the Big Cyborgs (Big Companies empowered by Citizen Big Data Machines).

companies increase disconnectivity but, despite the creation of economic inequality, a company like Facebook may have been the greatest when it comes to creating connectivity in the new medium environment (which also is their slogan), but also in creating disconnectivity (Tække 2019b). Filter bubbles connect like-minded people, just like conflicts integrate opponents (following Luhmann 1995), but with commercial algorithms programmed with the intention to *split* populations up into different interest groups with totally different knowledge and outlooks. Thus, *internal connectivity* also implies external *disconnectivity* on the societal level with big risk for societal disintegration (Tække 2019b).

Social Media Propels Populism

The globalisation of trade, the neoliberal deregulation of financial capitalism and the centralisation of democratic institutions, all driven by digitalisation, mean that populist fake news finds subscribers, for instance, in the Rust Belt in the US and in far-flung areas of Denmark (but also certain urban suburbs). This means that the shared identity of the western countries is weakened and there is an increased cognitive dissonance between different filter bubbles e.g., the educated and uneducated. In some way, this was already foreseen by Castells (2003) who distinguishes between *flow of space* and *place of space*. *Flow of space* connects the educated populations in and between the ('the centre of') big urban city areas and, at the same time, disconnects the populations living in the outskirts and deranged suburbs left with only *place of space*.

What Castells did not foresee was that the marginalised areas were also connected by digital media and interpellated by populist politicians. Populism works by a double distinction; first they claim that only they represent the people, second, they distinguish between those who belong to the people and those who do not (Müller 2016). As a consequence, we see a bifurcation in US society between citizens who believe in the institutions, that Biden won the election and, for instance, that COVID-19 is real and, on the other hand, citizens who, interpellated by populist politicians and opinion polls, do not believe in the institutions, but do believe that the election was stolen by the Democrats, and that COVID-19 is a fiction. In relation to filter bubbles and polarisation, social tumult and divisions facilitate our willingness to believe news that confirms our enmity toward another group (Edson et al., 2018), so we have a bad spiral of development where the medium environment plays a big and increasingly significant role.

The Bildung Approach to the Polarisation Problem

New norms and regulations have not yet been developed to handle the new communication situation. Big mass media, like Fox News and CNN are now actively helping to divide the US population (Jurkowitz et al., 2020), while social media platforms like Twitter and Facebook have begun to play the role of censuring authorities. Where not only illegal statements like threats of violence are censored by social media but also organisations and people who have expressed the 'wrong' message are filtered out by the search engines of social media platforms without democratic control, we have a huge democratic problem and risk even more radicalisation. We need new institutions to regulate social media such as those we put forward in relation to education in Chapter 5 (see Figure 5.7). As it is now, the big media corporations self-regulate and censor conspiracy theorists instead of conducting a democratic debate about, for example, COVID-19 with participation from those in the health institutions. We need transparency and democratic control grounded in a new kind of institution, at arm's length from the politicians and economic interests, that can regulate how the machine learning algorithms work.

We are in a dangerous situation and even though Bildung seems like a small actor, it is more important than ever for public educational institutions worldwide to work hard to support and challenge students to explore, evaluate and improve their *knowledge*, including, most importantly, what knowledge is, how it is produced in institutions, how we democratically can control institutions and the production of knowledge, how to make source criticism and how we control the Big Cyborgs (see Chapter 5).[4] However, they *also* need to work to support and challenge student's *attitudes* towards knowledge, encouraging them to see things from different perspectives, to think dialectically, not in black and white, to listen carefully to other people with different views, discussing these seriously in genuine dialogue; that is, encouraging students to treat others as colleages that can be wrong and should be corrected, but which could also be right and therefore call for correcting oneself.[5] Finally, this task also includes eye for student's *existence*, meaning that the critical work with knowledge should not be

---

[4] Thus, if search engines downplay different views on a subject, Bildung must be backed by a democratic, transparent institution that guarantees the full diversity of views – otherwise source criticism will be impossible.

[5] As we saw in Chapter 2, young people are not equipped with particularly good IT skills. As confirmed by Herrero-Diz et al., (2020) teens are more likely to share content if it connects with their interests, regardless of its truthfulness, that trust affects the credibility of information and the appearance of newsworthy information ensures that, regardless of the nature of the content, this information is more likely to be shared among young people.

something 'external', that students regard as only 'schoolwork' and without relevance for their own life. Thus, work with knowledge in the school should include and be based on actual experiences students have with knowledge-situations in their own life, of many different kinds, making it relevant to explore and improve their knowledge and their attitude towards knowledge, but also make knowledge into something existential, as was the main aim of Socratic dialogue, as portraited, for instance, in Plato's 'Meno'. If a student comes to this conclusion without much thought, that "I am so and so", it should be gently challenged in school: Is this really who I am? Or is it a result of parents, filter bubbles, populism, commercials etc? This also include a *deconstruction* of the populist distinction above, making the world black and white.

Taking Others Seriously

When it comes to the *attitude* dimension of Bildung it is the success criterium to take the perspective of the other and with impassion, empathy and knowledge to understand the other person in her own right as an unique being. This is, together with 'the passion for knowledge' (see above), the kit that keeps a good society together.

In the debates about #MeToo, the result of the American presidential election and whether COVID-19 is real, we see that discussions are going on in different echo chambers, in separated filter bubbles. In Facebook groups and comment fields of debaters and politicians, who actually give space for debate between different opinions, we see hate speech, accusations, prejudices, dehumanisation and a total lack of trying to understand each other. What has been the success criterium since the enlightening period, in connection to the idea of Bildung, namely, to try to understand the opponent and her motives, experiences and outlook, is under pressure or totally missing from the debates on social media.[6] Populist politicians are trying to use this to gain more followers by being most unnuanced and black and white. So, we have a situation where leaders show a role model that must be countered and challenged in the school. Here, again, the school looks little and without the necessary power, but it must keep on teaching in and about how a worthy debate could take place between two or more persons with mutual respect that tries to understand each other's outlook

---

[6] This is not necessarily the general picture: many interactions on social media are peaceful, dealing with topics like horses, food, theory and social relations, and there are also positive debates about politics, climate and health. The problem is that we miss norms and regulations in relation to conflicts, fake news and, e.g., populists. We also need regulation of the influence of money on search results and what is contained in our feed. We need democratic control and Bildung.

and situation. Overall, this is what holds society together and helps everyone to feel included.

When it comes to *existence*, the school must support, encourage and challenge students to become persons that are taking responsibility not only for one's own ego, but for the common good, the climate and people living in other places. The individual must be supported to become strong enough not to choose easy solutions running after the populistic notes in their networks and dehumanising people from other places, or those with another outlook or economic situation (e.g., religion or class).

All in all, the critical-constructive Bildung approach calls for good role models in the schools and if the politicians and opinion leaders cannot live up to the Bildung ideal presented in this book we really need the teachers to try to support and encourage their students to become true knowledge seekers and guards, experimenting in the school with correcting misinformation on the internet, improving dialogue in social media, breaking out of filter bubbles and caring about the common good.

The COVID-19 Lockdown and What It Shows Us About Digitally Mediated Education

In Denmark, a number of research reports have been published dealing with the state of the education system during the COVID-19 pandemic in the spring of 2020. For a number of reasons, it has not gone well, which shows that even in Denmark, one of the worlds most digitalised societies, success not only depends on hardware and software, but also on the development of new forms of teaching situated in a media environment that includes digital media. We now selectively pinpoint aspects from three research reports (in relation to primary schools, youth education and universities), then put the findings into perspective and discuss them.

Lockdown: Primary Schools

In primary school (which, in Demark, involves children from about six to fifteen/sixteen years old; thus, includes lower secondary schools), many children did not have contact with their teacher on a daily basis. No more than 34.1% of children completely or predominantly agreed that they had had daily contact with a teacher, while 48.9% predominantly or completely disagreed. In contrast, quite a few teachers stated that they did have daily contact with their students (Qvortrup et al., 2020: 38–39). It can be difficult to decide who is right (and perhaps both are to a certain extent, but experience and comprehend 'contact' differently), but it seems that many students in primary school did homework alone at home during the shutdown (81% of students state that they had, to some extent, worked with independent problem solving). They had not received instruction via, for instance, Zoom, done assignments with others via the internet (Qvortrup et al., 2020: 46), or completed assignments involving physical activity. The chairman of the Danish Teachers' Association, Anders Bondo Christensen, is quoted in Politiken (2020): 'the experiences from the closure demonstrate that nothing can replace good old, hand-held teaching in the classroom'. From a critical media perspective, this statement is at least partly wrong if it means, that in this extraordinary lockdown situation (see the beginning of this chapter), the incompetence of the school system is only blamed on problems with digital media. No matter how poorly it performed, it was only due to digital media that some kind of teaching was even possible, thus enabling the schools to get through lockdown.[7] Also, we should not forget that being physically present in a noisy classroom is not always good for all students. Further, there were also huge differences as to how different students evaluated their online teaching. A little more than half of students stated: 'I do well with this kind of [full online] teaching.' Some of the quieter students had a blast being at home in peace, while others such as weaker pupils, those from poorer socio-economic backgrounds and those who received no help from their parents, felt they struggled more than usual (Qvortrup et al., 2020).

Lockdown: Upper Secondary Schools

In upper secondary education, the common form of teaching has been teacher presentations (Zoom) followed by the students having to complete tasks. So lessons were comprised of 10 to 15 minutes of instruction and then work alone, or in groups, in front of a computer screen isolated from others at home. Only 25% of the teachers had experience with doing [full] online teaching and they expressed big differences in relation to how good their teaching was (Jørgensen et al., 2020: 32, 37). According to Andersen, every fourth teacher stated that their school, either to a small degree or not at all, 'has organised the sharing of

---

[7] In Denmark, all primary schools have Aula, a common online communication platform for employees, parents and students which was running long before the lockdown.

knowledge and experience with distance learning between colleagues'. Furthermore, about half of the teachers, stated that the school, to a low degree or not at all, 'has organised sharing of materials and/or teaching courses between colleagues'. In other words, for half of the teachers, the reorganisation was 'an uncoordinated matter' (Andersen 2020: 17). This means that in the upper secondary schools, there was little sharing of knowledge.

The students, too, experienced little plenary dialogue and community, too many submissions and too much monotony, while teachers found it difficult to help and guide (Jørgensen et al., 2020: 68). The teachers found it difficult to know whether the students understood their presentations (Jørgensen et al., 2020: 5). Some teachers stated that their teaching became monolingual, that they were met with a wall of silence and they found it difficult to identify those who could not keep up (Jørgensen et al., 2020: 101). While the teachers experienced a lack of response and had more assignments to correct and feed back, the students thought that they received a lot less attention than before – so it looks like a large workload with little result! Many teachers used 'video conferencing', but found it hard to observe whether the students kept up or understood and students became less motivated during the period. Teachers who acknowledged this and tried to think 'outside the box' did not have the time to pursue these options (Jørgensen et al., 2020: 5,6).

The researchers also found some nuances in the upper secondary education that probably also apply to primary school, namely that online sit-alone teaching is good for the quieter student, while, to a greater extent, the academically weakest have found it more difficult to keep up (Jørgensen et al., 2020: 11, 45).

Lockdown: Universities

Two-thirds of university students had problems with their motivation during the closure; the majority experienced increased stress, anxiety and loneliness (Jensen et al., 2020). Nine out of 10 missed informal gatherings with fellow students and six out of 10 missed conversations with their lecturer. A qualitative study from the IT University of Copenhagen (ITU) found a strong correlation between social aspects and motivation and identified that the stress, anxiety and loneliness probably connected with the missed informal gatherings is a huge problem (Andersen et al., 2020). Academically there was general satisfaction with the Zoom format when questions could be asked and the teaching was live or recorded. But many educators met a wall of turned off cameras and microphones with anxious students behind the black scenes.

Discussion

When looking at the educational problems experienced during the lockdown in Denmark in spring 2020 there are a number of explanations which are important to acknowledge if digitally mediated education – with a critical-constructive Bildung perspective – is to compensate for lockdown and the digitally development under normal conditions shall have a better direction in the times to come. Before discussing these explanations, it must be noted that the issue is complex and should be viewed in a nuanced way.

An Extraordinary Situation

First of all, it is important to take account of the extraordinariness of the lockdown situation. Neither the educational system, the teachers or other sectors of society were prepared for this specific situation; nor were individual citizens or students. In spring 2020, many institutions and individuals might have been in some kind of shock and did not know what to do. This was not what they had expected. Also, many non-formal institutions, like cultural institutions and concert halls etc., were more or less locked down, limiting the possibilities of social contact and informal interaction between students. The three reports we have presented above only deal with the first lockdown which took place in spring 2020. Thus, it would be hasty and wrong if one concluded from the reports above, that full online teaching is totally undesirable, because the *impact* has been overwhelmingly negative. Such conclusions rely on a deterministic view on media and education. Yet, what we argue against, is not that the effects were 'so and so' in spring 2020, but rather that these effects are not *unconditional*, but mediated through an extraordinary context, an unprepared society, including the educational systems and the responses that teachers, students and others formed during this special situation. Thus, it is likely, just as we have seen in general with regard to digitalisation, that the educational and societal 'response' to the first lockdown in spring 2020, is only the *first* response, while more elaborate, better developed and/or different responses might be expected from later periods of lockdown.

Development of Responses in Different Directions

Secondly, it should also be remembered, as we outlined in Chapter 3, that responses to digitalisation and thus also to lockdowns and extraordinary situations with full online teaching can evolve and develop in extremely different ways, depending on the basic societal and educational values teaching and schooling are based on. This is also not visible in the three reports, nor in hasty statements like the one we cited above about 'good old, hand-held teaching in the classroom', which implies that 'good teaching' means almost totally different things, depending on whether you have a technical, voluntaristic or critical-constructive Bildung outlook. Thus, we foreshadow that for educational systems and teachers that are based primarily on the technical outlook, full distance online teaching, if lockdowns continue in the future, will move in the direction of trying to obtain full control of students and their behaviour, through digital surveillance and control systems; and thus, also focus on problems like activating and controlling the students to do certain things, determined by the system. Thus, they will build up an educational Big Cyborg (see Chapter 5). On the other hand – and in the opposite direction – will educational systems and teachers that are based primarily on the voluntaristic outlook begin to integrate computer games, the interests of the students in their home settings, invent new games and plays, that can facilitate free development of the students´ own interests and abilities in a motivating way. Finally, we speculate, that educational systems and teachers that are based primarily on the critical-constructive Bildung outlook, will try to use digital media to enforce community support and challenge the students in many different ways to reflect on an extraordinary situation critically and constructively, to improve the situation, understand it better, experiment with different attitudes and care for each other as existential beings who are perhaps stressed by the new situation or perhaps enjoying it, depending on individual circumstances; supporting the students to (re)create themselves and the situation in different and, perhaps, better ways.

All in all, we should take care not to generalise too much from the reports above, because they might only give a glimpse of some of the effects of the first responses to the extraordinary lockdown situation.

Some Possible Explanations

With these precautions in mind, we now turn towards some possible explanations for the specific effects of the first educational responses to the lockdown situation.

Some of the responsibility for the negative effects, that the three reports indicate, probably lies with the politicians and the management of the educational institutions. They have invested huge amounts of money in hardware and software (including control systems), but not so much in supporting teachers and others in developing new forms of Bildung-orientated teaching that take account of and are situated in the new media environment that includes digital media.

Also, over the last 15 years, preparation time has gone down for all three levels of educational institutions. This means that at the same time as the digital media revolution and the investments in hardware, the educators have had less time to prepare, develop and reflect on their teaching. On top of this, the COVID-19 lockdown has shown that knowledge sharing between those who have actually developed new forms of teaching, got into teaching digitally, or just have experience with digital teaching, have not been used by the institutions to share knowledge with the rest of the teachers.

Further, in regard to social responsibility, the schools have failed. Schools have a huge social function which is the necessary foundation for teaching and learning. Students must find trust in themselves and in others and create a community in which they feel safe and know how to contribute. The children in primary school who are lucky to be in what, for the sake of simplicity, can be called 'surplus families' are looked after at home when they do homework and participate in online teaching; this also counts for the upper secondary schools where students with similar family situations are compensated and helped with their social relationships and self-esteem. Yet, for children and students for whom this is not the case, things might become more difficult, decreasing chances for equality. For university students, who often live by themselves, the problem might be even greater. Therefore, we especially see the problems at the university in regard to the social dimension. At ITU, some teachers facilitated informal social activities; their students felt better and were better able to hang on academically (Andersen et al., 2020). If such initiatives had been taken in the rest of the educational institutions, we would probably have seen a different picture. In the ITU study, the majority of students found it intimidating to ask questions, which is perhaps the case for all Danish universities – and something which should be high on the list of what the closure has clarified, which must be dealt with in the future. The students do not know each other well enough to feel safe and they need an appropriate habitus (Bourdieu) that they can trust. This must be supported through the educational system, by addressing what we have called the *existence* Bildung dimension (see Chapter 1).

Overall, it can be said that the closure has revealed a gigantic political and managerial failure: educators have not been supported enough to develop new forms of teaching through digital media.

Written Interaction

The reports show a strange kind of ignorance, like a form of educational research that somehow does not know about their topic. Obviously, they have produced a lot of usable knowledge like shown in this chapter, but the reports do not in any way deal with questions of how teaching can be developed and attuned to the new digital situation. As we have showed in previous chapters, especially in Chapters 3 and 4, many different approaches to and experiments with new forms of teaching have actually been developed by educators, to some extent in collaboration with researchers, but the reports don't say anything about whether these are known, applied or have been ignored by Danish teachers; nor does it seem that the authors of the reports are either aware of or interested in these.

It is striking that none of the reports look at the importance of the written interaction in relation to the closure and forced distance learning. As we discussed in Chapter 3, the parallel written interaction, significantly improves information clarity, depth and overview and social aspects such as phatic elements and the creation and affirmation of social relations. There are many qualities to mention, e.g., written interaction does not follow oral turn-taking (it has non-linear meaning cohesion, which is easy to understand and follow when reading, see Tække 2006). You can add links and criticise, enrich and deepen the oral interaction in the video conference in the parallel written interaction (and it can be saved and used as notes). The Socio Media Education experiment (SME) (see Chapter 3) showed that, for upper secondary school students, it takes about half a year to learn to interact in writing on academic topics and handle hashtags, tags, hyperlinks, etc. It is up to the schools and their management to start use the action research produced by us and other researchers and to support and enforce experiments by providing the teachers with knowledge, resources, space and time. Phenomenologically seen, teachers on all levels have practiced technics where they walk around the class and respond to movements, facial expressions and sounds from the students. Such a teaching technique is not one-to-one possible in pure digital teaching but, can to some extent, be functionally equivalated through experiments. For instance, turning on and off microphones and cameras for different groups in the online classes, using parallel written interaction, finding-solutions that work in the different classes and also including the social dimension and making informal activities for the students. Seen form a critical-constructive Bildung perspective, it is necessary that the social dimension is taken seriously to make a foundation for discussing knowledge, attitude and existence, in ways that genuinely engage the students and make it possible for them to participate fully in the teaching (see Chapter 4).

The Spanish Kitchen

Paradoxically, the teachers who seems to have strongest reservations towards digital media[8] are those who have been fiercely opposed to its introduction, who prefer a mechanical form of teaching (in the extraordinary full online situation in spring 2020), providing the students with instructions and then, with no process feedback or class discussions, have simply corrected submissions from their students. The students miss the community of the class and also the interaction with their teacher. At best, this can be seen as a very limited kind of second wave teaching in conditions where the classroom is now totally digital, but with the digital space being used only as a transmission channel.

In our action-based research going back to SME (see Chapter 3) it became clear that when students were different places in the geographical space while being together in the virtual space it provided new educational possibilities. Examples were that students on holiday in other countries, or sick at home could participate, but more on-the-spot examples were students on execution at e.g., business, reporting to the class community, or where the whole class were on educational journeys keeping in contact using organised and documented activities through written interaction.

In the present situation we have a documented teaching experiment from one of the teachers participating in the DUFA-project (see Chapter 4), carried out when all of the students at her upper secondary school stayed at home in the spring of 2020. Thus, Anne Lise Bennedsen, associate professor in Spanish and social studies at Rødkilde Gymnasium, came up with the idea that the students could cook Spanish food at home in their respective kitchens. The homework was that the students had to shop. The weakest students took pictures and wrote in their Facebook group in Spanish, the more skilled spoke Spanish on video in the kitchen. The activity also involved the parents/families. In addition, the teacher virtually visited the homes and families of her students which is of great importance in Spanish culture. Everyone thought it was funny that tortillas can fail and look funny. Via their Facebook group, all the students virtually came to each other's homes – and were together.

---

[8] See Chapter 2 in relation to 'media panics'.

Another Spanish teacher, probably inspired by Anne Lise who shared her idea on the Spanish teacher network, also experienced this as a great success, but varied the process in that the students stood at home in their kitchens and made tortillas according to Spanish recipe while on Microsoft Teams. As Rødkilde Gymnasium did not have a school kitchen, the repatriation provided an opportunity that otherwise did not exist. The cultural (culinary) aspect of the subject unfolded and all the senses came into play, something which the teacher hopes to be able to repeat and further develop after the lockdown. The activity also seems to be good for the class community and for the students' feelings of being seen and respected by the others and helped them to get to know each other and their respective homes. Such activities where students must go out and shop, cook, practice a foreign language and live out 'the culture' of their country, not to mention the social aspect, is in sharp contrast to the very limited second wave teaching described above. A theoretical lesson from the experiment with Spanish Kitchen is that when a class and its teachers only have the virtual space for their Bildung activities they must try to reclaim the physical space and use it educationally. Again, it is strange that none of the reports investigated such good examples and correlated them with the wellbeing and marks of the students (Anne Lise Bennedsen's students got better marks than usual in the spring of 2020). Also, the experiment could easily be expanded to become a full-blown third wave teaching experiment, in which students could take online contact to students in Spain (or other countries) and exchange culinary experiences, receipts and other cultural knowledge that could be educationally and socially relevant and also foster better social well-being both in Denmark and elsewhere.

Expanding Possibilities of Bildung in Online Teaching

It seems clear that the typical form of teaching during the lockdown described in the reports does not provide good conditions for Bildung. How can the teacher be said to put herself in play as otherness when only, if at all, providing short instructions and then correct assignments? Knowledge must be presented and discussed in plenum and in groups, perspectives and attitudes must be considered and otherness external to the class invited to participate and existence experimented with in the process. What we would suggest – if teachers were given the time and opportunity to develop their online teaching seen from a critical-constructive Bildung perspective – is to use the analytical 'Bildung and media' model from Chapter 4 and analyse the four media practices as explained in Chapter 2 under the new circumstances, with the current obstacle that it is not possible to be together physically:

1. *Participation practices* (interaction) relates to the educational understanding and application of new possibilities for interaction and participation in the new media environment. The design question could be: How can we develop ways of using online media that make as much interaction between students, students and teachers and between the class and otherness from outside the class possible? Perhaps students could also be invited into this design process, making use of their experiences with online interaction.
2. *Community practices* (organisation) also relates to participation, but at the organisational level. New forms of participation require the development of organisational forms, norms and ethics that enable participation. The design question could be: How could we, as teachers together with our students, develop an online organisation, that supports the teaching activities and the class community as much as possible?
3. *Expression practices* (production) relates to the area of expressing oneself in digitalised communities. It requires knowledge and skills to express oneself in new media both socially and professionally. The design question could be: how can we develop online teaching that makes it possible for students to express themselves and their knowledge products in as many different ways as possible? Perhaps the students could also be invited into this design process, making use of their experiences with expressing themselves in online media (e.g., making films)?
4. *Impression practices* (interpretation) relate to skills to search information and conduct source criticism, but now using the different locations of the students and what they have at hand. The design question could be: how can we develop an online teaching, that works critically constructively with as many different kinds of online content and formats as possible? This includes making use of extra online resources, like the physical surroundings of the students and the teachers, but also other persons around the world, who are contacted through online media. This could also include online mediated impressions of animals, plants and places.

Developing First, Second and Third Wave Online Teaching

The design and development of online teaching could make use of the analytical model of the three waves (see Chapter 3), which is also integrated in the analytical

'Bildung and media' model in Chapter 4. This can be seen as three levels of development through which teaching is transformed into new modes of communication and organisation that becomes possible with digital media. In relation to the lockdown, the teacher could develop her teaching wave by wave by getting along with new media that becomes relevant, for instance, to video conferences.

If this is done from a critical-constructive Bildung perspective, the first wave applies to the most basic steps of Bildung activities, not least to getting used to and finding yourself in the video-conference format, where one´s face, anxiety-provoking for some, is shown as a close-up picture. This must be supported for the most vulnerable and practised, for instance, in groups so the students find trust in themselves and each other; like they should practice how and when to turn on the microphone and camera, like the parallel written interaction. The first wave is analytically seen as a phase in which the school can begin to workout Bildung activities that address the main challenges of the new digital medium environment, such as anxiety in relation to showing one's face online or writing online. This must be practiced without prohibition and indifference (see Chapter 3), wave one lies beneath the other waves and is a prerequisite for moving the teaching along.

In the second wave, students must be encouraged, challenged and supported to handle, e.g., the videoconference media and the parallel written interaction on a higher and more academic level. Work is being done on building norms regarding the new interaction situations and the students must be supported to develop their own voice in this process. The transparency and registration that comes with digitalisation must also come into focus and be discussed critically, for example, in relation to commercial surveillance, but also in regard to shared documents that allow the teacher to provide process feedback. The new information situations regarding information search and source criticism are also formed at a basic level, in addition to work on processing, selection, storage, categorisation and retrieval in media chains including media platforms like Zoom, Twitter, shared documents and Wiki.

In the third wave, Bildung activities relates to the contact with the outside world, where the confidence with 'internal interaction' in the first two waves is put at risk in authentic transactions with otherness from the surrounding community, for instance with friendship classes, or geographically distributed activities like chemical experiments in the students' kitchens, physical education in nature, or a joint rehearsal of dance choreography in the living room.

Knowledge, Attitude and Existence in Online Teaching

Analytically, we see Bildung as the union of three inseparable elements, namely knowledge, attitude and existence, which we find in the middle of the analytical 'Bildung and media' model in Chapter 4. *Knowledge* denotes the question of *what* students need to know about themselves, society and the world to sustain and create a better world than the one we have today. Questions could be how to act on reducing loneliness in the class and in society or reduce infection. *Attitude* denotes the *question* of how students should relate to themselves, others and the world, in concrete matters of concern. Most students, for instance, could try to reach out to, say, their isolated grandparents. Another example is that they could create a project to fundraise to allow for vaccines to be sent to the Third World or other good causes, that do not directly benefit them, e.g., animals and nature in Brazil. *Existence* denotes the *question* of *who* the students can or ought to be; encouraging and challenging them to raise, develop and qualify their individual voices and ways of responding to others. In the first place the students could work with the epoch-typical key problems (see Chapter 4) in relation to the COVID-19 pandemic, such as how they can be someone that makes a difference to their classmates, teachers, parents, grandparents, children in refugee camps, endangered animals and plants etc.

Against the Technical Regime

Throughout the book and here in Chapter 6, we have criticised the technical understanding of teaching (including determinism, impact research, etc.). Against this background it seems fair to end this chapter with the following interpretations.

Firstly, it is worth noticing that the technical understanding of teaching (and media) has been mainstream and dominant for the last 30 years in Denmark, as in many other western countries, gradually displacing both the critical-constructive understanding of Bildung we have advocated in this book, as well as the progressive pedagogical tradition (i.e., the voluntarist understanding) (see Chapter 1).

Secondly, one could very well also conclude that our two analyses in this chapter indicate that the technical understanding (as the dominant educational regime) has failed. Why is that? Firstly, because when adults in Denmark (and other similar countries) are so bad at entering into a dialogue with otherness (see the first analysis of this chapter), then the education system must take some of the blame and not least the last 30 years where we have had mass education in Denmark, meaning that precisely in this (and only in this) period, the vast majority have gone to both primary school and secondary school (and thus have had at least 12 years of schooling) (Dolin et al., 2020). During the same period, 'democratic education' has actually been part of the purpose of the school, in Denmark (and elsewhere) in both primary and secondary school, in one way or another (Hansen et al., 2019), but it may not help if the educational structure itself is so hard wired to a technical (and thus reductive) understanding (that at its core is not compatible with democracy, because it does not treat students as free human beings, but things to be manipulated (reducing both people, culture and nature to mere resources), while democracy, on the other hand, is fundamentally based on the assumption of individual freedom). In addition, one might well reasonably hypothetically assume that the technical understanding simply does not really 'reach out' to students with particularly weak backgrounds in one way or another (Roy 2003; Petersen et al., 2021). But to that one could also say that when the school system has performed so poorly in relation to the COVID-19 lockdown, despite an excellent IT infrastructure, then it could be argued that a technical understanding (which has been dominant for almost all the time digitalisation has really gained a foothold in the schools) is one of the main reasons that schools have not been able to handle the lockdown very well. In a previous section we also said this indirectly by arguing that politicians and school leaders must have a main responsibility for the school not being better ready for online teaching – but the question is *why* have politicians and school leaders not made the right decisions? In our view, one reason might be that they did not precisely because they have strongly endorsed, de facto, the technical understanding of teaching and the media, which also explains why they have invested heavily in hardware and software, partly also under the influence of an industry with economic interests, but this would hardly have been the case if it were not for the dominance of the technical understanding.

So, the upshot is that the dominance of the technical understanding seems to undermine the opportunity for real democratic social development, as well as the opportunity to be able to develop and create meaningful teaching within the new media environment. With this, we have explained some important and serious societal trends and deficits in the current education system on a deeper level than just saying that school leaders and others have made wrong or bad decisions. This also implies that the current problems cannot just be solved with some kind of soft padding with moral formation thinking (e.g., if young people could just learn to behave better, then everything would be fine), because the problem goes deeper. And likewise, the problem is not just that politicians and leaders have idiosyncratically made the wrong decisions based on a desire for hardware: again, the problem goes deeper: it is because they have directly or indirectly endorsed a flawed, reductionist and socially problematic understanding of society, teaching and media, namely the technical. We have also seen the same problematic connection in research, which has also begun to talk about the impact and direct causality between media and teaching or learning, instead of going for the complicated and more thought-provoking detour around human actors, responses, developments, formation, reflection, etc. which has been the cornerstone of Western – especially, continental – thought, for centuries.

Conclusion

Throughout this book and in this final chapter, with regard to bubble filters and lockdowns, we have applied our action-based research and theories about teaching and Bildung in relation to digital media. Throughout we have advocated, experimented with and argued that a non-deterministic and critical-constructive Bildung perspective has something to say when it comes to teaching and digital media, in contrast to deterministic and technical research and views, that we have criticised for not properly understanding media and education, but also for promoting reductive views on humans, society and the world, seen from a critical Bildung perspective and, more generally, the tradition of continental thinking.

Yet, both media practices and Bildung are dynamic concepts that describe a never-ending effort to encourage, support and challenge the education system as (maybe the most) important societal institution, which aims to cultivate critical-constructive citizens that can and will try to improve humanity for the sake of the wellbeing of all people and living creatures on the planet. All this is brought together in the analytical model found in the beginning of Chapter 4 including both Bildung, media practices and the three waves. Thus, it is important to notice that it is not a mechanical model that can secure media practices and Bildung, but rather a reflective model that might help to form both an analytical tool to *reflect* on educational design (experiments and the development of teaching courses) and for the evaluation (and redesign) of existing courses. So, it is not – and should not be – used as a mechanical model for teaching which treats students and classes as trivial machines. Also, as we discussed at the end of

Chapter 3, the basic educational outlook is more important than anything else. If education is understood not only mechanically, like the 'engineer' but also totally voluntarily, like the 'gardener' (see also Chapter 3), it is not likely that teaching in digital age will contribute in any satisfactory way to encouraging, supporting and challenging new generations of newcomers to take up the fight for democracy, humanity and the wellbeing of all people and life on this planet, with the means, courage and power required for this task. In this chapter, we have tried to show that this is also the case when it comes to filter bubbles and lockdowns. Only 'the challenger' will both aim for and perhaps also manage to develop forms of teaching that can encourage, support and challenge the students to work critically and constructively together with their *knowledge*, *attitude* and *existence* in the media environment that includes digital media and also addresses the new forms of epoch-typical key problems adequately. This is, of course, a contestable statement in many ways, but we hope that this book has produced enough support for this statement to at least take it seriously and engage in further dialogue about how teaching and media can best be understood and pursued.

More concretely, we have supported the feasibility of the critical-constructive Bildung perspective in our present digital age, through our description of four paths if teaching in digital age should be Bildung-orientated (see Chapter 4). Looking at the first path, we generally see the school as a system that, in all school subjects and in its foundations, must seek to find itself in a world where digital media brings major challenges, but where these can be developed into tools that offer new possibilities to structure teaching and schooling in both better and different ways than before, when also seen from a Bildung perspective. Looking down the second path, we see that individual subjects have to find their reconfigured way into the digital world. They must keep themselves informed of the object in their environment that they address and develop means and aims so that they do not end up as anachronisms. Looking down the third path, we are reminded of our responsibility to work out what digitalisation itself means – as a main problem of our epoch – and to seek to encourage and support new generations of people to understand media critically and develop and alter digital and other media into something that can help us all to create a better world and help to fight surveillance capitalism. Looking down the fourth and final path, we see a crossroads where the other three roads can meet and begin a spiral that includes much more third wave teaching than we see today; helping new generations to become better at meeting and dealing with dialogical otherness than today's older generation. As we have argued in this chapter, one of the major problems today, is that social media propels filter bubbles and populism and many people don't have a friendly and collegial attitude towards others. Otherness, both human and more-than-human otherness (the other life creatures on this earth) might be the single most important issue to deal with in future education! And here, we have demonstrated and argued, that digital media and the Internet upholds radically new possibilities of challenging students and supporting and encouraging them to deal dialogically with otherness. For centuries, Bildung thinkers have argued that a dialogical meeting with otherness is one of the key aspects of a Bildung process; but not before digital media and the Internet, has it been possible to such a degree as it is now. What is still missing, however, is that schools and teachers are supported to develop a Bildung-orientated teaching, that brings out the prerequires for third wave education, otherwise, it is unlikely that the new potential for confronting otherness can be actualised in a manner that will do the job. The school in general, each of the subjects and our responsibility for digitalisation as an epochal key problem, can be part of the process of developing new forms of teaching. The development of the school becomes something that is continually revised and developed by processes that are reproduced and modified during each and every school hour executed in conjunction with the other three paths in third wave actions.

Lastly, in Chapter 5, we have also shown the risks of instrumentalising teaching using Big Data and machine-learning algorithms without democracy and Bildung. Here in Chapter 6, we have also argued, that democracy needs Bildung to challenge students to explore and improve their knowledge, attitude and existence, critically to stand up against conspiracy theories, fake news, polarisation, mistrust in institutions and their production of knowledge (not to mention that in many countries, with dictatorships and illiberal democratises, have malfunctioning institutions that must be criticised). After the dark analysis of the democratic problems in the digital age (see Chapter 5 and the beginning of Chapter 6), we have finally analysed how the education system in Denmark, one of the richest and most digitalised societies in the world, managed the COVID-19 lockdown in the spring of 2020. It has been rumoured that the second lockdown, in winter 2021, was managed better and we have also speculated, that the 'first' educational responses to the extraordinary lockdown situation, will be developed into something more concrete, when both teachers and researchers have had time to develop more detailed responses. Yet, if the reports analysing education in the spring are true, there is not much hope for democracy and social coherence in western societies, if we are relying on the education system to help new generations into the digital age. Anyhow, in our view, this only shows that there are strong reasons, together with all the other reasons we have put forward and discussed in this book, that a critical-constructive Bildung approach to teaching is both truly needed and *desirable*, in the digital age, in which we are now living. This is also *possible* – and we have given endless examples – but perhaps not likely – if our educational system and the beliefs it is based on, fail to *reorientate* away from the dominat technical understanding of education.

References

Aagaard, J. (2018). *Teknologier i klasselokalet - en magtfuld fristelse.* København: Unge Pædagoger, 2018(2), s. 48–57.

Al-Qallaf, C. L. and Al-Mutairi, A. S. R. (2016). Digital Literacy and Digital Content Support Learning – The Impact of Blogs on Teaching English as a Foreign Language. *The Electronic Library*, 34(3), 522–547.

Allcott, H. and Gentzkow, M. (2016). Social Media and Fake News in the 2016 Election. *Journal of Economic Perspectives* 31(2), 211–236.

Andersen, B. B. (2020). Analyse af omlagt undervisning i foråret 2020 på erhvervsskoler og gymnasier– forsknings–og datainfor. Forskningsrapport fra eVidensCenter.dk

Andersen, M. H., Gerwien R. G. and Kammer, A. (2020). Sammen, hver for sig: universitets-studerendes læringsstrategier under COVID19-nedlukningen. Tidsskriftet Læring og Medier (LOM), Nr. 23, 2020.

Andersen, Ø. (eds.) (1999). *Dannelse, Humanitas, Paideia.* Sypress forlag.

Anderson, Chris. 2008. "The End of Theory, will the Data Deluge Make the Scientific Method Obsolete?" *Edge [Online].* Available at: www.wired.com/2008/06/pb-theory/

Anderson, T. and Dron, J. (20101). Three Generations of Distance Education Pedagogy. *The International Review of Research in Open and Distributed Learning*, 12(3), 80–97.

Arendt, H. (1998). *The Human Condition.* Chicago: University of Chicago Press.

Beck, S., Beck S. and Paulsen, M (2014). Klassisk og moderne læringsteori. København: Hans Reitzels forlag.

Atkinson, C. (2010) *The Backchannel. New Riders, Peachpit.* Berkeley CA: Pearson Education.

Avram, E. M. (2014). Facebook Communication in Higher Education. *SEA – Practical Application of Science Volume II*, 2(3), 5.

Backer, Larry Catá. 2018. "Next Generation Law: Data Driven Governance and Accountability Based Regulatory Systems in the West, and Social Credit Regimes in China" 7 July 2018. Available at: https://ssrn.com/abstract=3209997 or http://dx.doi.org/10.2139/ssrn.3209997.

Bakshy, E., Messing, M. And Adamic, L. (2015). Exposure to ideologically diverse news and opinion on Facebook. *Political Science*, Vol 348(6239) 1130–1132.

Bardhi, F. J., Rohm, A, and Sultan, F. (2010). Tuning In and Tuning Out: Media Multitasking among Young Consumers. *Journal of Consumer Behaviour*, 9, 316–332.

Baumann, Z. (2009). *Fagre nye læringsliv – læring, pædagogik, uddannelse og ungdom i den flydende modernitet.* (red) Jacobsen. København: Unge Pædagoger.

Baym, N. (2010). Personal Connections in the Digital Age. Cambridge: Polity Press.

Beck, S. (2014). *Klassisk og moderne læringsteori*. Hans Reitzels forlag.

Biesta, G. (2006). *Beyond Learning – Democratic Education for a Human Future*. London: Paradigm Publishers.

Biesta, G. (2010). *Good Education in an Age of Measurement: Ethics, Politics, Democracy*. Boulder: Paradigm Publishers.

Biesta, G. (2011). *Learning Democracy in School and Society: Education, Lifelong Learning, and the Politics of Citizenship*. Rotterdam: Sense Publishers.

Biesta, G. (2017). *The Rediscovery of Teaching*. New York: Routledge.

Bijker, Wiebe E., Thomas P. Hughes and Trevor J. Pinch, (eds) (1987). *The Social Construction of Technological Systems: New Directions in the Sociology and History of Technology*. Cambridge, MA: MIT Press.

Bourdieu, P. (1977). Cultural Reproduction and Social Reproduction in J. Karabel and A. H. Halsey (eds) *Power and Ideology in Education*. New York, NY: Oxford University Press, pp. 487–511.

boyd, d. (2010). *Social Network Sites as Networked Publics: Affordances, Dynamics, and Implications. A Networked Self: Identity, Community, and Culture on Social Network Sites*. New York: Routledge.

boyd, d. (2014). *It's Complicated: The Social Lives of Networked Teens*. New Haven, CT: Yale University Press.

boyd, danah, and Kate Crawford. (2012). Critical Questions for Big Data. *Information, Communication & Society*, 15(5), 662–679.

Braidotti, R. (2011). *Nomadic Theory*. Columbia University Press.

Braidotti, R. (2013). *The Posthuman*. Cambridge: Polity Press.

Brauns, J. (2002). Die Metaphysik des Mediums. In Brauns, J. (eds), *Form und Medium* Weimar: VDG, pp. 9–20.

Bruford, W.H. (1975). *The German Tradition of Self-Cultivation: Bildung from Humboldt to Thomas Mann*, Cambridge: Cambridge University Press.

Brügger, N. (2002). Theoretical Reflections on Media and Media History. In *Media History, Theories, Methods, Analysis*. Edited by Brügger, N. and Kolstrup, S. Aarhus: Aarhus Universitetsforlag, pp. 33–66.

Bruns, A. (2008). *Blogs, Wikipedia, Second Life and Beyond: From Production to Produsage*. Oxford: Peter Lang.

Bryant, L. (2014). *Onto-Cartography – An Ontology of Machines and Media*. Edinburgh: Edinburgh University Press.

Burns, T. and F. Gottschalk (eds) (2019). *Educating 21st Century Children: Emotional Well-being in the Digital Age, Educational Research and Innovation*, OECD Publishing, Paris.

Buus, L. (2013). 'Perspectives on the Integration of Facebook Into Higher Education' in Proceedings of the 8th International Conference on e-Learning – Cape and Peninsula University of Technology, Cape Town, South Africa, (ed. Ivala, E.), pp. 437–443.

Caputo, John D. (2018). *Hermeneutics. Facts and Interpretation in the Age of Information*. Pelican Books. Penguin Random House UK.

Cassirer, E. (1970). *An Essay on Man*. New Haven and London: Yale University Press.
Castells, M. (2003). *Netværkssamfundet og dets opståen*. København: Hans Reitzels Forlag A/S.
Chen, Ying, Elenee Argentinis, and Griff Weber. (2016). IBM Watson: How Cognitive Computing Can Be Applied to Big Data Challenges in Life Sciences Research. *Clinical Therapeutics*. 38(4) 688–701.
Cinque, T and Brown, A. (2015). Educating Generation Next: Screen Media Use, Digital Competencies and Tertiary Education. *Digital Culture and Education*, 7(1), 1–18.
Cohen, S. (2002). *Folk Devils and Moral Panics*. London: Routledge.
Crook, C. (2008). *Web 2.0 Technologies for Learning: The Current Landscape – Opportunities, Challenges and Tensions*, Nottingham: Becta: Leading next generation learning.
Cuban, L. (2003). *Oversold and Underused: Computers in the Classroom*. Cambridge, MA: Harvard University Press.
Dall, S. (2015). Fælles onlinedokumenter i historie. In Paulsen and Tække (2015).
Debray, R. (1996). *Media Manifestos*. London: Verso.
Dede, C. (2016). Social Media and Challenges to Traditional Models of Education. In *Education and Social Media*. Greenhow, Christine et al (eds). London: MIT Press.
Deleuze, G. (1994). *Difference and Repetition*. Columbia University Press.
Deleuze, G. (2006). *Forhandlinger 1972–1990*. København: Det lille forlag.
Deleuze, G. and Guattari, F. (2000). *A Thousand Plateaus: Capitalism and Schizophrenia*. Continuum.
Deleuze, G., and Guattari, F. (1995). *What is Philosophy?* London: Verso.
Dewey, J. (1997). *Experience & Education*. New York: Touchstone.
Dewey, J. (2000). Erfaring og opdragelse i Hartnack and Sløk (eds) De store tænkere: John Dewey. København: Rosinante.
Dolin, J., Holten Ingerslev, G. and Jørgensen, H. S. (eds) (2020). *Gymnasiepædagogik: En grundbog*. 4. udg. København: Hans Reitzels Forlag
Drejer, C. M. (2014). Kampen om eleven – Hvordan skoler skaber elever. København: Unge Pædagoger.
Drotner, K. (1999). Dangerous Media? Panic Discourses and Dilemmas of Modernity *Paedagogica Historica*, 35(3) 593–619.
Dunlap, J.C. and P.R. Lowenthal. (2009). Tweeting the Night Away: Using Twitter to Enhance Social Presence. *Journal of Information Systems Education* 20(2), 129–135.
Dysthe, O., Bernhardt, N., and Esbjorn, L. (2013). *Dialogue-based Teaching*. Oslo: Fagbokforlaget.
Ebner, M., Kickmeier-Rust, M. and Holzinger, A. (2008). Utilizing Wiki-Systems in Higher Education Classes: A Chance for Universal Access? *Universal Access in the Information Society* 7(4), 199–207.
Echenique, E. G. (2014). An Integrative Review of Literature on Learners in the Digital Era. *Studia Paedagogica* Available at: https://doi.org/10.5817/SP2014-4-8.
Edson C. Tandoc Jr., Zheng Wei Lim and Richard Ling (2018). Defining "Fake News", Digital Journalism, 6(2), 137–153.

Eisenstein, E. (1983). *The Printing Revolution in Early Modern Europe.* Cambridge: Cambridge University Press.

Elavsky C., M., C. and Elavsky, S. (2011). When Talking Less is More: Exploring Outcomes of Twitter Usage in the Large-Lecture Hall. *Learning, Media and Technology* 36(3), 215–233.

Elavsky, C. M- (2012). You Can't Go Back Now: Incorporating "Disruptive" Technologies in the Large Lecture Hall. *Social Media.* Noor Al-Deen, Hana S. and Hendricks, John Allen (Rad). Lanham, Maryland: Lexington Books, pp 75–91.

Ellison, N., Steinfield, C., and Lampe, C. (2007). The Benefits of Facebook "Friends": Social Capital and College Students' Use of Online Social Network Sites. *Journal of Computer-Mediated Communication*, 12, 1143–1168

Engen, B. K., Giæver, T. H. and Mifsud, L. (2015). Guidelines and Regulations for Teaching Digital Competence in Schools and Teacher Education: A Weak Link? *Nordic Journal of Digital Literacy*, 10(2), 69–83.

Engeström, Y. (1987). *Learning by Expanding: An Activity-theoretical Approach to Developmental Research.* Orienta-Konsultit Orienta-Konsultit Oy.

Erstad, O., Eickelmann, B., and Eichhorn, K. (2015). Preparing Teachers for Schooling in the Digital Age: A Meta-perspective on Existing Strategies and Future Challenges. *Education and Information Technologies* 20, 641–654.

Esposito, E. (1999). 'Two-sided Forms in Language'. In Baecker, D. (ed.), *Problems of Form* Stanford, CA: Stanford University Press, pp. 78–98.

Fahey, C. and Meaney, T. (2011). Conversation is the New Attention. State of the Web, Business, 19 April 2011. Available at: www.alistapart.com/articles/conversation-is-the-new-attention/

Feng, S. F., Schwemmer, M., Gershman S. J., and Cohen, J. D. (2014). Multitasking vs. Multiplexing: Toward a Normative Account of Limitations in the Simultaneous Execution of Control-demanding Behaviors. *Cognitive Affective and Behavioral Neuroscience.* 14(1): 129–146.

Finnemann, N. O. (2008). 'The Internet and the Emergence of a New Matrix of Media.' Paper presented at AOIR 9.0, Copenhagen, Denmark.

Finnemann, N.O. (2005). Internettet i mediehistorisk perspektiv. Frederiksberg: Forlaget Samfundslitteratur.

Foucault, M. (2002). Overvågning og straf. Frederiksberg: Det Lille Forlag.

Frau-Meigs, D., Michel, J. F and Velez, I. (2017). *Public Policies in Media and Information Literacy in Europe Cross-Country Comparisons.* Abingdon: Routledge.

Frischmann, B. and Selinger, E. (2019). *Re-engineering Humanity.* Cambridge University Press.

Fu, Jo Shan (2013). ICT in Education: A Critical Literature Review and Its Implications. *International Journal of Education and Development using Information and Communication Technology* 9(1) 112–125.

Gadamer, H.-G. (2013). *Truth & Method.* London: Bloomsbury.

Giglietto, F., Iannelli, L., Rossi, L. and Valeriani, A. (2016). Fakes, News and the Election. (30 November 2016). Convegno AssoComPol (Urbino, 15–17 Dicembre 2016). Available at: https://ssrn.com/abstract=2878774.

Gottfried, J. and Shearer, E. (2016). 'News Use Across Social Media Platforms.' Pew Research Center. Available at: www.journalism.org/2016/05/26/news-use-across-social-media-platforms-2016/.

Gretter, S. and Yadav, A. (2016). Computational Thinking and Media and Information Literacy: An Integrated Approach to Teaching Twenty-First Century Skills. In *TechTrends* (2016) 60: 510–516.

Gustavsson, B. (1995). Almänbildning – bildung om alt och för alla. I Jacobsen, J. (ed.). Spor – en antologi om almendannelse. Vejle. Kroghs forlag a/s.

Gustavsson, B. (2017). *Bildningens dynamik*. Bokförlaget Korpen.

Habermas, J. (1976). *Borgerlig offentlighet – dens framvekst og forfall*. København: Fremad.

Habermas, J. (1992). *The Theory of Communicative Action*. Cambridge: Polity Press.

Han, B-C (2016). *Psykopolitik. Neoliberalisme og de nye magtteknikker*. Forlaget THP.

Hansen, D. et al. (2019). *Undervisning, dannelse og ungdomsliv*. Odense: Odense Universitetsforlag.

Hansen, D. R., Larsen, L., and Paulsen, M. (2019). *Undervisning, dannelse og ungdomsliv*. Odense: Syddansk Universitetsforlag.

Hansen, Thomas I. (2018). "Dannelse, digitalisering og dataficering – Hvad gemmer der sig bag begrebet digital dannelse?" [Bildung, Digitization and Datafication – What is behind the Concept of Digital Bildung?" *UP (Unge Pædagoger)* nr. 2.

Hattem, D. and Lomicka, L. (2016). What the Tweets Say: A Critical Analysis of Twitter Research in Language Learning from 2009 to 2016. *E-Learning and Digital Media*, 13(1–2) 5–23.

Havelock, E. A. (1982) *The Literate Revolution in Greece and its Cultural Consequences*. Princeton, NJ: Princeton University Press.

Heidegger, M. (2002). *The Essence of Truth*. London: Continuum.

Heider, F. (1959). *On Perception and Event Structure, and the Psychological Environment. Selected Papers by Fritz Heider*. New York: International Universities Press Inc.

Helsper, E and Eynon, R (2009). Digital Natives: Where is the Evidence? *British Educational Research Journal*, 36(3), 503–520.

Herrero-Diz P, Conde-Jiménez J, Reyes de Cózar S. (2020). Teens' Motivations to Spread Fake News on WhatsApp. *Social Media + Society*. July 2020.

Holotescu, C., and G. Grosseck. (2008). 'Using microblogging in education. Case Study: Cirip.ro'. Paper presented at the 6th Conference on E-learning Applications, January 2009, Cairo.

Hosterman, A. R. (2012). 'Tweeting 101: Twitter and the College Classroom' in *Social Media*. Noor Al-Deen, Hana S. and Hendricks, John Allen (eds). Lanham, Maryland: Lexington Books, pp 93–110.

Hutchins, E. (1995). *Cognition in the Wild*. New Haven, CT: MIT Press.

Hutchison, A. C., Woodward, L. and Colwell, J. (2016). What Are Preadolescent Readers Doing Online? An Examination of Upper Elementary Students' Reading, Writing, and Communication in Digital Spaces. *Reading Research Quarterly*, 51(4), 435–454.

Illeris, K. (2015). *Læring i konkurrencestaten – kapløb eller bæredygtighed*. Frederiksberg: Samfundslitteratur.

Innis, H. (1986). *Empire and Communications*. Victoria/Toronto: Press Porcépic.

Innis, H. (1991). *Bias of Communication*. Toronto: University of Toronto Press.

Islam, M. S., and Grönlund, Å. (2016). An International Literature Review of 1:1 Computing in Schools. *Journal of Educational Change* 17, 191–222.

Iversen, O.S., Smith, R.C. and Dindler, C.D. (2018). *Proceedings of the Participatory Design Conference*. New York: ACM Press.

Jaeger, W. (1973). *Paideia: De formung des grechischen Menschen*. Berlin: De Gruyter.

Jakobsen, K. A. (2016). Etter Charlie Hebdo – Ytringfrihetens krise i historisk lys. Trondheim: Forlaget Press.

Jenkins, H. (2008). *Convergence Culture: Where Old and New Media Collide*. New York: New York University Press.

Jenkins, H. et. al (2006) *Confronting the Challenges of Participatory Culture: Media Education for the 21st Century*. London: The MIT Press.

Jenkins, H, Ford, S., and Green, J. (2013). *Spreadable Media—Creating Value and Meaning in a Networked Culture*. New York: New York University Press.

Jensen, L. X., Karstad, O. M., Mosbech, A., Vermund, M. C., and Konradsen, F. (2020). *Experiences and challenges of students during the 2020 campus lockdown. Results from student surveys at the University of Copenhagen*. Copenhagen: University of Copenhagen, pp. 1–73.

Jørgensen S. L. et al [eVidenCenter & DEA]. (2020) Fjernundervisningstemperatur.dk. En rundspørge blandt elever og lærere på ungdomsuddannelser om erfaringer med fjernundervisning under Coronanedlukningen. Viby: eVidenCenter og København: DEA

Junco, R., Heibergert G and Loken E. (2010). The Effect of Twitter on College Student Engagement and Grades. *Journal of Computer Assisted Learning*. 27(2), 119–132.

Jurkowitz, M. et al. (2020). Media Polarization and the 2020 Election: A Nation Divided. Pew Research Center. Available at: www.journalism.org/2020/01/24/u-s-media-polarization-and-the-2020-election-a-nation-divided/

Kant, I. (1784). What is enlightenment? In the December 1784 publication of the *Berlinische Monatsschrift* (Berlin Monthly), edited by Friedrich Gedike and Johann Erich Biester, Kant replied to the question posed a year earlier, see: www.artoftheory.com/what-is-enlightenment_immanuel-kant/

Kant, I. (1803). *On Education* (über Pädagogik): Available at: http://oll.libertyfund.org/titles/356

Karlsen, C. D. (2015). Blogs og andre sociale medier i engelsk. In Paulsen and Tække 2015.

Kemp, P. (2013). *Verdensborgeren. Pædagogisk og politisk ideal for det 21. Århundrede*. 2.

Kergel, D. (2007). *Qualitative Bildungsforschung – Ein integrative Ansatz*. Springer Fachmedien Wiesbaden GmbH.

Kiili, C. (2012). *Online Reading as an Individual and Social Practice*. Jyväskylä: Publishing Unit, University Library of Jyväskylä.

Kiili, C., Leu, D. J., Marttunen, M., Hautala, J. and Leppänen, P. H. T. (2018). Exploring Early Adolescents' Evaluation of Academic and Commercial Online Resources Related to Health. *Reading and Writing*, 31(3), 533–557.

Kinsky, E. S. and Bruce K. (2015). 'It Throws you into the Ring': Learning from Live-Tweeting. *Teaching Journalism and Mass Communication*, 6(1), 36–52, Winter.

Klafki, W. (2005). Dannelsesteori og didaktik—nye studier. Århus: Forlaget Klim.

König C. J. (2005). Working Memory, Fluid Intelligence, and Attention are Predictors of Multitasking Performance, but Polychronicity and Extraversion are Not. *Human Performance*, 18(3), 243–266.

Koselleck, R. (2007). *Dannelsens antropologiske og semantiske struktur*. I Slagmark Nr. 48.

Krämer, S. (1998). Form als Vollzug oder: Was gewinnen wir mit Niklas Luhmanns Unterscheidung von Medium und Form? *Rechtshistorisches* 17, 558–574.

Krutka, D. (2015). Platforms, Purpose, and Pedagogy: Reclaiming Context and Resisting Technopoly with Participatory Media. *Journal of Thought* 49(3/4) 35–49.

Kuznekoff, J. H., Munz, S. and Titsworth, S. (2015). Mobile Phones in the Classroom: Examining the Effects of Texting, Twitter, and Message Content on Student Learning. *Communication Education*, 64(3), 344–365.

Larsen, J. (2014). Dannelse eller kompetence? *Kognition og Pædagogik* nr. 94.

Larsen, S. N. (2013). *Dannelse – en samtidskritisk og idéhistorisk revitalisering*. København: Fjordager.

Latour, B. (1994). On Technical Mediation – Philosophy, Sociology, Genealogy. In *Common Knowledge*. 3(2), 29–64.

Latour, B. (1999). *Pandora's Hope: Essay on the Reality of Science Studies*. Cambridge, MA: Harvard University Press.

Latour, B. (2008). *En Ny sociologi for et nyt samfund*. København: Akademisk Forlag.

Leaver, K and Kent, M. (2014). Introduction – Facebook in Education: Lessons Learnt. *Digital Culture & Education*, 6(1), 60–65.

Lee, J., Lin, L. and Robertson, T. (2012). The Impact of Media Multitasking on Learning. *Learning, Media and Technology*. 37(1), 94–104.

Li, J. and Su, M. (2020). Real Talk About Fake News: Identity Language and Disconnected Networks of the US Public's "Fake News" Discourse on Twitter. *Social Media + Society*. 6(2).

Liang, Fan, Vishnupriya Das, Nadiya Kostyuk, and Muzammil M. Hussain. (2018). Constructing a Data-Driven Society: China's Social Credit System as a State Surveillance Infrastructure. *Policy & Internet*, 10(4), 415–433

Liburd, J. J. og. Christensen, I. F. (2011). "*Web 2.0 i videregående uddan-nelser*" Idéhæfte fra eVidenCenter® – Det Nationale Videncenter for e-læring Århus Købmandsskole Viborgvej 159A, Hasle 8210 Århus V.

Linaa-Jensen, J. and Tække, J. (2018) *Sociale medier*. København: Samfundslitteratur.

Livingstone, S. (2012). Critical Reflections on the Benefit of ICT in Education. *Oxford Review of Education*, 38(1), 9–24.

Livingstone, S. (2014). *The Mediatization of Childhood and Education: Reflections on the Class*. In Kramp, L., Carpentier, N., Hepp, A., Tomanic-Trivundza, I., Nieminen, H., Kunelius, R., Olsson, T., Sundin, E., and Kilborn, R., (eds), *Media Practice and Everyday Agency in Europe*. Bremen: Edition Lumière, pp. 45–67.

Løvlie, L. Mortensen, K.P. and Nordenbro, S.E. (eds) (2003). *Educating Humanity – Bildung in Postmodernity*. Oxford: Blackwell Publishing.

Løvschall, S. (2015). Skriftligt arbejde i dansk med fælles online-processkrivning. In Paulsen and Tække (2015).

Lowe, B. and Laffey, D. (2011). Is Twitter for the Birds? Using Twitter to Enhance Student Learning in a Marketing Course. *Journal of Marketing Education* 33: 183.

Luhmann, L. (1998). Erkendelse som konstruktion. In Hermansen (ed.) *Fra læringens horisont – en antologi*. Aarhus: Klim, pp. 163–182.

Luhmann, L. (2006). *Samfundets uddannelsessystem*. København: Hans Reitzels Forlag.

Luhmann, N. (1979): *Trust and Power*. Chichester: John Wiley and Sons Ltd.

Luhmann, N. (1990). *Essays on Self-Reference*. New York: Columbia University Press.

Luhmann, N. (1993). Barnet som medie for opdragelsen. In *Læring Samtale Organisation*. Cederstrøm, J., Qvortrup, L. and Og Rasmussen, J. (eds) København: Unge Pædagoger pp 161–190.

Luhmann, N. (1995). *Social Systems*. Stanford, CA: Stanford University Press.

Luhmann, N. (2000a). *Art as a Social System*. Stanford, CA: Stanford University Press.

Luhmann, N. (2000b). *The Reality of the Mass Media*. Cambridge: Polity Press.

Luhmann, N. (2002). *Einführung in die Systemtheorie*. Heidelberg: Carl-Auer-Systeme Verlag.

Luhmann, N. (2012). *Theory of Society*. (vols 1 and 2). Stanford, CA: Stanford University Press.

Luhmann, N. (2017). *Education as a Social System*. Wiesbaden: VS Springer.

Luhmann, N. (2018). *Organization and Decision*. Cambridge: Cambridge University Press.

Lyotard, F. (1996). *Viden og det postmoderne samfund*. Århus: Forlaget Slagmark.

Lyotard, J. (1979). *The Postmodern Condition*. Manchester University Press.

Mackenzie, D. and Wajcman, J (eds) (1999). *The Social Shaping of Technology*. 2nd edn. Maidenhead: Open University Press,

Marciano, J. E. (2015). Becoming Facebook Friendly: Social Media and the Culturally Relevant Classroom. *English Journal* 104(5), 73–78.

Marner, A. (2013a). Digital Media Embedded in Swedish Art Education – A Case Study. *Education Inquiry*, 4(2), 355–373.

Marner, M. and Örtegren, H. (2013b). Four approaches to Implementing Digital Media in Art Education, *Education Inquiry*, 4(4), 671–688.

Mathiasen, H., Aaen J., Dalsgaard C. og Thomsen M. B. (2014). Undervisningsorganisering, –former og –medier – på langs og tværs af fag og gymnasiale uddannelser. Forskningsrapport 2014 Aarhus Universitet, Center for Undervisningsudvikling og Digitale Medier.

Mathiesen, K. (2015). Google Docs til mængdeberegningsopgaver i NF-kemi. In Paulsen and Tække (2015).

Matricciani, L. A., Olds, T. S, Blunden, S., Rigney, G. and Williams, M. T. (2012). Never Enough Sleep: A Brief History of Sleep Recommendations for Children. *Pediatrics* 129(3), 548–556.

McLuhan, M. (1967). Mennesket og Medierne. København: Gyldendal. Translated from: *Understanding Media: The Extension of Man*.

McLuhan, M. (1995). The Gutenberg Galaxy. The Making of Typographic Man. New York: New American Library.

McNely, B. J. (2009). Backchannel Persistence and Collaborative Meaning-Making. *SIGDOC'09*, 5–7 October, pp. 1–7.

Mead, G. H. (1934). *Mind, Self and Society*. Chicago: University of Chicago Press.

Menkhoff, T., Chay, Y. W., Bengtsson, M. L., Woodard, C. J. and Gan, B. (2015). 'Incorporating microblogging ("tweeting") in higher education: Lessons learnt in a knowledge management course'. In *Computers in Human Behavior* 1295–1302.

Menzies R., Petrie K. and Zarb M. (2017). A Case Study of Facebook Use: Outlining A Multi-Layer Strategy for Higher Education. *Education and Information Technologies* 22, 39–53.

Meyrowitz, J. (1985). *No Sense of Place: The Impact of Electronic Media on Social Behavior*. New York: Oxford University Press.

Montero-Fleta, B., Pérez-Sabater, C. and Pérez-Sabater, M. L. (2015). Microblogging and Blended Learning: Peer Response in Tertiary Education. *Procedia –Social and Behavioral Sciences* 191 1590–1595.

Moody, M. (2010). Teaching Twitter and Beyond: Tips for Incorporating Social Media in Traditional Courses. *Journal of Magazine and New Media Research*. 11(2) 1–9.

Mueller, J., Peruta, M.R. and Giudice, M. D. (2014). Social media platforms and technology education: Facebook on the way to graduate school. *International Journal of Technology Management*, 66(4).

Müller, J. W. (2016). *What is Populism?* Pennsylvania: University of Pennsylvania Press.

Nørreklit, L. (2017). Actor-reality Construction. In Nørreklit. H. (ed.), *A Philosophy of Management Accounting: A Pragmatic Constructivist Approach*. Abingdon: Routledge.

O'Brien, J. (2011). UCSF Study on Multitasking Reveals Switching Glitch in Aging Brain. Available at: www.ucsf.edu.

Oettingen, A (2001). *Det pædagogiske paradoks*. Forlaget Klim.

Ong, W. J. (1982). *Orality and Literacy*. Reprinted 2000. London: Routledge.

Pashler, H. (1994). Dual-task interference in simple tasks: data and theory. *Psychological Bulletin*, 16, 220–244.

Paulsen, M. (2020). 'The good, the bad and the ugly: how different teachers will construe digitalization differently'. In Kergel et al. (eds) *Communication and Learning in an Age of Digital Transformation* Abingdon: Routledge.

Paulsen, M. and Elf, N. (2020). Brug af it i gymnasiet—muligheder og umuligheder. In Dolin, J., Ingerslev, G. and Sparholt Jørgensen, H. (eds), *Gymnasiepædagogik*. København: Hans Reitzels forlag.

Paulsen, M. and Garsdal, J. (2017). Den lille og den store nytte: et interkulturelt perspektiv på forholdet mellem nytte og frihed. In Akademisk kvarter, 14. Available at: https://journals.aau.dk/index.php/ak/article/view/2705.

Paulsen, M. and Tække, J. (2009). Om den uformelle (mis)brug af medier i det formelle uddannelsessystem. i Mediekultur, *Journal of Media and Communication Research* 46, 56–72.

Paulsen, M. and Tække, J. (2010). Digitale medier og magt i undervisningen. *Dansk Sociologi* Nr. 3/21. årgang s. 29–48.

Paulsen, M. and Tække, J. (2010b). Trådløse netværk og sociale normer. *Norsk Medietidsskrift* 17, nr. 1, pp. 16–45.

Paulsen, M. and Tække, J. (2010c). Editorial: Luhmann and the Media. In *Journal of Media and Communication Research*. Mediekultur 49.

Paulsen, M. and Tække, J. (2013a). Sociale medier i gymnasiet – mellem forbud og ligegyldighed. København: Unge Pædagoger.

Paulsen, M. and Tække, J. (2013b). Social media and the Hybridization of Education. *Cybernetics & Human Knowing*, 20, 141–158.

Paulsen, M. and Tække, J. (2015a). Digital dannelse på HF og VUC – Udfordringer, erfaringer og perspektiver. København: Unge Pædagoger.

Paulsen, M. and Tække, J. (2015b). Steering of educational processes in digital medium environment. *Journal of Sociocybernetics*, 13(5), 72–83.

Paulsen, M. and Tække, J. (2016a). Bildung in the Era of Digital Media. *Journal of Sociocybernetics*, 14, 28–41.

Paulsen, M. and Tække, J. (2016b). 'Bildung in the Digital Medium Environment.' Paper for The Third ISA Forum 'The Futures We Want: Global Sociology and the Struggles for a Better World.' RC 51, Sociocybernetics. Vienna, Austria, 10–14 July 2016.

Paulsen, M. and Tække, J. (2016c). Steering of Educational Processes in a Digital Medium Environment. *Journal of Sociocybernetics*, 13(2), 72–83.

Paulsen, M, and Tække, J. (2016d). Sociale medier og ulovlige netværk i gymnasieskolen. *MedieKultur*, 31(59), 115–132.

Paulsen, M. and Tække, J. (2016e). Undervisningsfællesskab og læringsnetværk i det digitale samfund. København: Unge Pædagoger.

Paulsen, M. and Tække, J. (2017a). 'Main Features in the Concept of Digital Bildung.' Paper for the NordMedia 2017 conference 'Mediated realities – Global Challenges' Division 5: Media Literacy and Media Education at the University of Tampere, School of Communication, Media and Theatre. 17–19 August.

Paulsen, M. and Tække, J. (2017b). Digitalization of education: The theory of the three waves. In Skrifter fra Center for internetforskning, 17. Available at: http://cfi.au.dk/fileadmin/www.cfi.au.dk/publikationer/cfis_skriftserie/017_Taekke_Paulsen.pdf.

Paulsen, M. and Tække, J. (2018). Digitalt understøttet faglighed og almendannelse – Bog 1: et overblik. København: Unge Pædagoger.

Paulsen, M. and Tække, J. (2019a). Digitalt understøttet faglighed og almendannelse. Bog 2: analyser og indblik. København: Unge Pædagoger.

Paulsen, M. and Tække, J. (2019b). Distraction and digital media – Multiplexing, not Multitasking in the Classroom. Tidsskriftet Læring og Medier (LOM), Nr. 21, 2019ISSN: 1903-248X.

Paulsen, M. and Tække, J. (2019c). Bildung through Social Media. NETCOM— *Networks and Communication Studies*. Available at: https://pure.au.dk/ws/files/54508198/Social_Media_and_Teaching._Taekke_and_Paulsen.pdf.

Paulsen, M. and Tække, J. (2020). Acting with and against Big Data in School and Society: The Big Democratic Questions of Big Data. *The Journal of Communication and Media Studies* 5(3): 15–31. doi:10.18848/2470-9247/CGP/v05i03/15-31.

Pedersen, O. K. (2011). *Konkurrencestaten*. København: Hans Reitzels forlag.

Pennycook, G, McPhetres, J., Zhang, Y. Lu, J. G. and Rand D. G. (2020). Fighting COVID-19 Misinformation on Social Media. *Psychological Science*, 31(7) 770–780.

Petersen, K. et al. (2021). *Rethinking Education in Light of Global Challenges: Scandinavian Perspectives on Culture, Society and the Anthropocene*. Abingdon: Routledge.

Pietersma, H. (2000). *Phenomenological Epistemology*. Oxford: Oxford University Press.

Pool, I. S. (1983) *Technologies of Freedom*. Cambridge: MA: Harvard University Press.

Poshka, A. (2014). Digital Culture and Social Media versus the Traditional Education. *Journal of Education Culture and Society* 1, 201–205.

Postman, N. (1993). *Technopoly*. New York: Vintage Books.

Qvortrup, A., Qvortrup, L., Wistoft, K. & Christensen, J. (2020). Nødundervisning under coronakrisen – et elev- og forældreperspektiv. Available at: https://ncs.au.dk/projekter/noedundervisning-under-corona-krisen/

Reagan, T. (2018). *Non-Western Educational Traditions*. Abingdon: Routledge.

Reid, Crystal (2018). Chinese schools make pupils wear micro-chipped uniforms to thwart truancy. *The Telegraph*. 26 December 2018. Available at: www.telegraph.co.uk/news/2018/12/26/china-schools-make-pupils-wear-micro-chipped-uniforms-thwart/

Reid, J. (2011). "We don't Twitter, we Facebook": An Alternative Pedagogical Space that Enables Critical Practices in Relation to Writing. *English Teaching: Practice and Critique* 10(1), 58–80.

Rekart, J. (2012). Taking on Multitasking. I Kappan December 2011/January 2012. V93 N4 pp. 60–63.

Rorty, R. (1989). *Contingency, Irony, and Solidarity*. Cambridge: Cambridge University Press.

Rorty, R. (1999). *Philosophy and Social Hope*. London: Penguin Books.

Roy, K. (2003). *Teachers in Nomadic Spaces*. Oxford: Peter Lang.

Schreiber, T. (2017). Hvad er digital dannelse. Fra bogen: *Biblioteksdidaktik*. (ed.) Laskie, C. København: Hans Reitzels Forlag.

Selwyn, N. (2014). *Distrusting Educational Technology: Critical Questions for Changing Times*. Abingdon: Routledge.

Selwyn, N. (2017). *Education and Technology*. 2nd edn. London: Bloomsbury.

Sen, A. (2005). *The Argumentative Indian: Writings on Indian History, Culture and Identity*. New York: Penguin.

Shannon B. R., Tapp, S., and A. Laverie, D. (2011). Learning by Tweeting: Using Twitter as a Pedagogical Tool. *Journal of Marketing Education* 33(2), 193–203.

Sims, C. (2017). *Disruptive Fixation – School Reform and the Pitfalls of Techno-Idealism*. Princeton NJ: Princeton University Press.

Sivarajah, U.R, Muhammad M.K., Zahir I. and Vishanth W.. (2017). Critical Analysis of Big Data Challenges and Analytical Methods. *Journal of Business Research* 70, 263–286.

Sorkin, D. (1983). 'Wilhelm Von Humboldt: The Theory and Practice of Self-Formation (Bildung), 1791–1810'. *Journal of the History of Ideas* 44(1) 55–73.

Spencer-Brown, G. (1969): *Laws of Form*. London: George Allen and Unwin Ltd.

Straume, I. (ed.) (2019). *Danningens filosofihistorie*. Copenhagen: Gyldendal.

Sundén, J. (2003). *Material Virtualities: Approaching Online Textual Embodiment*. Oxford: Peter Lang.

Tække, J. (2002). 'Cyberspace as a Space Parallel to Geographical Space' in *Virtual Space: The Spatiality of Virtual Inhabited 3D worlds*. Lars Qvortrup (ed.), New York: Springer Publishers, pp. 25–42.

Tække, J. (2006). *Mediesociografi*. København: Innovative Communication (InC).

Tække, J. (2007). Selvets dannelse – 6 stadier på vejen mod selvrefleksivitet. in Paulsen & Qvorteup: *Luhmann og dannelse*. Unge Pædagoger 2007.

Tække, J. (2011). 'Media as the mechanism behind structural coupling and the evolution of the mind.' Paper presented at Luhmann in Action: Empirical Studies of Structural Couplings, International University Centre of Post-graduate studies (IUC), Dubrovnik, Croatia.

Tække, J. (2014). 'Twitter as equipment for educational interaction: The struggle between efficiency and being.' Paper presented at 27th Nordic Sociological Association conference: Exploring Blind Spots, 14–16 August 2014 in Lund, Sweden.

Tække, J. (2019a). 'Big Data in the School – a Systems and Media Theoretical Discussion.' Paper for the conference: Politics of Communication – *Observed with Social Systems Theory*. Croatia, Dubrovnik: International University Centre.

Tække, J. (2019b). Acquisition of New Communication Media and Social (Dis) Connectivity in *Current Sociology*, Mongraph. SAGE.

Tække, J. (2021). "Systems-theoretical observations of moral media panic debates", *Kybernetes*, Vol. ahead-of-print No. ahead-of-print. https://doi.org/10.1108/K-11-2020-0724.

Toffler, A. (1980). *The Third Wave*. New York: Bantam Books.

Turan, F. (1993). Addiction as a Social Construction. *Journal of Psychology* 127(5), 489–499.

Wang, R., Scown, P., Urquhart, C. and Hardman, J. (2014). Tapping the Educational Potential of Facebook: Guidelines for use in Higher Education. *Journal of Education and Information Technologies* 19: 21–39.

Webb, L. M. (2012). Facebook–How College Students Work It. I *Social Media*. Noor Al-Deen, Hana S. and Hendricks, John Allen (Rad). Lanham, Maryland: Lexington Books, pp. 3–23.

Wegerif, R. (2013). *Dialogic: Education for the Internet Age*. London: Routledge.

Williamson, B. (2017). *Big Data in Education*. London: SAGE.

Wong, K. and Dobson, A. (2019). We're just Data: Exploring China's Social Credit System in Relation to Digital Platform Ratings Cultures in Westernised Democracies. *Global Media and China 2019*, 4(2) 220–232.

Wright, N. (2010). Twittering in Teacher Education: Reflecting on Practicum Experiences. *Open Learning* 25(3), 259–265.

Yaros A., R. (2012). Social Media in Education: Effects of Personalization and Interactivity on Engagement and Collaboration. *Social Media*. Noor Al-Deen, Hana S. and Hendricks, John Allen (eds). Lanham, Maryland: Lexington Books, pp. 57–75.

Young, K. (1999). Fanget i Nettet. Copenhagen: INTROITE.

Zeng, L., Hall, H. og Pitts, M. (2012). Cultivating a Community of Learners: The Potential Challenges of Social Media in Higher Education *Social Media*. Noor Al-Deen, Hana S. & Hendricks, John Allen (eds). Lanham, Maryland: Lexington Books, pp. 93–110.

Zuboff, S. (2019) *Overvågningskapitalismens tidsalder*. [The Age of Surveillance Capitalism – The Fight for a Human Future at the New Frontier of Power] København: Informations Forlag.

Index

The letter *f* following an entry indicates a page that includes a figure.
The letter *t* following an entry indicates a page that includes a table.

abduction 60
academic collaboration 113
accessibility 20–1, 22
action 3
addiction 55, 81
adding 71
affinity rooms 65
Al-Qallaf, C. L. 68
ambivalence 81–3, 99
   of action 82
   of interaction 82
   of responsibility 82
America. *See* USA
Anderson, T. and Dron, J. 79
Anglo-American world 148–51, 152
Anthoni, Kasper 88–9
appropriation 70–1, 72 n.17, 115–16
art education 70
attention 59–60, 77–8, 101–2
attitude 36, 108, 117, 152
   Big Data 154
   design and visual arts 120
   history 121
   information search and source criticism course 125–7
   online teaching 175
   polarisation 162
   taking others seriously 163
authenticity 91
Avram, E. M. 67

BDMs (Big Data Machines) 135, 138–40, 153–4, 155
behaviourism 153
Bennedsen, Anne Lise 171–2
Biesta, G. 19, 36 n.13
Big Cyborgs 141–5*f*, 147–8, 155, 256
Big Data 135–7

Big Cyborgs 141–5*f*, 147–8, 155, 156
Big Data Machines 135, 138–40, 153–4, 155
Citizen Big Data Machines 136, 140–5, 153–4, 155
definitions 135, 137–8
democratic models 136, 151–54, 155–6
machine assemblage 144–4
market models 136, 148–51, 155
media ecologies 146–54
responding to 145–54
Small Cyborgs 147, 155
state models 136, 146–8, 155
states/companies 138, 142*f*–4
Student Big Data Machines 149–50*f*, 153*f*–4, 155
Big Data in Education (Williamson, Ben) 149
Big Data Machines (BDMs) 135, 138–40, 153–4, 155
Bildung approach 4, 8, 14 n.1, 30–42 *see also* Big Data *and* DUFA project
   actualisation 35
   analytics 108
   critical approach 5
   as critical exploration of ways of being in the world 31, 35–9*f*
   critical knowledge 159–60
   as experimental and creative transgression of the existing order 31, 39–41*f*
   experimental approach 5
   as external shaping of the individual by society 31, 32–3*f*
   as facilitated internal self-development 31, 33–5*f*
   four ways of working with 111–30
   media, and the 7–8

online teaching 172–5
paradoxes 41 n.15
polarisation 162–3
reflective ideas about education 13–14, 30–2, 35–41
socialisation/indoctrination 35
teaching practices 72–3f, 95
theory of the three waves 95–104, 173–4
three classical dimensions of 36 n.13, 37f, 152 *see also* attitude *and* existence *and* knowledge
tradition of 5–7, 13
vulgar ideas about education 13–14, 30–5, 151
BIT (IT for all) project 68, 76–7
blogs 67–8
bodily oral language 21–2
Bryant, L. 25–6

Cambridge Analytica 140
capacity 22 n.5, 24
 extending 25
 teaching 26
Castells, M. 161
CBDMs (Citizen Big Data Machines) 136, 140–5, 153–4, 155
challenger teachers/teaching 5, 95–7, 100–1, 102, 178
cheating 94
China/Chinese 122–4t, 128, 129
 Big Data 146–8
Cinque, T. and Brown, A. 57
Citizen Big Data Machines (CBDMs) 136, 140–5, 153–4, 155
classrooms 45–6, 47–9, 50–2
 closed 45–6, 47–9, 103
 contact-seeking 88–92, 128–30
 intensified 84–7
 open 50–2, 55, 56, 80, 97
 penetrated 80–3
 social media in 84–7, 88–91
 third wave activities 127–30, 132–3
closed classrooms 45–6, 47–9, 103
collaboration 113
Comenius, Iohannes Amos 45
 Orbis Sensualium Pictus 45
commercial systems 114
community 117, 171

community practices (organisation) 65–7, 109, 173
computational empowerment 58
concentration 93
Confucianism 34
connectivity 160–1
contact-seeking classrooms 88–92, 128–30
copying/copyright 113–14, 115–16
COVID-19 pandemic 157–8
 Danish primary schools lockdown 164–5, 169, 176, 179
 Danish universities lockdown 166, 169, 179
 Danish upper secondary schools lockdown 165–6, 169, 171–2, 176, 179
 lockdown as extraordinary situation 167
 lockdown responses 167–71, 176, 179
creator teachers/teaching 5, 95
critical-constructive Bildung approach. *See* Bildung approach
critical hermeneutics 37
critical knowledge 159–60

Dall, S. 68
dark posts 143 n.3
debates 52–5
democracy 143–4, 151, 156, 176, 179
Denmark 175–7
 schools in lockdown 164–6, 169–72, 176, 179
design and visual arts 118–20, 124t
determinism 24–5, 52
dialogical teaching 37–8
digital media *see also* media
 before/after 44 n.1 *see also* theory of the three waves
 criticism 53, 64–5, 75, 101
 as dominant 72
 educational responses to. *See* theory of the three waves
 literacy in 70
digital natives 57, 69
digital revolution 43
digital timelines 121
digitalisation 114 n.3
digitalisation as a Bildung-relevant, epoch-typical, key issue 125–7, 132, 178

digitally supported disciplines and common Bildung (DUFA) project. See DUFA
disconnectivity 161
distance teaching 157–8, 164–6, 168, 170–1, 172–5
distraction 60, 93
document sharing 68, 86, 113–17
Drotner, K. 54
DUFA (digitally supported disciplines and common Bildung) project 10, 77
   analytical model 106–10
   Bildung analytics 108
   digitalisation as a Bildung-relevant, epoch-typical, key issue 125–7, 132, 178
   four ways of working with Bildung 111–33
   framework 105–10
   media analytics 108–9
   new special subject matter Bildung practices 118–25, 131, 132, 178
   new transdisciplinary Bildung practices 112–18, 131, 132, 178
   third wave activities that transform classroom teaching and Bildung 127–30, 132–3, 178
   wave analytics 109–10

echo chambers 47
education 3 *see also* schools *and* teaching
   art 70
   Biesta, G. 36 n.13
   Bildung approach. *See* Bildung approach
   critical and challenging understanding of 48, 136
   critical-constructive Bildung approach. *See* Bildung approach
   Denmark 175–7
   digital media, responses to. *See* theory of the three waves
   experimental and creative understanding of 48–9
   historical medium perspective 44–52
   progressive model of 34
   reflective ideas 13–14, 30–2, 35–41
   role of 18–19
   technical and causal approach 4, 6, 7, 47, 136
   technological expectation of 32
   traditional 32
   voluntaristic and facilitating approach 4, 6, 7, 48, 136
   world-orientated view on 37
education system, the 17
   positivistic understanding of 47–8
   vulgar ideas 13–14, 30–5, 151
   technical and causal approach 4, 6, 7, 47, 136
   voluntaristic and facilitating approach 4, 6, 7, 48, 136
electronic analogue media 27
Ellison, N. 66
embedding 71
Emile (Rousseau, Jean-Jacques) 7, 35
engineer teachers/teaching 5, 95–8, 102, 178
epoch-typical key problems 125–7, 132
equality 18
EU (European Union) 151–4
existence 36, 37, 108, 117–18, 152
   Big Data 154
   design and visual arts 120
   information search and source criticism course 125–7
   online teaching 175
   polarisation 162
   taking others seriously 164
expression practices (production) 67–8, 109, 173

Facebook 66–7, 94, 140, 148
   filter bubbles 160, 161
facts 158–9
fake news 159–60, 161
feedback 113, 114–15
filter bubbles 160–1
flexibility 20–1, 22
flow of space 161
friendship classes 129–30
Fu, Jo Shan 58
functionalism 18

Gallardo Echenique, Eliana 56–7
gardener teachers/teaching 5, 95–7, 99–100, 178

geography 171
globalisation 122–4
good citizens 6, 32–3
governmental psycho-policy 150
Gretter, S. and Yadav, A. 57
group work 60
growth mindset 149

Habermas, J.
  Theory of Communicative Action, The 97
Hattem, D. and Lomicka, L. 64
history 121, 124*t*
homework 86, 87
humanity 29–30, 36–7
  actions 26
  actualisation 35
  definition 35
  innate abilities 33–5*f*
  socialisation/indoctrination 35
  world relationship 106
Hutchison, A. C. 70

identity 91, 117–18
immigrants 57
impression practices (interpretation) 68–9, 109, 173
indifference strategies 82, 83*f*, 94
Innis, Harold 20–1
interdisciplinary studies 58
Internet, the 69 *see also* social media
  control 97–8
  ignoring 99
  information search and source criticism course 125–7
  protection from 99
  truth 126
involvement 93
IT-boosters 52
IT for all (BIT) project 68, 76–7
IT-sceptics 52, 53
IT University of Copenhagen (ITU) 166, 169
Iversen, O.S. 57–8

Kant, Immanuel 18, 35
Kapital, Das (Marx. Karl) 51
Klafki, W. 125–7
knowledge 7–8, 36, 108, 117, 152, 158–9

Big Data 154
  communicating 44–5
  critical 159–60
  design and visual arts 119–20
  education system 17
  history 121
  information search and source criticism course 125–7
  new expression practices (production) 67
  online teaching 175
  polarisation 162–3
  production 72
  social sciences 120
König, C. J. 59
Krutka, D. 64, 65

language 3, 89 *see also* writing
  Chinese 122–4*t*, 128, 129
  oral 23, 44
  Spanish 171–2
Leaver, K. and Kent, M. 67
literacy 70
lockdown 167
  in Danish schools 164–6, 169–72, 176, 179
  responses to 167–71
Luhmann, N. 17

machine learning algorithms 126, 139, 141, 149
McLuhan, M. 25, 26
Marner, A. 70–1
Marner, M. and Örtegren, H. 70, 71–2
mass media 162
mastery 70–1
mathematical drawing programs 118–20
mathematics 121–2, 124*t*
media *see also* media concept, the *and* technology
  accessibility 20–1, 22
  bias 20
  bodily oral language 21–2
  changing 111
  determinism 24–5
  expansion 22
  flexibility 20–1, 22
  history 22–4
  human actions and 26

impact of 13
interaction 62–3
new media situation 55–6
revolutions 1–2, 26–7
space-bias 20–1
teaching and 8, 13–14, 20–2
time-bias 20–1
transformation and 53–4
media analytics 108–9
media chains 66 n.16
media concept, the 19–30
media ecologies 22–4, 25–6, 26, 146–54
media epochs 22–4
media matrices 22–4
media of teaching 20–1
media panic 54
media revolutions 1–2, 26–7
   digitalisation 43
   humanity 29–30
   society 28–9
medium theory 3 n.2
memory 29, 59–61
Mencius 34
Menkhoff, T. 63–4
Meyrowitz, J. 26–8
moral media panic 54
multi-tasking 59–61, 80–1, 83
multiplexing 61, 85 n.6, 87, 101–2

new community practices (organisation) 65–7, 173
new expression practices (production) 67–8, 173
new impression practices (interpretation) 68–9, 173
new media situation 55–6
new participation practices (interaction) 62–5, 173
non-deterministic approach 2–4, 53
non-linguistic teaching 22 n.7
nudgeocracy 150

online shared documents 68, 86, 113–17
online teaching 157–8, 164–6, 168, 170–1, 172–5
onto-cartography 138
   of Teaching, Media and Bildung 15, 26
open classrooms 50–2, 55, 56, 80, 97
openness 73–4, 78–9

orality 23
Orbis Sensualium Pictus (Comenius, Iohannes Amos) 45
originality 113–14, 115–16
otherness 64, 79, 101, 110, 118, 174, 178–9

participation 78, 100
participation practices (interaction) 62–5, 109, 173
peer feedback 113
physics 121–2, 124t
place of space 161
plagiarism 115, 116
Plato 29, 39 n.14, 60–1
polarisation 157, 159–63 *see also* filter bubbles
politics 120, 128, 129, 143, 146–54
   polarisation 159
populism 161–4
post-human media ecology 25–6
post-modernism 39–41
Postman, N. 64–5
   Technopoly 29
primary schools lockdown 164–5, 169, 176, 179
printing 7, 45, 54
problem-based learning 37
problematic fields 24
programming 57–8, 122
progressive model of education 34
prohibition strategies 82, 83f, 94
psychographic segmentation 140
psychological governmentality 150

reading 54
reflexivity 72, 101–2
research 52–5, 75–7, 98 *see also* SME
resistance 71
response 3
Rousseau, Jean-Jacques
   Emile 7, 35

SBDMs (Student Big Data Machines) 149–50f, 153f–4, 155
school information management systems 98
school trips 86
schools 15–16, 17, 45 *see also* education *and* teaching

classrooms. *See* classrooms
constraints 58
COVID-19 lockdown 164–6, 169–72
equality 18
historical medium perspective 44–52
society and 34
Spanish kitchen, the 171–2
subjects, transformation of 70–2, 118–30, 171–2
subjects as part of DUA project 105–6, 108, 118–30
Scratch program 121
search engines 69
shared online documents 68, 86, 113–17
single-tasking 60
SketchUp program 119
sleep 54–5
SME (Socio Media Education experiment) 9–10, 63, 76, 83, 84–91, 129–30
  obstacles 93–5
  reflexivity 101–2
social behaviour 27
social identity 91
social media 62–4, 65, 66–7 *see also* Facebook
  cheating 94
  in China in Chinese 122–4, 128, 129
  in classrooms 84–7, 88–91
  dark posts 143 n.3
  existence in 117–18
  polarisation 157, 159–60, 162 *see also* filter bubbles
  politics 120, 128, 129
  populism 161, 163–4
  strategies 66
  teachers 83
  Twitter 63–4, 65, 84–6, 87, 88–91
  weblogs 67–8
social sciences 120, 124*t*, 128
society
  alterations in 1
  education, role of 18
  external shaping of the individual by 31, 32–3
  hierarchies 46
  polarisation of 157, 159–60 *see also* filter bubbles
  protection from 34

schools 34
  transforming 26–9
Socio Media Education experiment (SME). *See* SME
sociotechnical imaginary 149
soft skills 67
soft values 66
source criticism 69
space-bias media 20–1
Spanish kitchen, the 171–2
special subject matter Bildung practices 118–25, 131, 132, 178
stimulation 54–5
Student Big Data Machines (SBDMs) 149–50*f*, 153*f*–4, 155
students 6–8
  ambivalence 81–2
  behaviourism 153
  cheating 94
  classrooms 45–6, 50–1
  competencies 56–8, 87
  COVID-19 lockdown 165–6, 169, 171–2
  critical and challenging teaching 48
  digital media, responses to. *See* theory of the three waves
  experimental and creative teaching 48–9
  facilitative and voluntaristic teaching 48
  home life 46
  interaction with 16
  machine learning algorithms 149
  multi-tasking 59–60
  new media situation 55–6
  online teaching 165–6, 171–2, 174
  performance 150–1
  social activities 169, 171–2
  social media 9–10, 84–91
  Socio Media Education experiment (SME) 9–10, 84–91
subjects, transformation of 70–2, 118–30, 171–2
supersynchronous 114 n.4
surveillance 98, 146–50, 153 *see also* CBDMs

teacher-process feedback 113
teachers 5 *see also* teaching

actor types 95–103
ambivalence 81–2
challenger 5, 95–7, 100–1, 102, 178
classrooms 45–6, 47, 50–1
combined strategies 101–2
constraints 58
creator 5, 95
digital age, response to 51, 82
digital media, responses to 51, 121 *see also* theory of the three waves
DUFA (digitally mediated Bildung in different schools subjects) 10
engineer 5, 95–8, 102, 178
gardener 5, 95–7, 99–100, 178
as mediators 101
prohibition/indifference strategies 82, 83*f*, 94, 99
social media 83, 84–9
Socio Media Education experiment (SME) 9–10, 84–90
trans-epochal 97
trans-individual 97
teaching 43–4 *see also* education *and* schools
after Internet and digital medial 49–50
aims and means 70–1
before Internet and digital media 45–9
Bildung 72–3*f*, 95
bodily oral language 21–2
capacity 26
challenger 5, 95–7, 100–1, 102
creator 5, 95
critical and challenging understanding of 48, 136
as critical exploration of ways of being in the world 36–7, 39*f*
dialogical 37–8
distance 157–8, 164–6, 168, 170–1, 172–5
engineer 5, 95–8, 102
as experimental and creative transgression of the existing order 40, 41*f*
experimental and creative understanding of 48–9
facilitative and voluntaristic understanding of 48, 136
to facilitate internal self-development 33–5*f*

gardener 5, 95–7, 99–100
infrastructures of 23*f*–4
interaction level 15, 16
media and 8, 13–14, 20–2, 43–4
media of 20–1
new community practices (organisation) 65–7, 173
new expression practices (production) 67–8, 173
new impression practices (interpretation) 68–9, 173
new media situation 55–6
new participation practices (interaction) 62–5, 173
new practices 61–73
non-linguistic 22 n.7
online 157–8, 164–6, 168, 170–1, 172–5
organisational level 15, 17
to produce good citizens 32–3*f*
semiotic accessibility and flexibility 20–1, 22
societal level 15, 17
society and 8, 28
specialised media 68–9
teaching concept, the 15–19
technical and causal understanding of 47, 136, 175–8
third wave activities 127–30, 132–3, 173–4, 178
two-chamber system 45
technological expectation of education 32
technology 3
alliances with 4
impact of 13
Technopoly (Postman, N.) 29
television 27, 28
theoretical framework 8–9
Theory of Communicative Action, The (Habermas, J.) 97
theory of the three waves 10, 75, 77–104
activities that transform classroom teaching and Bildung 127–30, 132–3
Bildung 95–104
first wave 78, 80–3, 92–3, 109–10, 174
online teaching 173–4
second wave 78, 80, 83*f*–7, 92–3, 110, 174

SME experiment obstacles 93–5
third wave 78–9, 80, 88–92–3, 110, 174
upshot 92–3
variants 79–80
wave analytics 109–10
3D mathematical drawing programs 118–20
three generations of distance education 79
time-bias media 20–1
timelines 121
traditional education 32
transactional relations 3
transdisciplinary Bildung practices 112–18, 131, 132, 178
transparency 116
transverse inspiration 113
trust 159
truth 126 *see also* facts
Twitter 63–4, 65, 84–6, 87, 88–91
two-chamber system of teaching 45

understanding-seeking attitudes 117
universities lockdown 166, 169, 179
upper secondary schools lockdown 165–6, 169, 171–2, 176, 179
USA 148–51, 152, 161

wave analytics 109–10
weblogs 67–8
WeChat 147
wikis 86–7
Williamson, Ben 150–1
  Big Data in Education 149
world-orientated view on education 37
writing 3, 7, 29, 44–5, 60–1
  digitalisation of 113
  interaction 84–6, 113, 170–1

Zeng, L. 66
Zuboff, S. 67

www.ingramcontent.com/pod-product-compliance
Lightning Source LLC
Chambersburg PA
CBHW061826300426
44115CB00013B/2270